HARLEM

❧ TRAVEL GUIDE ❧

CAROLYN D. JOHNSON

VALERIE JO BRADLEY

❧ www.welcometoharlem.com ❧

Published by:
Welcome to Harlem
www.welcometoharlem.com

Publisher/Writer
Carolyn D. Johnson

Writer/Editor
Valerie Jo Bradley

Graphic Design
Total Design Freedom

Printed in the United States of America

Every effort has been made to ensure that the information in this book is as up-to-date as possible at press time. However, many details can and will change. The publisher cannot accept responsibility for any consequences arising from the use of this book.

Welcome to Harlem does not solicit individuals, organizations, or businesses for listings inclusion in this guide, nor do we accept payment for inclusion in the editorial portion of this book. We have tried to provide a fair representation of Harlem sites, but all sites are not listed because of space constraints. We always welcome communications regarding anything having to do with this book. Please contact us at:

Welcome to Harlem
2360 Frederick Douglass Blvd., Suite D
New York, NY 10027
Tel: (212) 662-7779
Toll Free: (888) 391-7480

Fax: (646) 216-8644
www.welcometoharlem.com

Follow us on:
Facebook – http://www.facebook.com/welcometoharlem
Twitter – http://www.twitter/welcometoharlem

ACKNOWLEDGMENTS

Harlem Travel Guide was born out of our frustration that New York travel guides did not feature more of the wonderful sites that exist in Harlem. It is easy to be critical of someone else's work and much harder to actualize your own vision of what a guide about Harlem should be. But, we bit the bullet, and as we worked to document the Harlem we love, we were encouraged by our terrific and patient family members and friends who simply had our backs. It was their support that kept us going, and we are eternally grateful to those who believed in us.

The creative eye of graphic designer Michael Lawrence of MasTypography Studio helped us imagine the possibilities by encouraging us to obtain "strong" photographs that say something. Jasmine Wong's early research was invaluable. Our colleagues in the Travel Professionals of Color (TPOC) were generous in sharing information about what tourists are looking for. Our parents, Nola Johnson, and Ernestine and Roger Bradley, were incredibly understanding, as we were "missing in action" during most of the time we worked to produce this guide. We thank Michael Henry Adams for his perseverance over the years to convince others that Harlem has value as a tour destination if its historic buildings are cherished and not destroyed, and for enhancing the guide with his strong endorsement of our work in his introduction. A. Peter Bailey's support was invaluable because he dug in his extensive Harlem archive to conjure up relevant facts that are too often forgotten, but are terribly important to provide a perspective that only a person who really knows the political and cultural history of Harlem could produce, which is what he did in his Glimpse of Harlem's Fascinating History.

And then there are our new friends found on Flickr who generously supplied us with phenomenal photographs that document the beauty of Harlem. We would be remiss if we did not thank old friends too—like Jacquie Connors, Keith Debetham, Kevin McGruder, and Yuien Chinn—for sharing their photographs or for helping us obtain needed photographs. We also feel honored that Harlem organizations, businesses, and institutions took the time to send a photograph or read a passage for accuracy. And kisses to all those who let us know when a restaurant or store closed, opened, or reopened so that we could pull it from or add it to the guide.

If we had any doubts about our work, these were erased after we heard from our editor, Jenny W. of CreateSpace, who in her editorial letter confirmed that "The information in this book is detailed and well researched, and clearly stems from an intimate knowledge of the neighborhood and its best-kept secrets." She went on to say, "The primary objective of *Harlem Travel Guide* is clear and succinct: to give readers an authentic, diverse, and enjoyable experience in Harlem. This objective is more than fulfilled in the engaging and informative pages of this book."

Now that we have tooted our horn, we thank you for purchasing *Harlem Travel Guide*, and we hope that your expectations have been satisfied. If not, we would love to hear from you. Just contact us at www.welcometoharlem.com.

FOREWORD

WELCOME TO OUR HARLEM!

Harlem Travel Guide is a tour book exclusively about Harlem, the Black and Latino Cultural Capital of the World. Finally, all things tourists want to know about Harlem are organized in one book—no more surfing the Web for hours to organize a day or a week in Harlem. The variety of Harlem tour destinations provided in this book is phenomenal—there is something for everyone, from being directed to Harlem's hidden architectural wonders to enjoying first-class jazz performances.

This one-of-a-kind book is conveniently organized into distinct sections because the areas are uniquely distinct: Central Harlem, where African Americans first settled in the early 1900s; East Harlem or El Barrio, which is home to Latinos, with Puerto Ricans first migrating to the enclave after WWI; and West Harlem, which includes a diverse population of African Americans, West Indians, Latinos, and whites. Clubs, restaurants, places to shop, libraries, museums, galleries, churches, landmarks, parks, monuments, and much more are listed and described with uncommonly known cultural and historical facts that underscore why these sites are even more interesting to visit. The book also lists exciting annual events that heretofore only Harlem "insiders" knew about and suggests unique "things to do."

Many come to Harlem seeking the nostalgia of its past, and this book puts that history in focus while also concentrating on the "new" Harlem, which has undergone a housing and economic development renaissance that makes the area an even more engaging tourist destination. Now visitors can find banks that provide foreign exchange services, free Internet access and Internet cafes, authentic tours, and guest accommodations. The "real" Harlem unfolds in the pages of *Harlem Travel Guide* in a way never presented before.

Harlem was home to four New York City mayors, the first African American from New York elected to Congress, six Manhattan borough presidents, scores of past and present musicians, actors, internationally celebrated intellectuals, celebrities, and social activists, and they appear larger than life between the pages of *Harlem Travel Guide*. Harlem's rich history is unparalleled by any other New York City neighborhood. Its ethnic diversity makes it a fascinating place to visit and this book helps visitors navigate its nooks and crannies with user-friendly guide maps and directions.

The definitive reference to all things Harlem, *Harlem Travel Guide* is a must-have. It certainly will make an impact on Harlem's economic boom because it has opened greater access to a thriving and growing section of Manhattan. It's about time!

Carolyn D. Johnson
Publisher/Writer

Valerie Jo Bradley
Editor/Writer

CONTENTS

INTRODUCTION

WELCOME TO HARLEM'S LONG-AWAITED GUIDE

By Michael Henry Adams

Here at last is the informative, authoritative, and authentic guidebook so many of us have long awaited. For the past four centuries, fabled Harlem, USA, has been a section of New York renowned throughout the world as a special destination. Helping to give it a distinctive character, more even than a textbook-like array of nineteenth-century architecture, are a host of incomparable twentieth- and twenty-first-century Harlem people, as wise, welcoming, confounding, and beautiful as any on the globe. Helping one to better appreciate these citizens and their environment, and to discover their most distinguished artistry, comfortable lodgings, and superb cuisine, is *Harlem Travel Guide*.

In turn a Native American seasonal settlement, a Colonial-Dutch outpost, a rural retreat, the city's first suburb, a middle-class enclave of competing white Protestants and Catholic immigrants, where former Lower East Side residents became proud and prosperous Uptown Jews—today's Harlem is someplace else again. At some Victorian churches, later turned into synagogues, which are now evangelical houses of worship, one encounters the same layering of history upon history that makes places like Rome or Cairo so evocative of the past.

Accidentally Black America's capital for roughly the past one hundred years is the Harlem of greatest fame. Poised again at a point of pivotal transition, depending on events over the next generation, Harlem's identity as a uniquely African American place may soon come to be as tenuous a memory as its once-strong association with settlers from the Netherlands has become.

Themselves latter-day Harlem settlers, the eminent publisher, Welcome to Harlem Tours owner, and Harlem-born and -bred Carolyn Johnson, and her collaborator/editor and Harlem activist Valerie Jo Bradley, know all about this varied Harlem history—its ins and outs, multicultural quirks, offbeat byways, and hidden historic crannies. In an accessible, engaging narrative, they relate much of what they have learned over the decades, both by the trial and error of living here, as well as through prodigious research. Through these means and more they not only enlighten the reader, but they also make one as eager as an inquisitive tourist during the Harlem Renaissance of the 1920s to come, to see, to explore, to taste, to hear, to dance, and to experience this familiar, but strange, all-American place like nowhere else.

Discouraged by friends and family from buying a house in Harlem in the 1980s, Valerie Jo Bradley smiles pensively, satisfied by the substantial brownstone house won by determination, but slightly saddened that she "didn't buy three more! So much has changed since I moved here. It seems like only yesterday, but it's more than a quarter century, and that's brought exciting shops, superb restaurants, and charming inns we once only dreamed of..." Equipped with this marvelous new resource, wherever one hails from, all these new amenities plus a score of unexpected or difficult-to-find hideaways and traditional delights await all in pursuit of incredible Harlem, both the lost and the found and the here and now.

Michael Henry Adams is an architectural historian who conducts unique Harlem tours and is the author of Harlem Lost and Found *and* Style and Grace: African Americans At Home.

I

A GLIMPSE OF HARLEM'S FASCINATING HISTORY

By A. Peter Bailey

October 31,1919, was a bright, sunny fall day in Harlem, a perfect day for the historic launching of the maiden voyage of Marcus Garvey's ship, the *Frederick Douglass*.

In the book *Marcus Garvey and the Vision of Africa*, edited by renowned historian John Henrik Clarke, with the assistance of Amy Jacques Garvey, the charismatic Black leader describes the excitement and sense of pride generated by the launching. "On a day in October 1919, we launched in the New York Harbor, the first boat of the line [Black Star Line]. That was a day never to be forgotten. Hundreds of thousands of people gathered at the foot of the 125th Street Pier at the North River to see the boat sail under the Black captain. People also gathered in the thousands on Riverside Drive to witness the spectacle…" It was an auspicious entry of Harlem on the national and international stages. Harlem has been there ever since.

The launching was the first of numerous historical events to take place in Harlem, which at the time was still at the beginning of its transition into an overwhelmingly Black neighborhood. Harlem had been the home of Native Americans, who were defeated by the Dutch in 1658; the Dutch in turn lost control to the British in 1664. When the latter took over, they attempted to change the neighborhood's name from the Dutch "Nieuw Haarlem" to Lancaster. Because of strong resistance, the British just anglicized the name by dropping one *a*.

When Blacks began settling in Harlem in 1904, inhabitants were mostly Jewish and Italian according to Jeffery S. Gurock in his book, *When Harlem was Jewish: 1870–1930*. "In the late 1800s and early 1900s Temple Israel was at 125th Street and Fifth Avenue. In 1903 it was moved to 120th Street and Lenox Avenue." The first is now the site of the National Black Theatre and the second is the site of Mount Olivet Baptist Church. Among congregants of Temple Israel was a branch of the Sulzberger family, owner of the *New York Times*.

As for Harlem's Italian Americans, E. Idell Zeisloft in his book, *The New Metropolis*, noted that "Little Italy, one of the most flourishing and picturesque Italian colonies in New York, commences at 104th Street to the east of Second Avenue. It extends to the river and has gradually swept uptown until it has reached 116th Street." Legendary New York City Mayor Fiorello LaGuardia was a Harlemite.

White Harlemites strongly resisted the coming of Black folks in 1904, who were spurred by the opening up of residences for Blacks on 135th Street, east of Lenox Avenue, by Black real estate broker Phillip A. Payton Jr. Between 1910 and the 1930s thousands of Black folks fleeing white supremacist terrorism in the South poured into Harlem, along with people from the Caribbean seeking better economic opportunities. Among the early newcomers were three institutions that are still major forces in Harlem— Mother A. M. E. Zion Church, Abyssinian Baptist Church, and St. Philip's Episcopal Church.

By World War II Harlem had become the political and cultural (not economic) capital of Black America. Many of the most creative, visionary, talented, exciting, and dynamic people that this country has ever produced either lived in, worked in, performed in, or had strong connections to Harlem. These include Garvey, Adam Clayton Powell, Jr., A. Phillip Randolph, Paul Robeson, Langston Hughes, Zora Neale Hurston, J. A. Rogers, Malcolm X, James Baldwin, Madame C. J. Walker, Ruby Dee, Ossie Davis, Billie Holiday, Miles Davis, Duke Ellington, Jackie Robinson, and Romare Bearden, among many, many others.

It was in Harlem that Sugar Ray Robinson owned a bar; that Lewis Michaux and Richrd B. Moore each owned memorable bookstores; that Oscar Micheaux set up his film industry; that boxing champion Jack Johnson owned a club (which later became the Cotton Club); and that J. Raymond (The Fox) Jones displayed his superb political skills.

It was in the Harlem YMCA's Little Theatre that artists such as Alvin Ailey, Cicely Tyson, Eartha Kitt, and James Earl Jones found a venue early in their careers on which to display their talent. It was in Harlem that Abram Hill and Frederick O'Neal launched the American Negro Theatre, which played a pivotal role in the early performing careers of Harry Belafonte, Sidney Poitier, and Isabel Sanford. It was Harlem nightclubs and theatres, including the Savoy Ballroom, the Cotton Club, the Apollo Theatre, the Renaissance Ballroom, and Minton's Playhouse that advanced the performing careers of Thelonius Monk, Ella Fitzgerald, Cab Calloway, Aretha Franklin, James Brown, and a host of others.

Because of this illustrious history, Harlem can justifiably do more name-dropping than any other neighborhood in the country, if not the world.

Other Harlem facts and nuggets:

1. One reason that Harlem has always played a significant role in New York City's history is that, contrary to popular belief, it is not uptown Manhattan but midtown Manhattan, since the borough goes up to 230th Street.

2. Harlem's 125th Street has for many years been a major transportation hub in Manhattan, being one of the few streets in the city that runs straight from river to river.

3. Harlem was annexed to New York City in 1873 as the city's first suburb. This explains why it has more brownstones than any other neighborhood in Manhattan.

4. Harlem's foreign visitors have included Fidel Castro, whose stay in the Theresa Hotel in 1960 attracted visits by prominent world leaders, including the Soviet Union's Nikita Khrushchev, India's Jawaharlal Nehru, and Egypt's Gamal Abdel Nasser. For a few dazzling days, Harlem was the center of the world's attention.

5. It was in Harlem in the late 1950s that the African Jazz Arts Society (AJASS) and its Grandassa Models introduced the cultural movement that led to the natural hairstyles and the wearing of African-influenced clothing, including dashikis.

6. It was also in Harlem that the first of the urban uprisings of the 1960s erupted (1964).

7. Columbia University will now admit that it's in West Harlem. Until recently, the university fiercely resisted any connection with Harlem, insisting it was in Morningside Heights.

8. The name Harlem has been included in the titles of at least thirty-five books, seventy-four songs, and twenty-six movies. No other neighborhood in the country can match this recognition.

Harlem, as a neighborhood, has come a long way since the launching of the *Frederick Douglass* in October 1919 dramatically introduced it to the nation and world as an emerging Black neighborhood. Through much pain and equal amounts of glory, the neighborhood pressed on.

A. Peter Bailey is a journalist, lecturer, and author of Harlem: Precious Memories…Great Expectations; *he can be reached at apeterb@verizon.net.*

USEFUL INFORMATION

NYC & Company is New York City's official marketing, tourism, and partnership organization. NYC & Company information centers and kiosks offer free brochures and discount coupons to a diverse selection of destinations throughout the city. Learn about hotels, culture, dining, shopping, sightseeing, events, attractions, tours, and transportation.

NYC & Company Official Visitor Information Center
810 Seventh Ave., between 52nd and 53rd Sts. (212) 484-1222. www.nycvisit.com. Mon–Fri 8:30am–9pm, Sat and Sun 9am–5pm. Bus—M6, M7, M10, M20, M30, M31, M57, M104. Subway—B, D, E to Seventh Ave.; N, Q, R, W to 57th St.

Harlem Information Center
The Studio Museum in Harlem. 144 W. 125th St., between Adam Clayton Powell Blvd. and Malcolm X/ Lenox. (212) 222-1014. Mon–Fri 12pm–6pm, Sat and Sun 10am–6pm (closed holidays). Bus—M2, M7, M60, M100, M101, M102, BX15. Subway—A, B, C, D, 2, 3 to 125th St.

Federal Hall Information Center
26 Wall St., at the Federal Hall National Memorial. Mon–Fri 9am–5pm (closed federal holidays). Bus— M1, M6, M9, M15. Subway—J, M, Z to Broad St.; 2, 3 to Wall St.

City Hall Visitor Information Kiosk
Located on the southern tip of City Hall Park. Mon–Fri 9am–6pm; Sat and Sun 10am–5pm; Holiday Hours: 10am–5pm. Bus—M1, M6, M15, M20, M22, M103. Subway—1, 2, 3, 4, 5, 6, A, C, E to Chambers St.; J, M, N, R, Z to City Hall.

Chinatown Visitor Information Kiosk
Located at the triangle where Canal, Walker, and Baxter Sts. meet. Daily 10am–6pm. Bus—M1, M51. Subway—J, M, N, R, Q, W, Z, 6 to Canal St.

Times Square Information Center
1560 Broadway, between 46th and 47th Sts. (212) 869-1890 www.timessquarenyc.org; http://www. timessquarebid.org/visitor. Daily 8am–8pm. Bus—M6, M7, M10, M27, M42, M104. Subway—1, 2, 3, 7, N, R to 42nd St./Times Square.

Everyone wants to visit Times Square—especially on a first visit to New York! Visit the Information Center to obtain assistance in navigating this exciting destination. You can purchase books about Times Square as well as posters and memorabilia. Services offered include multilingual citywide information, discount tickets to Broadway shows, Gray Line/Circle Line bus or boat sightseeing tours, and free access to the Internet.

Welcome to Harlem
2360 Frederick Douglass Blvd., between 126th and 127th Sts. (212) 662-7779. www.welcometoharlem.com. Mon–Fri 10am–5pm, Sat 10am–3pm and Sun 9am–1pm (closed holidays). Bus—M2, M3, M60, M100, M101, BX15. Subway—A, B, C, D, 2, 3 to 125th St.

Information center for visitors and residents that offers information on accommodations, culture, dining, shopping, sightseeing, events, attractions, tours, and transportation. Provides walking, shopping,
soul food and jazz, gospel and brunch, and custom tours.

TRAVEL RESOURCES

Web Sites
New York City: www.nyc.gov—Official New York City Web site
New York State Division of Tourism: www.iloveny.com—Official New York State Web site
Travel Insurance: www.securemytravelonline.com—Do you need travel insurance?

News
New York 1: www.ny1.com—New York City's 24-hour local news channel

Weather
National and local weather: www.weather.com

Phone Numbers
Emergencies (police, fire or ambulance): 911
New York City government agencies (non-emergency): 311
Directory assistance: 411

Holidays
New Year's Day—January 1
Martin Luther King Jr. Day—third Monday in January
Presidents' Day—third Monday in February
Memorial Day—fourth Monday in May
Independence Day—July 4
Labor Day—first Monday in September
Columbus Day—second Monday in October
Veterans Day—November 11
Thanksgiving Day—fourth Thursday in November
Christmas Day—December 25

Map Icons

⚐	Accomadations	≋	Books
Y	Bars & Lounges	✎	Cigars
⚲	Church	◉	Cosmetics-Salons-Spas
⛪	Cultural Center	₵	Discount Store
X	Dining	☜	Fabric Store
⚲	Educational Institutions	≋	Food
▦	Gallery	☜	Home Furnishings
▣	Garage	✪	Music
((•))	Internet wi-fi	✓	Recreation
☙	Library	!	Sneakers-Shoes

♪	Live Entertainment	°	Toys
🏛	Museum-Historic Sites	⍦	Wines-Liquors
✉	Postal Services	🏛	Fire Watch Tower
⛽	Service Station	⊕	Hospital
☙	Theater	☪	Mosque
🎭	Theatre	✿	Synagogue
♠	Apparel		

Sales Tax

New York City sales tax is 8.825%. There is no city sales tax on clothing and footwear items under $110. A New York State tax of 4.375% is charged when the total exceeds $110.

Smoking

Smoking is prohibited in all public areas throughout New York City, including subway stations, taxis, restaurants, and bars.

Tipping

Hotel doorman: $1 for hailing a cab
Porters and bellhops: $1–$2 per bag
Maids: $1–$2 per day of your visit, or as much as $5 per day
Wait staff and bartenders: 15%–20% of total bill
Restaurants: double the sales tax of 8.825%. In most restaurants, with a party of five or more there is an 18% gratuity factored into the bill
Taxi drivers: 15%–20% of total bill

Credit Cards Information

Listed for your convenience are the telephone numbers and Web sites for major card companies, should your card(s) be lost or stolen.

Name	Telephone # in U.S.	Web Site	Abbreviation
American Express	(800) 992-3404	www.americanexpress.com	**AmEx**
Discover	(800) 347-2683	www.discovercard.com	**Dis**
MasterCard	(800) 622-7747	www.mastercard.com	**MC**
Visa	(800) 847-2911	www.visa.com	**V**

Banks

Most banks open at 8am and have extended hours up to 6pm–8pm depending on the bank.

Foreign Currency Exchange

Chase Bank locations: Mon–Fri 8am–6pm, Sat 9am–3pm
103 E. 125th St., at Park Ave.
106 E. 125th St., at Lexington Ave.
179 E. 116th St., between Lexington and Third Aves.
1924 Third Ave., at 106th St.
2195 Frederick Douglass Blvd., at 119th St.

2218 Fifth Ave., at 135th St.
2824–26 Broadway, at 110th St.
2875 Broadway, at 112th St.
300 W. 135th St., at Frederick Douglass Blvd.
322 W. 125th St., between St. Nicholas Ave. and Frederick Douglass Blvd.
350 W. 125th St., at St. Nicholas Ave.
55 W. 125th St., between Malcolm X/Lenox and Fifth Ave.

Do not forget to bring your passport.

Significant Faith-Based Institutions & Burial Grounds

Often tourists come to Harlem in search of "gospel" music, and we have provided you with that list-ing. However, we would be remiss if we did not include a category of places of worship significant for their architectural beauty outside and inside. All sections of Harlem have a phenomenal collection of faith-based institutions that are both architecturally engaging and culturally significant. Many of these structures are legacies left by previous residents of Harlem before African Americans moved "Up-town." These grand buildings of neo-Gothic, Romanesque Revival, and Italianate Revival were built in the late 1800s by proud Protestant or Jewish congregations that moved on to other locations in Manhattan or the Bronx. Some structures were built for other uses, such as movie palaces, and were converted to places of worship, while still others were built from the ground up by prominent African American congregations who followed their flocks in the migration up Manhattan Island. In East Harlem, congregations of Irish and Italian residents built imposing Catholic churches that are now attended by Spanish-speaking residents who moved to the area after World War I. In the *Harlem Travel Guide* is a sampling of the vast collection of places of worship in Harlem. It doesn't represent all that could be mentioned—such as in Central Harlem the marble-faced **Greater Metropolitan Baptist Church** built for a Lutheran German congregation, or **Metropolitan Baptist Church** that was built as the **New York Presbyterian Church**, or **Mount Morris Baptist Church** now **Mount Moriah Baptist Church**. In West Harlem there is **St. James Presbyterian Church** or the unfinished **Our Lady of Lourdes Roman Catholic Church**, which incorporated materials from landmarks further downtown, or **St. Mary's Episcopal Church**, which sits next to its clapboard rectory in a garden that gives it an ambience of an old English village church. We recom-mend you visit some of the institutions in this listing to experience even more of Harlem's diversity.

Churches with Gospel Services

Visiting Harlem church services is encouraged, and the congregations are warm and welcoming. It is suggested that visitors respect church worship services by dressing appropriately (no shorts or halter tops, and men must wear shirts), turning off cell phones during service, and **arriving at least fifteen minutes prior to the start of service and remaining until the service has ended**. Most churches do not allow picture taking, videoing, or recording during services. You should check with the church you intend to visit in advance to understand its visitor guidelines.

Accommodations (*Home Away in Harlem*)

In addition to its outstanding nightlife, world-renowned down-home cuisine, and eclectic cultures, Har-lem also has a number of places to stay—some of which are owned and operated by recognized artists, musicians, writers, or photographers. Unique in design and ambience, many of the locations spotlight the stars of Harlem's glorious past in décor and other inspirations. More than the traditional hotels elsewhere throughout the city, these B&Bs, inns, and hostels bring your Harlem experience full circle.

NOTE: We have tried to be as accurate as possible in our representation of these establishments and believe the information we've provided to be correct as of our publication date. To avoid inconvenience, however, please check with the specific locations or go to their Web sites for any changes in rates, service, availability, or other details.

For more hostels and other affordable short-term accommodations in Harlem, you can visit: New-York50.com.

Electrical Current—In the U.S. 110–120V, 60-cycle.

Area codes—212, 718, 646, 347, and 914. They are interchangeable for home and cell numbers. In New York when placing a call, first dial "one" (1), then the area code, and last the telephone number: 1-212-555-1212.

Direct International—call 011 plus the country code, city code, and telephone number.

Restaurant Legend

$	Less than $7
$$	$7.01–$12
$$$	$12.01–$18
$$$$	$18.01–$25
$$$$$	Greater than $25

Useful Conversions

Weight
1 pound = 0.454 kilogram
1 ounce = 28.350 grams

Length
1 mile = 1.609 kilometers
1 yard = 0.9144 meter
1 foot = 30.48 centimeters
1 inch = 2.54 centimeters

Area
1 acre = 4,047 square meters

Liquid measure
1 pint = 0.473 liters
1 quart = 0.946 liters
1 gallon = 3.785 liters

Temperature Conversion
$°C = (°F - 32) / 1.8$
$°F = (°C \times 1.8) + 32$

Transportation

New York is probably the most accessible city in the world, primarily because of its efficient and 24-hour public transportation system. Private automobile travel is discouraged by extremely high fees in midtown parking garages, the prohibition of street parking in especially commercial areas during business hours, and traffic-congested streets. It is best to leave the car at home, or if you just have to drive, park it in a neighborhood that allows street parking and enjoy using the public transportation to travel around the city.

Metropolitan Transportation Authority (MTA)

The MTA's Web site, http://www.mta.info, is a key source for getting around via local transportation during your stay in the city of New York. While we strongly believe the best way to see the city is on foot, we recognize the need for the occasional subway or bus ride. The site includes information on city buses and subways, as well as the Long Island Railroad and Metro-North Railroad. Key features include schedules, maps, and service advisories. We've laid out some basic information that we hope will make getting around easier, but urge you to visit the site for more detailed information.

QUICK FACTS/DID YOU KNOW
THAT THE NEW YORK CITY SUBWAY SYSTEM:

» Is one of the oldest and most extensive public transportation systems in the world—468 stations serving 26 subway lines, covering 229 miles of routes.
» Carries more passengers than all other rail mass transit systems in the United States combined.
» Trails only the metro systems in Tokyo, Moscow, and Seoul in annual ridership.
» Is the only metro system that runs 24 hours a day, 365 days a year. *Source:* bullets 1-4 en.wikipedia. org.

MetroCard is a bright yellow plastic card with a black strip on the back which you must swipe in a subway turnstile or dip in a fare box on the bus in order to gain access to the transit system. MetroCard may be purchased at subway station booths, MetroCard vending machines, neighborhood merchants, and MetroCard buses and vans. There are a few ways to buy a MetroCard but Pay-Per-Ride (regular) and Unlimited Ride seem to give you the best bang for your buck, especially if you're just visiting.

Fares: The fare for a one-way subway or local bus ride is $2.25, payable with MetroCard. Up to three children 44 inches tall and under ride for free on subways and local buses when accompanied by a fare-paying adult. Express bus fare one-way is $5.50.

TIP

» Senior citizens 65 and older pay a reduced rate of $1.10 on buses (cash only) and receive a free transfer (must show a valid Medicare card). Reduced fare is not available during peak periods, 6am–10am and 3pm–7pm.
» With an unlimited MetroCard the more you ride, the less it costs.
» Buses only accept MetroCard or exact change.
» Free transfers are included, but must be used up to two-hours after your MetroCard is initially swiped.
» An unlimited MetroCard can only be used by one person at a time, and cannot be used again at the same station or bus route for eighteen minutes.

Subway Station Globes
Green lamps indicate the entrance is open 24 hours and a station clerk is on duty. Red lamps indicate the entrance is not open 24 hours and MetroCard must be used for entry, as there is typically no clerk on duty.

Pay-Per-Ride MetroCard	Unlimited Ride MetroCard
Buy rides anywhere from $4.50 to $80.00. Receive a 15% bonus when you put $8.00 or more on your card. You'll receive an automatic free transfer between subway and bus, or between buses. These transfers are good for up to 2 hours. *There are no transfers from subway to subway or to the bus route on which you started on Pay-Per-Ride MetroCard.* *Up to four people can ride together on a single Pay-Per-Ride MetroCard. There is no penalty wait time after each swipe, as with the Unlimited MetroCard.*	This MetroCard gives you several options to buy an unlimited number of subway and bus rides for a fixed price. They are: 1-Day Fun Pass – $8.25. Good until 3 a.m. the following day. 7-Day – $27.00. Good for unlimited rides until midnight on the 7th day. 14-Day – $51.50. Good for unlimited rides until midnight on the 14th day. 30-Day – $89.00. Good for unlimited rides until midnight on the 30th day. 7-Day Express Bus Plus – $45.00. Good for unlimited express bus, local bus, and subway rides until midnight on the 7th day. *Unlimited Ride MetroCard cannot be used again at the same station or same bus route until 18 minutes after each use.*

Online Travel Tools

If you're looking for detailed travel directions because you're not quite comfortable reading the subway and bus maps, or you're just into the details, we recommend the following sites.

Google Maps: http://maps.google.com
Trip Planner: http://tripplanner.mta.info
HopStop: http://www.hopstop.com

Getting Around the City

Manhattan streets are easy to navigate once you learn a few rules—like "downtown" means south and "uptown" means north. For the most part, streets are laid out as a grid. Numbered avenues run north-south and numbered streets run east-west. Fifth Avenue divides the city into East and West. Avenues with numbered names less than five are east of Fifth Avenue and those greater than five are west of Fifth Avenue.

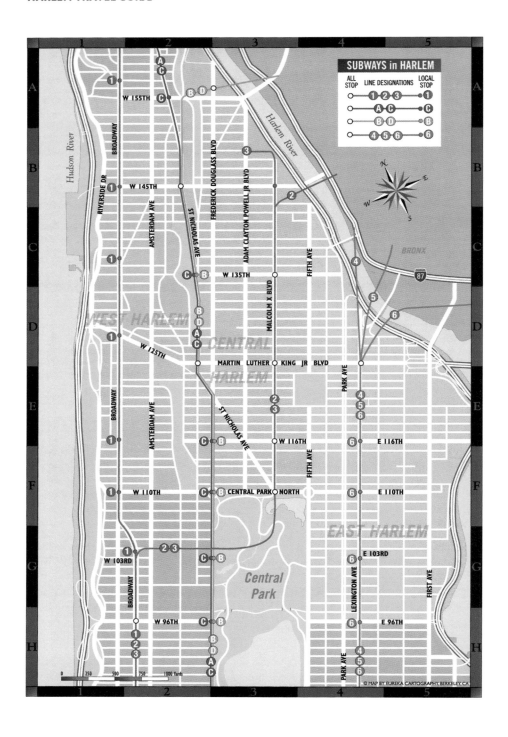

SUBWAYS in HARLEM

Renamed Streets

Harlem streets, like streets in other parts of New York City, have seen their share of renaming, and this can be a bit confusing for visitors.

Malcolm X/Lenox Ave. is **Sixth Ave.** The signage is there for both **Malcolm X Boulevard** and **Lenox Avenue**. The Avenue was renamed Lenox in 1887 after millionaire philanthropist and book-collector **James Lenox**, who donated his private collection as part of the founding material of the New York Public Library. In 1988, the street was again renamed, in honor of slain Black nationalist and human rights activist **Malcolm X**.

Adam Clayton Powell Blvd. is **Seventh Ave.** In 1974 it was renamed in honor of Harlem's first congressman, who was responsible for getting fair employment practices legislation passed, and who also was minister of the esteemed **Abyssinian Baptist Church**.

Frederick Douglass Blvd. is **Eighth Ave.** In 1977 it was renamed in honor of a man born into slavery, who rose to become a noted abolitionist, orator, editor, author, and statesman.

Martin Luther King Jr. Blvd. is the famous **125th Street**, the primary commercial corridor in Central Harlem. It was renamed in honor of the slain civil rights leader and Nobel Peace Prize winner.

Cathedral Parkway is 110th St. It was renamed, from Seventh Avenue to Riverside Dr., in 1891 in honor of **Cathedral Church of St. John the Divine**, which is located on Amsterdam Ave. between 110th and 112th Streets.

Key Transportation Locations in Manhattan

Pennsylvania Station, commonly known as Penn Station, is located at 33rd St. between Seventh and Eighth Avenues. A major commuter rail hub in midtown, the station serves commuters from Long Island and New Jersey as well as subway riders in New York City connecting with the 1, 2, 3, A, C, and E subway lines. It is also a major intercity rail station serviced by Amtrak. A number of businesses ranging from convenience stores to newsstands, quick-service food shops, and retailers call it home. What you'll find:

Amtrak Tel: (800) USA-RAIL, (800) 872-7245. Web: www.amtrak.com
Long Island Railroad Tel: (718) 217-LIRR. Web: www.mta.info/lirr/
New Jersey Transit Tel: (973) 275-5555. Web: www.njtransit.state.nj.us
Port Authority Trans-Hudson (PATH) Tel: (800) 234-PATH. Web: www.panynj.gov/path

QUICK FACTS/DID YOU KNOW:

» Penn Station is the busiest passenger transportation facility in the United States and the busiest train station in North America. It serves 600,000 passengers a day.
» Penn Station is the busiest Amtrak station in the United States. There were 4.3 million boarding in 2004.

The Port Authority Bus Terminal, located between Eighth and Ninth Avenues and 40th to 42nd Streets, serves approximately 55 million riders each year. The terminal is within walking distance of Times Square and the Theatre District. Close to three dozen bus lines operate from the Port Authority and the terminal connects with underground passageways to the A, C, E, N, Q, R, S, W, 1, 2, 3, and 7 trains. A number of businesses ranging from convenience stores to newsstands, quick-service food shops, and retailers call the terminal home.
Location: 625 Eighth Avenue
Automated bus information: (212) 564-8484 (Provides bus carrier telephone numbers only)
General Information: (212) 502-2200
Web: www.panynj.gov/commutingravel/bus/html/pa.html

Grand Central Terminal, simply called Grand Central or Grand Central Station by most New Yorkers, is located in midtown Manhattan at 42nd Street and Park Avenue. It serves commuters traveling on the Metro-North Railroad to Westchester, Putnam, and Dutchess counties in New York State, and Fairfield and New Haven counties in Connecticut. The Harlem line begins at Grand Central and ends in Dutchess County. The terminal also connects to the 4, 5, 6, and 7 subway lines. Aside from the tracks, Grand Central is home to restaurants, fast-food outlets, delis, bakeries, newsstands, a gourmet and fresh food market, and retail stores.
Location: 87 E. 42nd Street

Metro-North Railroad: Travel Information (800) METRO-INFO from New York City (212) 532-4900; outside New York City (800) 638-7646.
Web: www.mta.info/mnr

The Bryant Park locations are used by various bus services to the airports.
Bryant Park (1)—42nd St. and Sixth Ave., across the street from the W. R. Grace Building
Bryant Park (2)—42nd St. and Fifth Ave., across the street from the New York City Public Library (Newark)

Tip: Tickets should be purchased online for discounts or prior to departure to avoid additional fees.

Other bus services—the following bus services have gained popularity for their relatively inexpensive fares:
Megabus: www.megabus.com
BoltBus: www.boltbus.com
GotoBus: www.gotobus.com

GETTING INTO THE CITY FROM THE THREE MAJOR AIRPORTS

There are several options available when traveling to and from the three major airports. We've outlined some of the options available to you for coming into Manhattan. There are transportation counters at each airport for your convenience and safety. Please use uniformed dispatchers only.

	LaGuardia Airport	Newark Liberty International Airport	JFK International Airport
Public Transportation	**New York City's Metropolitan Transit Authority (MTA)** operates 24 hours a day. (718) 330-1234 Q33 bus from all terminals except the Marine Air Terminal to Jackson Heights in Queens, with connections to the E, F, R, V, and 7 subway lines. Coins or MetroCard required. Q47 bus from the Marine Air Terminal. Connects with E, F, R, V, and 7 subway lines. Coins or MetroCard required. M60 bus from all terminals to Manhattan, with connections to the N, W (both in Queens), 1, 2, 3, 4, 5, 6, A, B, C, and D subway lines and local bus lines. Coins or MetroCard required. Bus and Subway – $2.25	**AirTrain Newark** provides easy connections to and from NJ Transit and Amtrak through Newark Liberty. Tickets purchased from NJ Transit or Amtrak will include the $5.50 AirTrain fare. Children under 5 ride for free. 1-888-EWR-INFO When leaving the airport take AirTrain to the Airport Station. Once you've exited the AirTrain follow the signs to NJ Transit and purchase your tickets. You must have an Amtrak ticket before boarding Amtrak from Penn Station. Amtrak – $15.00 Penn Station in New York **New Jersey Transit** Take Bus 107 from the Port Authority to Bus 37. Tickets can be purchased at the Port Authority or on the bus. The buses accept bills and exact fare only. Bus 107 $5.50 & Bus 37 $1.70	**JFK's AirTrain** operates 24 hours a day. The AirTrain connects with Long Island Rail Road, subways, and local buses via Howard Beach and Jamaica Stations. 1-877-JFK-AIRTrain At Jamaica Station AirTrain connects with the E, J, and Z subway lines. At Howard Beach Station, AirTrain connects with the A subway line. AirTrain – $5.00 Subway – $2.25 From Penn Station take the LIRR to Jamaica Station. $12.00 (includes AirTrain fare)
Bus Service	**New York Airport Express** (718) 875-8200. Departure every 20 – 30 minutes. Port Authority, Grand Central Station, Penn Station, Bryant Park, and Midtown hotels between 31st and 60th Sts. Bus stop located at the Express Bus Stop at each airline terminal. Fare is $12.00. Provides bus service between LaGuardia and JFK Airports. Fare is $13.00.	**Newark Liberty Airport Express** (877) 8-NEWARK. Departure every 15 minutes. Port Authority, Grand Central Station, and Bryant Park. Bus stop located at the Express Bus Stop at each airline terminal. Fare is $12.00.	**New York Airport Express** (718) 875-8200. Departure every 20 – 30 minutes. Port Authority, Grand Central Station, Penn Station, Bryant Park, and Midtown hotels between 31st and 60th Sts. Bus stop located at the Express Bus Stop at each airline terminal. Fare is $15.00. Provides bus service between LaGuardia and JFK Airports. Fare is $13.00.

14

	LaGuardia Airport	Newark Liberty International Airport	JFK International Airport
Bus Service	Bus Services Web Sites and additional information: **New York Airport Express** 125 Park Ave. (Between 41st and 42nd Sts.). (718) 875-8200. http://www.nyairportservice.com. Discounted rates for students and senior citizens and can be purchased only at their office every day from 9:00 a.m. – 5:00 p.m. **Newark Liberty Airport Express** (877)-8-NEWARK. http://www.coachusa.com/olympia/ss.newarkairport.asp. Purchase tickets at area hotels.		
Taxi	$24.00 to $28.00	$50.00 to $75.00	$45.00 flat rate
	Note: Fares do not include tolls and tips. Please use a Uniformed Taxi Dispatcher.		
Van Service	The following companies provide shared door-to-door van service to the three airports. Prices vary. **Airlink New York** – Any location between Battery Park and 125th St. 1-800-498-9676. http://www.goairlinkshuttle.com **Super Shuttle Manhattan** – Any location between Battery Park and 227th St. (including all hotels). 1-800-258-3826. http://www.supershuttle.com **ETS Air Shuttle** – Any location in Manhattan. They also provide shuttle service between LaGuardia and JFK and between LaGuardia and Newark Airports. 718-221-8344. http://www.etsairshuttle.com		
Car Rentals	**Avis** – (800) 230-4898. www.avis.com **Budget** – (800) 527-0700. www.budget.com **Dollar Rent a Car** – (866) 434-2226. www.dollar.com **Enterprise** – (800) RENT-A-CAR. www.enterprise.com **Hertz** – (800) 654-3131. www.hertz.com **National Car Rental** – (800) CAR-RENTAL. www.nationalcar.com **Zip Car** – (617) 995-4306. www.zipcar.com		
Car Service	The following companies provide car service in Harlem. **Harlem Car Service** – (212) 663-8080 **Kennedy Car Service** – (212) 283-1111 **Premium Car Service** – (212) 694-2222 **Riverside Car Service** – (212) 923-1111 **Seaman Car Service** – (212) 304-1515		

TIP:

If you've had a truly delightful experience, or you've misplaced your belongings during your cab ride, you can call **311,** New York City's phone number for government information and non-emergency services. Outside of New York City, dial (212) NEW-YORK.

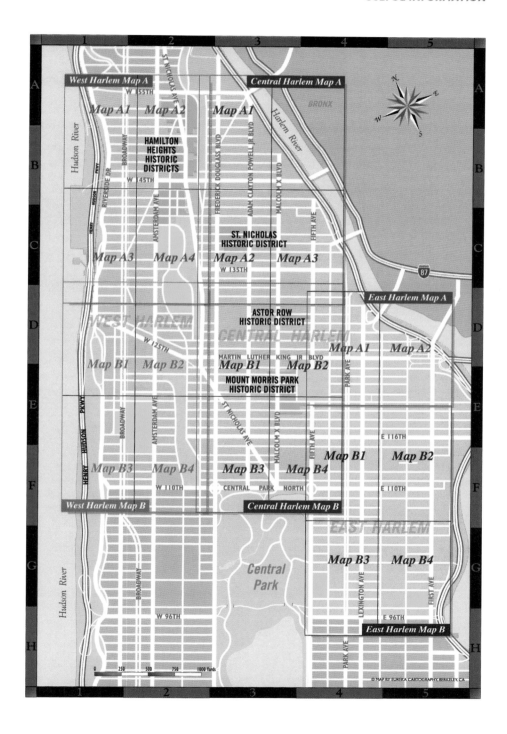

SPIRIT OF HARLEM MURAL

INTRODUCTION

Central Harlem occupies approximately 1.5 square miles of relatively flat land and is often referred to as "the Valley" by long-term residents. It stretches from Central Park North (110th Street) to the Harlem River (155th Street) between the west side of Fifth Avenue to the east side of St. Nicholas Avenue. It is in Central Harlem that African Americans initially settled, starting in 1904 east of Lenox Avenue. Many of the cultural and faith-based institutions and entertainment establishments here have for decades formed the central tourist destinations for visitors to Harlem. In the 1920s and 1930s, between Lenox and Seventh Avenues, over 125 entertainment places operated, including speakeasies, cellars, lounges, cafes, taverns, supper clubs, rib joints, theaters, dance halls, and bars and grills. Not only is Central Harlem associated with the **Harlem Renaissance** but it was also the center for political movements like **Marcus Garvey**'s **Universal Negro Improvement Association, A. Phillip Randolph**'s **Brotherhood of Sleeping Car Porters** (which was the first Black labor union formed in the United States), and **Malcolm X**'s **Organization of Afro American Unity**. Also, the phenomenon of "Star Evangelist" was introduced in Central Harlem when **Rev. George Wilson Becton** paved the way in the early 1930s. Soon after, evangelists **Father Divine** and **Daddy Grace** launched their national charismatic ministries that also fed, clothed, and housed those in need during the Depression. Daddy Grace's legacy survives in the **United House of Prayer for All People** (Frederick Douglass Blvd., between 124th and 125th Streets), which owns substantial commercial real estate on 125th Street and operates a popular cafeteria that serves up low-priced soul food meals upstairs above the church. Note that it's a treat to hear the **McCollough Sons of Thunder Brass Band** that replaced the church's shout bands.

ADAM CLAYTON POWELL, JR.
STATE OFFICE BUILDING

The major commercial strip for Central Harlem is 125th Street, which also runs through West Harlem to the Hudson River and through East Harlem, where it leads directly to the Triborough Bridge to New York City's two major airports—LaGuardia and Kennedy. It's on 125th Street that the **Adam Clayton Powell, Jr. State Office Building**, the tallest building in Harlem (which was designed by the African American architectural firm **Ifill, Johnson & Hanchard**), is located, on the site where **Lewis Michaux's National Memorial African Bookstore** was the epicenter of Black literary life and was the rallying point for political speeches, often delivered in front of the store by nationalist and Pan-African proponents. Today the building's plaza, which is also known as **African Square**, features a 12-foot bronze statue of New York City's first Black congressman, **Adam Clayton Powell Jr.**, which was created by Haitian American sculptor **Branly Cadet**. Various rallies are still held here, in-

cluding a massive spontaneous outpouring to memorialize pop music icon **Michael Jackson**, a welcome rally for former South African President **Nelson Mandela**, who visited the USA after he was released from Robben Island Prison, and the presidential election returns watch when **Barack Obama** won the nation's highest office. All through the summer, the 125th Street Business Improvement District sponsors free lunchtime and evening music and dance performances here. Don't miss the colorful artwork on the roll-down metal security gates of storefronts on 125th Street that were painted by **Franco Gaskin**, better known as "Franco the Great," who has been dressing up gates since the 1970s.

MICHAEL JACKSON MURAL
BY FRANCO GASKIN ON 125TH STREET

ADAM CLAYTON POWELL, JR. STATUE

HARRIET TUBMAN STATUE BY ALISON SAAR

In Central Harlem the street names change—Sixth Avenue (Malcolm X/Lenox), Seventh Avenue (Adam Clayton Powell Jr. Blvd.), Eighth Avenue (Frederick Douglass Blvd.), and 125th Street (Martin Luther King Jr. Blvd.), which can confuse visitors, but street name change is a tradition followed in every New York City neighborhood to memorialize significant members of the community. Memorial sites to see in Central Harlem include the statue of famous Underground Railroad conductor **Harriet Tubman** by African American artist **Alison Saar** at 122nd Street where Frederick Douglass Blvd. and St. Nicholas Avenue meet. It is the only statue of a Black woman erected in New York City. On June, 2010, a statue of **Frederick Douglass** by artist **Gabriel Koren** was unveiled at 110th St. and Frederick Douglass Blvd., inside Frederick Douglass Circle. The plaza features a complex colored paving pattern that alludes to traditional African American quilt designs by Harlem-based artist **Algernon Miller**. Enjoy the serenity of relaxing in **Malcolm X Plaza** (110th Street and Malcolm X/Lenox), which is landscaped as a replica of an Islamic garden, with benches, chairs, and tables amid trees, shrubs, and white roses, and will one day include a statue of Malcolm X and his wife, **Betty Shabazz**.

FREDERICK DOUGLASS STATUE BY GARIEL KOREN

CRAIG S. HARRIS

Currently Central Harlem is home to writers/poets **Quincy Troupe** and **Maya Angelou**, hip-hop music producer and Wu Tang Klan founder **Tru Master**, world-renowned jazz trombonist **Craig S. Harris**, choreographers **George Faison** (who is a Tony Award winner) and **Abdel Salaam** (co-founder of **Forces of Nature Dance Company**), the **Bill T. Jones/Arnie Zane Dance Company** administrative offices, actresses **Marcella Lowery** and **Billie Allen**, theater producer **Vy Higginsen**, interior designer **Sheila Bridges**, basketball legend **Kareem Abdul-Jabbar**, the office of **President Bill Clinton** at 55 W. 125th Street, and many other noted celebrities.

LANDMARK DISTRICTS

stor Row Historic District
Boundaries: Southside of W. 130th Street from Malcolm X/Lenox to Fifth Avenue.

Astor Row is a one-block area of row houses that are distinct for their wooden porches and front yards which are unique to New York. The smallest historic district in Harlem, this area was designated a landmark in 1981. The architect **Charles Buek** designed a tight row of twenty-eight semi-detached three-story brick dwellings with ample front gardens on the south side of W. 130th Street as rental properties for the **William Waldorf Astor** estate. Completed in three campaigns from 1880 to 1883, these moderately Italianate structures introduced striking broad front porches. Instead of the usual wooden, cast-iron, and galvanized-tin cornices, their friezes and cornices were made of brick. In 1992, the New York Landmark's Conservancy, in association with the Landmarks Preservation Commission and the Abyssinian Development Corporation, began an ongoing project to reverse serious deterioration and restored the porches of these extraordinary houses and developed some into limited-equity cooperatives for moderate-income families. The houses on the north side of the street are large, attractive brownstones of a more common design. In 1932, Father Divine, leader of Father Divine's **International Peace Mission Movement**, lived on the north side of Astor Row.

ount Morris Park Historic District
Boundaries: North between W. 118th Street to W. 124th Street and west from Mt. Morris Park West and Fifth Avenue to the east side of Malcolm X/Lenox.

This historic district was designated a landmark in 1971, primarily because of the almost unaltered streetscapes of late nineteenth-century and early twentieth-century brownstone townhouses interspersed with institutions representing the eclectic styles of the Gilded Age. Almost every street in the district contains houses designed in the neo-Grec, Romanesque Revival, neo-Renaissance, and Queen Anne styles, designed primarily by architects who specialized in the creation of speculative row houses. Initial development of the area is tied to Mount Morris Park, a village green for which the neighborhood was named and one of the oldest parks in Manhattan. The park was renamed Marcus Garvey in 1973 to honor Black nationalist leader Marcus Garvey who

advocated Black self-determination. The neighborhood was built up by affluent white Protestant families following the extension of rapid transit in 1880
on Park Avenue and Lenox Avenue in the early 1900s. Later, Irish Tammany
Hall bosses and affluent Western European Jews moved to the area. Next,
less affluent Eastern European Jews moved from the Lower East Side to the
area prior to African Americans moving in around 1930. Notable sites are
"Doctor's Row," 4–16 W. 122nd Street east of Malcolm X/Lenox. These
brownstone-fronted and intricately carved facades were developed by real
estate tycoon **Henry Morgenthau** and were designed by **William
Tuthill**, who two years later designed Carnegie Hall. On the uptown side
of the street Nos. 7 through 19 were designed by **Cleverdon & Putzel**,
the most prolific architectural firm in the Mount Morris area. Some of the
houses on this side of the block contain stoops that have multiple turns and
massive newel posts. A larger area, encompassing sixteen blocks, is listed
on the National Register of Historic Places and extends the boundaries of
the area over to the east side of Adam Clayton Powell Blvd. between 118th and 124th Streets. Of
note are houses at 133 through 143 W. 122nd Street, between Malcolm X/Lenox and Adam Clayton Powell Blvd., which were designed by **Francis Kimball**. Noted for his theater designs, he
designed the Rhinelander mansion on Madison Ave. and was one of the first architects to extensively
employ terra-cotta for ornamental detail, which allowed the creation of complex facade decoration at
a modest cost. Some notable early residents of this area include famed composer of Broadway musicals
Richard Rodgers (3 W. 120th Street) and his lyricist partner **Lorenz Hart** (59 W. 119th Street).
Also, the last **CCC Studio** of acclaimed photographer **James VanDerZee** is located at 272 Lenox
Avenue. Notice that a portion of the studio's signage was uncovered when the building was renovated
in 2005.

Saint Nicholas Historic District

Boundaries: North between W. 138th Street to W. 139th Street between Adam Clayton
Powell Blvd. and Frederick Douglass Blvd.

Designated a landmark in 1967, this
historic district is home to the famous
Striver's Row, a name which refer-
ences many of the aspirations of African Americans who purchased these
homes in the 1920s. Created by developer **David King Jr.**, in 1891, the
four block fronts each have a unified
streetscape which is an outstanding
example of late nineteenth-century
urban design. Three distinguished architectural firms were hired to design
the 146 row houses and three apartment buildings. On the south side of
138th Street, **James Lloyd Brown**
designed the red brick Colonial Revival/Georgian–inspired houses with white limestone and
terra-cotta trim and typical brownstone stoops. **Bruce Price** was designer of the yellow
brick Colonial Revival houses with shorter stoops on the north side of 138th Street and the
south side of 139th Street. **McKim, Mead & White** partner **Stanford White** designed the
Italian Renaissance–inspired row in dark ochre-colored brick with brownstone and terra-cotta
trim that features the American basement entrance on the north side of 139th Street. What is unique about
these two blocks is that service alleys, which are extremely rare features in New York, run behind each row.

Also notice the sign mid-block on 138th Street that advises "Private road, walk your horses" etched in a stone column to the service road. Due to an economic depression, few of these houses sold in 1895 and the mortgagor, the Equitable Life Assurance Company, foreclosed on the properties. They remained empty until 1919–20 when they were sold to African Americans. Many were home to prominent people, including: 138th Street—surgeon **Louis T. Wright** (No.218), who fought to practice in **Harlem Hospital** and later became its administrator; composer, and mentor to many jazz musicians, **Will Marion Cook** (No. 221); singer and songwriter **Eubie Blake** (No. 236), who created *Shuffle Along* on Broadway; **Harry Pace** (No. 257), the founder of Black Swan Record Company, which was a pioneer in recording African American singers and musicians; and **Alpha Phi Alpha House** (No. 203), the oldest African American fraternity in the country, founded at Cornell University in 1905, with the New York chapter organized in 1908. 139th Street—architect **Vertner Tandy** (No. 221), musician and "Father of the Blues" **W. C. Handy** (No. 232), bandleader **Fletcher Henderson** (No. 228), and boxer **Harry Wills** (No. 245). Most houses, however, were owned by hardworking people striving to survive.

HISTORIC SITES NOT TO MISS

3 69ᵀᴴ Regiment Armory

2360 Fifth Ave., between 142ⁿᵈ and 143ʳᵈ Sts. (212) 281-9474.
http://369historicalsociety.org. 369ᵗʰ Historical Society, (212) 926-6401 Armory.
Museum store Mon–Fri 10am–4pm, Sat–Sun by appointment. Bus—M1, M7, M102. Subway—3 to 145ᵗʰ St.

369TH REGIMENT ARMORY

The 369ᵗʰ Regiment Armory, one of the last armories erected in New York City, combines both medieval motifs common to armory designs and Art Deco influences. The drill shed, which was designed by **Tachau & Vought**, was built between 1921–24. The massive administration building, which was designed by **Van Wart & Wein**, was erected between 1930–33. The complex, which was designated a landmark in 1985, is constructed of brick and the administration building embellished with prominent terra-cotta parapets. The Armory is the home of the renowned **Harlem Hellfighters**, the first African American regiment to fight in World War I, but with the French Army because white American soldiers did not want to fight next to Blacks. Their bravery won them France's highest honor, the Croix de Guerre with silver star, for the taking of Séchault in Northern France. Upon returning home, the 369ᵗʰ Regiment received a heroes' parade marching from the Washington Square Park Arch to Harlem, but received no recognition from the U.S. government. The 369ᵗʰ Historical Society was founded in 1960 to organize and showcase the merits of African Americans who served in the U.S. military from World War I to the present through its collection of hundreds of photographs and dozens of artifacts, papers, and other items, including bugles from the 369ᵗʰ Regimental Band led by **James Reese Europe**, which introduced jazz to Europe, and a copy of the 1920 book *From Harlem to the Rhine: The Story of New York's Colored Volunteers*, which gives a chronology of the 369ᵗʰ Infantry. In the 369ᵗʰ Hall of Fame stands a replica of the monument that was dedicated in memory of the 369ᵗʰ Harlem Hellfighters and erected in Séchault, France, in 1997. Across the street from the Armory stands a memorial to the Harlem Hellfighters—a black granite obelisk replica of the one erected in France. Unveiled on September 29, 2006, the 88ᵗʰ anniversary of that battle, the obelisk is 12 feet high and features gilded inscriptions, the 369ᵗʰ's crest, and its coiled rattlesnake insignia. The Armory also houses the Harlem Tennis Center, where aspiring U.S. Open players hone their skills on professional courts.

4 West 123ʳᵈ St.

Between Mt. Morris Park West and Malcolm X/Lenox. Bus—M1, M2, M7, M60, M100, M101, M102, BX15. Subway—2, 3 to 125ᵗʰ St.

This lovely house was built in 1882 as part of a group, Nos. 2 through 26. Located in the Mount Morris Park Historic District, this house was designed by **Charles Baxter** in the neo-Grec mode. By the end of 1870, both the style, characterized by incised linear decoration and abstracted neo-Classical ornamentation, as well as the facade's brownstone cladding, was considered old-fashioned by more innovative designers. This fact might be what caused the original owners to hire **Edgar K. Bourne** to "dress up" the front in 1885. An elaborate cast-iron fence and gate and a stamped, galvanized tin oriel window at the second story were added. The best alterations by far are the mahogany and beveled glass storm door, with an elegant arcade above a bull's-eye window. Notice the mounting block and hitching post with the number of the house carved on it in the entryway to the garden level. The mounting block originally was located at the curb to allow ladies to alight from high carriages onto its step. Of course, the horses were hitched to the post. Another surviving mounting block can be found at **104 W. 121ˢᵗ Street** in the garden area entryway. The block is carved in imitation of a tufted cushion.

Alhambra Ballroom

2110 Adam Clayton Powell Blvd., at 126ᵗʰ St. (212) 222-6940 or 6941. www.alhambraballroom.net. Bus—M2, M7, M60, M100, M101, M102, BX15. Subway—A, B, C, D, 2, 3, to 125ᵗʰ St.

ALHAMBRA BALLROOM

Most nightclubs that were popular during the Harlem Renaissance have been demolished and only a few remain standing. The Alhambra stood empty for decades after it closed in the austere 1960s. It was restored in 2003 and contains a great deal of its original beauty, like its overhanging balcony, bandstand and stage, and crystal chandeliers. Now a special events venue, the structure was originally built as a vaudeville house in 1905 and designed by movie theater architect **John B. McElfatrick**. When the ballroom opened in the penthouse in 1926, it was an architectural jewel. It was generally occupied by whites and Blacks on different nights, unlike other clubs that catered exclusively to a white clientele. It played host to legendary performers such as **Bessie Smith**, **Jelly Roll Morton**, and **Frank Manning**, who at age thirteen used to dance the Lindy Hop here before eventually graduating to the Savoy. **Billie Holiday** headlined here in the 1930s. Later, the Alhambra, under the management of RKO Pictures, Inc., offered a three-in-one show: a movie, a musical revue (cabaret), and a dramatic sketch.

Graham Court

1927 Adam Clayton Powell Blvd., between 116ᵗʰ and 117ᵗʰ Sts. Bus—M2, M7, M116. Subway—B, C, 2, 3 to 116ᵗʰ St.

GRAHAM COURT

Graham Court, which was designated a landmark in 1984, was commissioned by William Waldorf Astor and is one of New York's grandest courtyard apartment houses. Designed by **Clinton & Russell** right before they undertook the more imposing Apthorp on 79ᵗʰ and Broadway, this building was completed in 1899–1901. It features a landscaped courtyard entered through an arch that is clad in Guastavino tile. Most apartments contain six to ten rooms—some having a music room and a maid's room and grand fireplace mantles, proving intent for the affluent families that first occupied them. The apartments are now home to African American writers and artists and have served as a popular movie location for such films as *Jungle Fever* and *New Jack City*.

Theresa Hotel

2090 Adam Clayton Powell Blvd., between 124th and 125th Sts. Bus—M2, M7, M60, M100, M101, M102, BX15. Subway—A, B, C, D, 2, 3 to 125th St.

THERESA HOTEL

The Theresa Hotel, known later as the *Waldorf of Harlem*, opened in 1913 to a white-only clientele. Designed by the architectural firm **George & Edward Blum**, the white brick and terra-cotta facade was adorned with distinctive geometric ornamentation. It was designated a landmark in 1993. The Theresa remained segregated until 1940, when it became the favorite accommodation for Harlem sports and entertainment personalities such as boxing champions **Joe Louis** and **Sugar Ray Robinson**, crooner heartthrob **Billie Eckstein**, dancer and actor **Bill "Bojangles" Robinson**, comedian **Jackie "Moms" Mabley**, and **Grace Nail Johnson**, widow of writer, civil rights activist, and statesman **James Weldon Johnson**. **U.S. Congressman Charles B. Rangel** at one time was a desk clerk at the hotel. **Charlie "Yard Bird" Parker** performed at the rooftop ballroom at campaign benefits for Harlem Communist Party leader **Benjamin Davis**, who served as New York City Councilman from 1943 to 1947. And every year the Communist Party USA held its national convention at the Theresa. This was the childhood home of **Ron Brown**, whose father, **William Harmon Brown**, was the second manager of the hotel when it desegregated. Ron Brown later became chairman of the Democratic National Committee and was Secretary of Commerce during the Clinton Administration. The hotel, which is now an office tower, served as the office space for Malcolm X after he left the **Nation of Islam** and formed the Organization of Afro American Unity. It also contained the offices of A. Phillip Randolph's 1963 March on Washington. Cuban leader **Fidel Castro**, while attending the UN General Assembly, moved to the Theresa in 1960 after he was insulted at a midtown hotel.

Tree of Hope Marker

Adam Clayton Powell Blvd., between 131st and 132nd Sts. Bus—M2, M7, M10, M102, BX33. Subway—B, C, 2, 3 to 135th St.

The legend and tradition of the Tree of Hope, which stood between the famous **Harlem Lafayette Theatre** (now a church) and **Connie's Inn** (now a store), began when aspiring actors, dancers, and performers who gathered there believed the tree brought good luck to those who stood beneath its branches. Seventh Avenue was then known as the *Boulevard of Dreams*. The Lafayette was the first New York Theatre to integrate, as early as 1912, and hosted the history-making **Orson Welles'** production of Shakespeare's *Macbeth* or the *Voodoo Macbeth* in the 1930s. Connie's Inn was the **Cotton Club's** only real competition and hosted great bands led by **Luckey Roberts** (who headed the house band), **Louis "Satchmo" Armstrong**, and **Fats Waller**. Around the time that the **Apollo Theater** first opened to Blacks in 1934, the City of New York widened Seventh Avenue and the majestic elms that lined the boulevard were removed, including the Tree of Hope. The tree was cut up and pieces were sold as good-luck souvenirs. Apollo Amateur Night host **Ralph Cooper Sr.** purchased a piece of the tree that measured 18 inches across and was about a foot high. He had it sanded and shellacked and mounted it on an iconic column. The column pedestal was placed stage right, just outside the curtain so the audiences could see it. Since then, every single performer who has appeared on **Apollo Amateur Night** has touched that log for good luck. In 1972 an impressive sculpture by the artist **Algernon Miller** was erected as a marker where the tree once stood.

YMCA, Harlem Branch
180 and 181 W. 135th St., between Adam Clayton Powell Blvd. and Malcolm X/Lenox.
(212) 912-2100. Bus—M2, M7, M102, BX33. Subway—B, C, 2, 3 to 135th St.

The first of two Harlem Y buildings opened in 1919 at 181 W. 135th Street on the north side of the street. Now the **Jackie Robinson Youth Center**, the Italian Renaissance–style building was designed by **John F. Jackson**. To encourage youth participation in sports, **Jackie Robinson** and **Roy Campanella** of the Brooklyn Dodgers coached boys here in athletics and calisthenics in 1948. Eventually outgrowing the space, a new monumental Colonial Revival structure was erected across the street at 180 W. 135th Street in 1932. This structure was designed by **James C. Mackenzie, Jr.**, and was listed on the National Register of Historic Places in 1976. It received landmark designation in 1998. This structure houses a hotel where many migrants stayed upon their arrival to New York, including writers **Claude McKay** (for whom the residence is named), **Langston Hughes**, and **Ralph Ellison**. The Harlem YMCA also served as a well-respected showcase for local talent. The stage of the **"Little Theatre,"** which still exists, was the site of **Cicely Tyson's** professional acting debut. Other performers included **James Earl Jones, Isabel Sanford, Esther Rolle, Alvin Ailey, Sidney Poitier, Eartha Kitt, Roscoe Lee Brown**, and **Danny Glover**. *Evolution of the Negro Dance*, an **Aaron Douglass** mural commissioned in 1933 by the WPA, is still housed here.

MUSEUMS

G enesis II Museum of International Black Culture
2376 Adam Clayton Powell Blvd., at 139th St. (212) 690-3800. Suggested Admission:
Adults $5.50, Children under 12 $3. Thu–Sun 11am–7pm. Bus—M2, M7, M10, M102.
Subway—B, C, 2, 3 to 135th St.

Genesis II Museum of International Black Culture was founded in 1972 by **Andi Owens**, who is also the curator. Over the years, it has been a museum-in-residence at **The City College of New York** and was a Museum Resource Center for Harlem's Community School Board #5 and P.S. 125. Since 2001, when it moved to its permanent space, it has quietly mounted important exhibitions on works by African, African American, African-Caribbean, and Afro-Latin artists. There are also five visual presentations which are historical in nature, including: Black Presence in the era of the American Revolution 1700–1800; Malcolm X: The Man and His Times; **The Duke Ellington Orchestra**; Africa Unadorned: A Celebration of the Quiet and Serene Strength of African Women; and African Americans and the Constitution: The Black Presence in America. The museum houses multiple galleries, including the African Sculpture Court, and the Egyptian and Haitian Galleries.

M useum of African American Cinema, Inc.
163 W. 125th St., Ste. 903, between Adam Clayton Powell Blvd. and Malcolm X/
Lenox. (212) 749-5298. www.moaac.org. Mon–Fri 9am–6pm. Wheelchair accessible.
Bus—M2, M3, M7, M10, M60, M100, M101, M102, BX15. Subway—A, B, C, D, 2, 3 to 125th St.

The Museum of African American Cinema, Inc. was founded to collect, preserve, and interpret objects related to the African American presence in cinema, theatre, and television, and to research, document, and disseminate this information. This is being achieved by assembling, preserving, and interpreting through research, exhibits, workshops, publications, and public screenings. Currently the collection has over 35,000 items, which includes films, videos, posters, and other items, and it is continuously growing. You can purchase movies, posters, and other items online or at the museum.

S tudio Museum in Harlem
144 W. 125th St., between Adam Clayton Powell Blvd. and Malcolm X/Lenox. (212) 864-
4500. www.studiomuseum.org. Suggested Admission: Adults $7, Students and Seniors
$3, Members and Children under 12 Free, Admission Free on Target Free Sundays 12pm–6pm.
Wed–Fri 12pm–6pm, Sat 10am–6pm, and Sun 12pm–6pm. Guided tours and a gift shop.
Wheelchair accessible. Bus—M2, M3, M7, M10, M60, M100, M101, M102, BX15. Subway—A, B,
C, D, 2, 3 to 125th St.

Founded in 1968, the Studio Museum of Harlem was the first museum in the United Stated that was totally dedicated to Black art. With 60,000 square feet of space, the museum has become a major hub for the nineteenth-, twentieth- and twenty-first-century works of famous Black artists. The museum's permanent collection contains over 1,800 works of art, including drawings, pastels, prints, photographs, mixed-media works, and installations from artists representing the United States, the Caribbean, the Americas, and Africa. Among its Harlem Renaissance artists the museum features an extensive archive of the work of photographer James VanDerZee, the quintessential chronicler of the Harlem community from 1906 to 1983. The museum continuously sponsors workshops, readings, concerts, lectures, symposia, seminars, a museum/school cooperative program, community outreach lectures, and film screenings.

Canvas Paper and Stone

2611 Frederick Douglass Blvd., Studio 2N, between 139th and 140th Sts. (212) 694-1747. www.canvaspaperandstone.com. By appointment. Bus—M2, M3, M10. Subway—B, C to 135th St.

Located in the Bradhurst Condominiums along with an online presence, Canvas Paper and Stone Gallery features contemporary fine art created by emerging and mid-career artists of color in all media. Artwork prices range from $20 to over $5,000—there is something for everybody. Online purchases can be made, frames selected, and framed artwork delivered.

Casa Frela Gallery

47 W. 119th St., between Malcolm X/Lenox and Fifth Ave. (212) 722-8577. www.casafrela.com. Mon–Sat 12pm–4pm. Bus—M1, M7, M102, M116. Subway—2, 3 to 116th St.

Casa Frela Gallery is committed to the community of Harlem and the enrichment of cultural life throughout New York City. The gallery creates and produces programs that connect the inhabitants of Harlem with local and international art, music, and culture. Casa Frela also runs programs that trace local culture and history through written research and the oral stories of lifelong residents. Through these activities and programs, the gallery hopes to elevate the cultural standard of living and provide a comfortable, social place to experience art and music.

Connections Fine Arts Gallery

3 Mt. Morris Park West, Suite A, between 120th and 121st Sts. (347) 439-1322. www.connectionsconsultingcompany.com. By Appointment. Bus—M1, M7, M102. Subway—2, 3 to 116th St.

Located in a restored brownstone garden condominium across from Marcus Garvey Park, Connections Fine Art Gallery features the work of world-renowned artist and spiritual healer, **Zaccheus Oloruntoba** of Nigeria, who produces silk tapestries on canvas. Also on exhibit are Kilims from the Sahara, flat tapestry-woven carpets and rugs skillfully handwoven by the Berbers of northern Morocco.

Gadson Gallery

225 W. 134th St., between Frederick Douglass and Adam Clayton Powell Blvds. (212) 694-0262. www.gadsongallery.blogspot.com. By appointment. Bus—M2, M10, BX33. Subway—B, C to 135th St.

Quilt and craft artist **Laura R. Gadson** lives, works, and exhibits her work in her Harlem brownstone. Affiliated with several arts organizations, she is a member of the Harlem Girls Quilt Circle, National Quilt Association, and Harlem Arts Alliance, and she works with Harlem Needle Arts.

Gallery M

Weston United Community Renewal, Inc., 123 W. 135th St., between Adam Clayton Powell Blvd. and Malcolm X/Lenox. (212) 234-4106. www.westonunited.org/retail.html. Tue, Wed, Fri, Sat, 12pm–6pm, and Thu 12pm–8pm. Bus—M2, M7, M102, BX33. Subway—2, 3 to 135th St.

Gallery M, a contemporary fine arts gallery, exhibits art by emerging and established African American and Latino artists. Past exhibitions have included the works of A. A. Bronson, John Bankston, Larry Clark, Ellen Gallagher, David Hammons, Adrian Piper, Howardena Pindell, Malick Sidibe, Kara Walker, Andy Warhol, and Carrie Mae Weems. Owned by Weston United, a not-for-profit social services organization, once a year the gallery presents works by artists who are mentally challenged.

Haile King Rubie

124 W. 121st St., between Adam Clayton Powell Blvd. and Malcolm X/Lenox. (646) 261-5334. www.hailesimo.org. By appointment. Bus—M2, M7, M102. Subway—2, 3 to 125th St.

Haile King Rubie, twenty years old, has Down syndrome and often functions on the level of a ten-year-old. But give him brushes, canvas, and vibrant paints and he transforms into an accomplished artist. Painting since the age of six, Haile has created a world of art with no formal training, in his studio located in his parents' brownstone home. His work has been exhibited at various galleries in New York City.

Harlem Arts Salon

1925 Adam Clayton Powell Blvd., at 116th St. (212) 749-7771. www.harlemartssalon.com. By appointment. Bus—M2, M7, M10, M102, M116. Subway—2, 3, B, C to 116th St.

Harlem Arts Salon provides an exclusively private setting in a tastefully and eclectically furnished apartment in the landmark Graham Court, where cultural soirees reminiscent of Harlem Renaissance gatherings are held. Book readings and signings, art exhibitions, and salon talks with distinguished artists from the African Diaspora usually end with a fabulous supper. These intimate events are hosted by **Margaret Porter Troupe**, former owner and director of Porter Troupe Gallery in San Diego, California. Admittance is by invitation or appointment only. To find out about upcoming events, please email to join the mailing list.

Heath Gallery

24 W. 120th St., between Malcolm X/Lenox and Fifth Ave. (212) 427-0057. http://heathgallery.squarespace.com. By appointment. Bus—M1, M7, M102. Subway—2, 3 to 116th St.

The Heath Gallery, co-founded by artist **Thomas Heath**, who has exhibited his works in New York for over seventeen years, is located in his brownstone townhouse in the Mount Morris Park Historic District. Works by established and emerging contemporary painters, sculptors, photographers, textile, and mixed-media artists fill the space.

ndasa Fine Art Gallery

11 W. 121st St., between Malcolm X/Lenox and Fifth Ave. (212) 289-5032. www.indasafineart.com. By appointment. Bus—M1, M2, M7, M102. Subway—2, 3 to 116th St.

Indasa offers its clients an opportunity to collect contemporary to abstract art, and intuitive to folk art. Among the gallery features are serigraphs, giclees, and limited/open edition artworks by local and national artists. Principals of Indasa are the co-founders of **Harlem Open Artist Studio Tour, HOAST.**

enaissance Fine Art

2075 Adam Clayton Powell Blvd., at 124th St. (212) 866-1660. www. therfagallery.com. Wed–Sat 11am–7pm. Bus—M2, M7, M10, M60, M100, M101, M102, BX15. Subway—A, B, C, D, 2, 3 to 125th St.

One of the newest art galleries to open in Harlem, Renaissance Fine Art, which conjures up the Harlem Renaissance of the past while embracing the New Harlem Renaissance, is fast becoming the "in" gathering place for community artists and creative visionaries to explore artistic inspirations of the past and present. The gallery displays the works of contemporary painters, sculptors, and photographers, specializing in the works of artists from the Diaspora. To support other artistic expressions, the gallery provides a venue for film screenings, book signings, educational workshops, and seminars. The gallery is also available for event and meeting rental.

THEATERS AND CULTURAL INSTITUTIONS

Schomburg Center for Research in Black Culture
515 Malcolm X Blvd., at 135th St. (212) 491-2200. www.nypl.org/research/sc/sc.html. Mon–Wed 12pm–8pm, Thu and Fri 11am–6pm, Sat 10am–5pm. Free tours and gift shop. Wheelchair accessible. Bus—M2, M7, M102, BX33. Subway—2, 3 to 135th St.

One of the world's leading research libraries, the Schomburg Center for Research in Black Culture is devoted to collecting and preserving materials on the global experiences of people of African descent. The center contains over ten million holdings and provides services and programs for users worldwide. The collection is named for **Arturo Alfonso Schomburg** (1874–1938), a scholar and bibliophile whose collection provides the backbone for the center's holdings. After coming to New York from Puerto Rico in 1891, Schomburg began amassing items that documented the history and culture of Blacks from around the world. This extensive collection was purchased in 1926 by the New York Public Library with funds from the Carnegie Corporation for the newly formed Division of Negro Literature, History and Prints that was housed in the 135th Street Branch of the Library. Schomburg served as curator of the division from 1932 until his death in 1938. Renamed in his honor in 1940, it was then designated one of the research libraries of the New York Public Library.

There are two exhibition spaces at the Schomburg, and a wide range of educational and cultural programs—including concerts, film screenings, panel discussions, performances, forums, and staged readings—are presented on a year-round basis in the renowned Langston Hughes Auditorium. A wonderful jazz series is presented annually in honor of Women's History Month.

The ashes of Langston Hughes (1902–1967), a celebrated Harlem Renaissance writer who immortalized Harlem and its people in his work, are interred beneath a floor medallion in the middle of the lobby leading to the auditorium named after him. The terrazzo floor plan, an African cosmogram titled *Rivers,* was designed by noted artist **Houston Conwill** in collaboration with writer **Estella Conwill Majozo** and architect **Joseph DePace**. The title is taken from Hughes' popular poem, "The Negro Speaks of Rivers."

AMC Magic Johnson Harlem 9 Theater
2309 Frederick Douglass Blvd., at 124th St. (212) 665-6923. Wheelchair accessible. Bus—M2, M3, M7, M10, M60, M100, M101, M102, BX15. Subway—A, B, C, D, 2, 3 to 125th St.

In June 2001, the Magic Johnson Harlem 9 Theater opened its 60,000-square-foot state-of-the-art movie theater, with nine screens and 2,000 seats for visitors to enjoy first-run releases of the hottest movies. The movie theater was developed by Johnson Development Corporation, the business holding company of the famed former professional basketball player/entrepreneur **Magic Johnson**.

Apollo Theater

253 W. 125th St., between Frederick Douglass and Adam Clayton Powell Blvds. (212) 531-5300. www.apollotheater.org. Box Office Hours: Mon and Tue 10am–6pm, Wed 10am–8:30pm, Thu and Fri 10am–6pm, Sat 10am–5pm. Historical tours and gift shop. Wheelchair accessible. Bus—M2, M3, M7, M10, M60, M100, M101, M102, BX15. Subway—A, B, C, D, 2, 3 to 125th St.

Undoubtedly the most celebrated of Harlem's landmarks, the Apollo Theater captures the imagination of every visitor. Built in 1914, the **"Hurtig and Seamon's New Burlesque Theatre"** did not allow African Americans in its audience. In 1934, the theater was sold to **Frank Schiffman** and **Leo Brecher**, who renamed the hall the **125th Street Apollo** and the rest, as they say, is history. Apollo Amateur Night remains to this day a venue in which amateur performers grace the stage every Wednesday night in hopes of launching a successful career. Among the Apollo's success stories are some of the entertainment industry's most influential and legendary artists, including jazz singers **Ella Fitzgerald**, **Sarah Vaughan**, and **Billie Holiday**; the King of Soul, **James Brown**; R&B singers **Jackie Wilson** and **Luther Vandross**; and hip-hop artists **Lauryn Hill** and **Blu Cantrell**, to name a few.

Dwyer Cultural Center

258 St. Nicholas Ave., at 123rd St., (212) 549-1854. www.dwyercc.org. Mon–Wed 10am–5pm, Sat 1pm–5pm. Wheelchair accessible. Bus—M2, M3, M7, M10, M60, M100, M101, M102, BX15. Subway—A, B, C, D, 2, 3 to 125th St.

Opened in June 2009, the Dwyer Cultural Center is located in a 7,000-square-foot state-of-the-art multimedia facility devoted to the culture, traditions, and history of Harlem. The Dwyer Cultural Center offers live theater, music, and dance, documentary and independent film screenings, conferences, panels, and symposia, educational and community workshops, and guided tours.

Faison Firehouse Theatre

Six Hancock Place, at 124th St., between Morningside and Manhattan Aves. (212) 531-3185. www.faisonfirehouse.org. Bus—M2, M3, M7, M10, M60, M100, M101, M102, BX15. Subway—A, B, C, D to 125th St.

A vintage firehouse was converted into the Faison Firehouse, a state-of-the-art performance space founded by Tony Award–winning director/choreographer George Faison. The Firehouse is home to the **American Performing Arts Collaborative (APAC)**, a not-for-profit organization organized in 1997 to develop theatrical, educational, and entertainment events in Harlem. APAC developed and nurtures the Respect Project, which is made up of primarily high school youth who are encouraged to transcend their environments through the performing arts.

IMPACT Repertory Theatre

253 W. 138th St., Ste. 100, between Frederick Douglass and Adam Clayton Powell Blvds. (212) 926-4516. www.impactreptheatre.org. Bus—M2, M10. Subway—B, C, 2, 3 to 135th St.

The dynamic IMPACT Repertory Theatre is a not-for-profit performing arts youth development organization that trains and empowers young people ages twelve to nineteen. This is accomplished in a nurturing and challenging environment. In addition to benefiting from performance opportunities, its members receive instruction in arts and leadership, participate in community service activities, and are tutored and mentored. In 2008, IMPACT was nominated for an Oscar for the song "Raise It Up," which is featured on the Grammy-nominated soundtrack for the film *August Rush*. All the material produced by IMPACT is developed by IMPACT members, through creative workshops where the kids transform their daily experiences into song, spoken word, short stories, and performance pieces. IMPACT is their reality, communicated through creativity.

Jazzmobile

154 W. 127th St., 2nd Fl., between Adam Clayton Powell and Malcolm X/Lenox. (212) 866-4900. www.jazzmobile.org. Bus—M2, M3, M7, M10, M60, M100, M101, M102, BX15. Subway—A, B, C, D, 2, 3 to 125th St.

ARTURO O'FARRILL JAMS AT JAZZMOBILE/
CENTRAL PARK CONSERVANCY CONCERT

Founded in 1964 by the legendary jazz pianist and scholar **Dr. William "Billy" Taylor**, Jazzmobile provides free outdoor summer concerts in New York City and its outlying areas. Its mission is to bring "America's classical music"—jazz—to the largest possible audience. During the months of July and August, the Jazzmobile mobile cart winds through the streets and parks of Harlem providing free performances by some of the most respected jazz recording artists and emerging talents. To experience the true flavor of Harlem, start with a Jazzmobile performance every Wednesday at **Grant's Tomb** (122nd and Riverside Dr.) and every Friday at the **Marcus Garvey Park Amphitheater** (Mt. Morris Park West at 122nd St., behind **Pelham Fritz Recreation Center**) at 7pm.

LonGar Ebony Ensemble

119 W. 119th St., between Adam Clayton Powell Blvd. and Malcolm X/Lenox (212) 749-5500. longarebonyensemble@hotmail.com. Bus—M7, M102, M116. Subway—2, 3 to 116th St.

Harlem's own LonGar Ebony Ensemble provides opportunities for classically trained musicians to increase their public exposure and to create performance events that showcase classical works by African American composers. The organization was founded by a family of classically trained musicians, including soprano **Roberta Long**, who has made numerous appearances at concert halls and on Broadway, and her daughters: violist **Crystal Garner**, a Fulbright scholar who is a member of the American Symphony Orchestra, and percussionist/timpanist **Yvonne Garner**, who has performed with many celebrity orchestral musicians and artists. LonGar also sponsors chamber and symphonic orchestral concerts, music festivals, and other events that showcase chamber ensembles, string quartets, duos, and soloists. In addition, the organization serves as a performance booking clearinghouse for African American classical music artists. Email to get a performance schedule.

Mama Foundation for the Arts

149 W. 126th St., between Adam Clayton Powell and Malcolm X/Lenox. (212) 280-1045. www.mamafoundation.org. Bus—M2, M3, M7, M10, M60, M100, M101, M102, BX15. Subway—A, B, C, D, 2, 3 to 125th St.

The Mama Foundation of the Arts was established by author, playwright, and radio and TV personality Vy Higginsen in 1998 after the successful run and international tour of the musical *Mama, I Want to Sing*. Higginsen co-wrote and produced the musical, which ran for eight years and enjoyed 2,200 performances at the Off-Off-Broadway **Heckscher Theater** in East Harlem. The newest production, *Sing Harlem Sing*, is an uplifting, inspiring, and emotionally satisfying amalgam of R&B, soul, and gospel music that can be seen at the **Dempsey Theater** (127 W. 127th St., between Adam Clayton Powell Blvd. and Malcolm X/Lenox).

Maysles Cinema

343 Malcolm X/Lenox, between 127th and 128th Sts. (212) 582-6050. www.mayslesinstitute.org/cinema. Bus—M2, M7, M102. Subway—2, 3 to 125th St.

The Maysles Cinema is a new sixty-seat not-for-profit theater in Harlem dedicated to the exhibition of documentary film and video. The aim is to expose viewers to independent documentaries and feature films that would not ordinarily be seen by the masses. The **Maysles Brothers**, for whom this theater is named, garnered acclaim for such documentaries as *Salesman* (1968), *Gimme Shelter* (1970), and *Grey Gardens* (1976). The Maysles brothers' principle that the lives of ordinary people deserve and demand attention in film is also shared by Maysles Cinema, which presents movies in collaboration with independent filmmakers, programmers, critics, local film clubs, and organizations to ensure a democratic viewing experience.

The H.A.D.L.E.Y Players

207 W. 134th St., between Frederick Douglass and Adam Clayton Powell Blvds. (212) 926-0281. www.hadleyplayers.org. Bus—M2, M3, M7, M10, M102, BX33. Subway—B, C to 135th St.

Established in 1980, the Harlem Artist's Development League Especially for You (the H.A.D.L.E.Y.) is dedicated to bringing professional theater at reasonable prices to the community. At such affordable prices, entire families have the opportunity to experience dramas, mysteries, comedies, and educational theatre.

EDUCATIONAL INSTITUTIONS

College of New Rochelle-Rosa Parks

144 W. 125th St., between Adam Clayton Powell Blvd. and Malcolm X/Lenox. (212) 662-7500. www.cnr.edu/SchoolofNewResources/RosaParksCampus. Bus—M2, M3, M7, M60, M100, M101, M102, BX15. Subway—A, B, C, D, 2, 3, Metro North to 125th St.

The College of New Rochelle is the first Catholic college for women founded in New York State in 1904 by the Order of St. Ursula. In 1987 the Rosa Parks campus, named in honor of civil rights icon and "Mother of the Civil Rights Movement" **Rosa Parks**, was opened in a space at the Studio Museum in Harlem building. This campus operates under the School of New Resources, which is a recognized leader in adult higher education. The school provides a BA degree in liberal arts tailored for today's adults.

Touro College of Osteopathic Medicine

230 W. 125th St., between Frederick Douglass and Adam Clayton Powell Blvds. (646) 981-4500. www.touro.edu/med. Bus—M2, M3, M7, M60, M100, M101, M102, BX15. Subway—A, B, C, D, 2, 3, Metro North to 125th St.

Touro College of Osteopathic Medicine (TOUROCOM), which opened in the fall of 2007, is New York's first new medical school in nearly thirty years and the first osteopathic college of medicine with a special emphasis on training minority doctors. TOUROCOM is also committed to improving medical care in the Harlem community and to increasing the number of minorities practicing medicine. This school is located in the former Art Nouveau/Art Deco **Blumstein Department Store** building, where in 1943 the first Black Santa Claus was hired and where in 1958 **Dr. Martin Luther King Jr.**, was stabbed while there on a book tour. This 75,000-square-foot space contains state-of-the-art features, including amphitheater-style lecture halls, classrooms, offices, support and clinical skills training facilities, as well as technologically advanced laboratories. More than 50,000 e-books and 26,000 e-journals, sophisticated virtual resources, more than eighty computer workstations, multimedia areas, and comfortable reading spaces are available in the school's library.

ACCOMMODATIONS

Harlem 144 Guest House

144 W. 120th St., between Adam Clayton Powell Blvd. and Malcolm X/Lenox. (212) 749-7289. valbradley@aol.com. Bus—M2, M7, M102. Subway—B, C, 2, 3 to 116th St.

To experience authentic Harlem, start at Harlem 144 Guest House. Built in 1888 and on the National Register of Historic Places, this brownstone townhouse contains most of its original detail—from the elaborate wainscoting that runs from the parlor floor to the second floor, intricately carved fireplace mantles, to the parquet oak and yellow pine wood floors. There are two rooms on the third floor—a two-bedroom and a one-bedroom—that share a kitchen and bathroom; and a private apartment on the garden level. All rooms are furnished with original African, Caribbean, and African American fine art, antiques, and collectibles, and first-edition African American books. Each space is air-conditioned, has cable TV with premium channels, a DVD player, and wireless Internet access. The garden apartment's country kitchen leads to a Zen garden. All kitchens are fully outfitted and there is free washer and dryer use. A healthy continental breakfast of fresh berries, yogurt, breakfast breads, orange juice, coffee, and tea is provided. The proprietor loves to recommend restaurants and clubs and can arrange authentic Harlem tours, order door-to-door car service, book Broadway/Off-Broadway plays, arrange reservations for one-of-a-kind Harlem events, and refer you to free outdoor summer events from swing and salsa dancing, major jazz and film festivals, to dance performances. Rates range from $100 to $225 a night. Discounts are offered for stays of seven nights and more. Also, favorable rates can be arranged for monthly stays.

51 West 120th Street Brownstone

151 W. 120th St., between Adam Clayton Powell Blvd. and Malcolm X/Lenox. (212) 749-7289. www.151west120brownstone.com. Bus—M2, M7, M102. Subway—B, C, 2, 3 to 116th St.

To guarantee a memorable experience in Harlem, choose 151 West 120th Street Brownstone, which is an elegant duplex apartment located in a brownstone townhouse in the Mount Morris Park Historic District. The apartment contains three bedrooms, including a master bedroom with private deck and bathroom on the parlor floor, and two rooms on the garden level that have access to a landscaped garden. This comfortable accommodation features a full kitchen with dishwasher, two full baths, luxury queen-sized beds in each room, complimentary high-speed Internet, cable TV and DVD player in the common room, and a business space with fax machine, computer, and printer. Conveniently located, 151 West 120th is a block and a half from **Marcus Garvey Park**, where Tony and Oscar award–winning composer Richard Rodgers played in the early 1900s, ten blocks from the north end of **Central Park**, and a short subway ride from midtown Manhattan and the famous Times Square. Rates are based upon occupancy, either single or double, depending on the season and day of week. Please email to obtain additional information.

BED AND BREAKFASTS

C asa Tua-Harlem
2 W. 131st St., between Malcolm X/Lenox and Fifth Ave. (917) 346-4345.
www.casatua-harlem.com. Bus—M1, M7, M102. Subway—2, 3 to 125th St.

This unique penthouse apartment is perfect for small groups or families. Located in a renovated brownstone just west of Fifth Avenue, the tri-level apartment includes two separate bedrooms and a bathroom downstairs plus a sleeping mezzanine with separate bath on the top floor and a terrace that overlooks the garden. In between is a large loft-like living room with double-height cathedral ceiling and vast skylight, and an open dining/kitchen area. The apartment is fully stocked with cooking equipment, utensils, dishes, glasses, linens, and towels. There is also a TV with cable and a DVD player, Internet access, and a washer and dryer. Casa Tua-Harlem generally rents at $2,500 per week for six people and can sleep a few more with special accommodations. Ask about discounts for fewer people or shorter stays.

C rystal's Castle Bed & Breakfast
119 W. 119th St., between Adam Clayton Powell Blvd. and Malcolm X/Lenox. (212) 865-5522. Bus—M2, M7, M102. Subway—B, C, 2, 3 to 116th St.

If you want to stay where you'll be treated like family, you'll love Crystal's Castle. This bed-and-breakfast, located in one of the beautiful brownstones of the Mount Morris Park Historic District, lets you feel at home—only better. The owners are professional musicians, so they know what it's like to be on the road. They're committed to providing the ambience that so often is missing from chain establishments, which includes a backyard (yes, in NYC!) and a lovely common room. Please call for room rates and availability.

E furu Guest House & Suites
106 W. 120th St., between Adam Clayton Powell Blvd. and Malcolm X/Lenox. (212) 961-9855. www.efuru-nyc.com. Bus—M2, M7, M102. Subway—B, C, 2, 3 to 116th St.

The Efuru, the Eastern Nigerian Igbo word for Daughter of Heaven, Guest House and Suites is located in two beautifully restored late nineteenth-century brownstone townhouses in the historic Mount Morris Park Historic District. Accommodations include furnished studio apartments with private bath and kitchen; deluxe suites with kitchenette and shared bath; and deluxe rooms that share a kitchenette and bath. Efuru's amenities include queen-sized beds, air-conditioning, cable TV, private phone, wireless Internet service, hair dryer, AM-FM radio alarm, and fully equipped kitchen, as well as personal code/keyless self-entry. Guests rave about the gardens, which are a retreat after an active day in the hustle and bustle of the city. Also, there are Jacuzzis in selected suites. Rates range from $95 to $155.

Harlem Flop House

242 W. 123rd St., between Fredrick Douglass and Adam Clayton Powell Blvds. (212) 662-0678. www.harlemflophouse.com. Bus—M2, M3, M10, M60, M100, M101, BX15. Subway—A, B, C, D to 125th St.

Belying its name, this is a charming 1890s Victorian brownstone located on a quiet, tree-lined block in Central Harlem. The Flop House is owned and operated by an artist who has generously displayed his work along with the beautiful original architectural details throughout the house. There are four rooms furnished with full-sized beds and two full bathrooms (shared) complete with antique claw-foot tubs. Please note that there are two resident cats on the premises. Rates range from $100 to $175, depending on the season and day of the week.

Harlem Renaissance House

237 W. 139th St., between Frederick Douglass and Adam Clayton Powell Blvds. (212) 226-1590. www.harlemrenaissancehouse.com. Bus—M7, M10. Subway—2, 3 to 135th St.

This Renaissance Revival bed-and-breakfast is located in one of the elegant townhouses on landmark Striver's Row. Created in a neo-Italian style in 1890 by the renowned architect Stanford White, who designed the first Madison Square Garden, there are two bedrooms and several parlor rooms that can be booked, along with several public rooms, including a living/dining room and kitchen that are free to use during your stay. The bedrooms come with full private baths as well as twenty-four-hour concierge service, Wi-Fi, iPod music port, and in-room continental breakfast. Generally room rates range from $200 to $220, depending upon length of stay, but ask about special recession rates.

Harlem's In at Carmen's Bed & Breakfast

8 W. 121st St., between Malcolm X/Lenox and Fifth Ave. (646) 468-0308. www.harlemsin.com. Bus—M1, M2, M7, M102. Subway—2, 3 to 116th St.

This is a family-run space situated in a Victorian row house-style brownstone in the Mount Morris Park area, convenient to new and long-established restaurants as well as museums, public parks, and shopping areas. The guest accommodation is a fully furnished studio apartment with private bathroom, equipped kitchen, and washer and dryer. A continental breakfast is provided each morning and there is access to a private garden. Room rates start at $160 per night for single occupancy, with no charge for children under six.

Indigo Arms Guest House

181 Lenox Ave., at 119th St. (212) 316-9122. www.indigoarms.com. Bus—M2, M7, M102. Subway—B, C, 2, 3 to 116th St.

Since the Indigo Arms opened its doors in June 2009 it has been the hidden gem chosen by sophisticated travelers from around the world who seek an atmosphere of warmth, privacy, culture, and authentic luxury. The high-end bed-and-breakfast is housed in a remarkable brownstone in the heart of the Mount Morris Park Historic District. Its 15-foot-high ceilings, vintage hardwood floors, and African mahogany wood detailing, coupled with modern amenities provide the perfect marriage of Harlem

Renaissance charm and contemporary refinement. This recently renovated family-run establishment operates: five guest rooms, including three suites over two floors that have their own private bathrooms with a common bathroom on the third floor; common room areas on each floor; private guest kitchen on the third floor; central air and heat; free Wi-Fi Internet access; and continental breakfast served each day with an extended Southern-influenced breakfast on Sundays. Indigo Arms also rents its elegant parlor floor reception area with full kitchen on the garden floor for elite gatherings, location shoots, weddings, and other unique events. Guest room rates range from $125 to $500, but call about recession-friendly rates that are offered off-season.

Mount Morris House Bed and Breakfast
12 Mt. Morris Park West, between 121st and 122nd Sts. (917) 478-6214. www.mountmorrishouse.com. Bus—M2, M7, M60, M100, M101, M102, BX15. Subway—2, 3 to 125th St.

Built in 1888 at the height of New York's Gilded Age, Mount Morris House is a fine example of that period's splendid architecture and extravagant lifestyle at the turn of the twentieth century. In addition to the grand reception rooms and private garden are guest accommodations that include spacious bedroom suites with dressing rooms, private baths, and wood-burning fireplaces as well as the modern conveniences of plasma HDTV cable television, DVD players, radio alarm clocks, and Wi-Fi. There is in-house maid service and breakfast is served daily in the dining room, with kitchen facilities for guests' use. Room rates range from $150 to $295.

Hostels

5th Avenue Spot
35 W. 126th St., between Malcolm X/Lenox Blvd. and Fifth Ave. (212) 289-6405. www.spothostels.com. Bus—M1, M7, M60, M100, M101, M102, BX15. Subway—2, 3 to 125th St.

Spot hostel is located right off Fifth Avenue in a renovated Harlem brownstone, complete with backyard. A variety of air-conditioned room configurations are available, including four-, six-, and eight-bed dorms that share bathrooms and showers, or private rooms with private baths and their own TVs. Among the other amenities are a self-catering kitchen, laundry machines, a guest lounge with flatscreen TV, free Wi-Fi, and Internet kiosks. Rates start at about $27, depending upon configuration and occupancy, and seasonal rates may apply.

Jazz on Lenox
104 W. 128th St., between Adam Clayton Powell Blvd. and Malcolm X/Lenox. (212) 222-5773. www.jazzhostels.com/jazzonthelenox.php. Bus—M2, M7, M60, M100, M101, M102, BX15. Subway—2, 3 to 125th St.

Part of one of the largest independently owned hostel chains in North America, Jazz on Lenox is located in a classic Victorian-style brownstone that has been fully renovated to meet the needs of youthful, adventurous travelers—all in the epicenter of the neighborhood but still just fifteen minutes from Times Square! This location has a range of air-conditioned rooms, from ensuite dorms to private rooms. They offer a free light breakfast, twenty-four-hour reception and security services, a guest kitchen, plus free linens, towels, and housekeeping service. There is also a TV/Internet lounge and a huge backyard. Room rates vary according to room configuration, so please check the Web site or call for details. Group discounts are available.

The Harlem YMCA's Claude McKay Residence

180 W. 135th St., between Adam Clayton Powell Blvd. and Malcolm X/Lenox. (212) 281-4100 x210. www.ymcanyc.org. Bus—M2, M7, M102, BX33. Subway—2, 3 to 135th St.

Named after Claude McKay, a famous Harlem Renaissance writer, the Harlem YMCA, which once housed famous writers Langston Hughes and Ralph Ellison, has 235 rooms and offers reasonable rates for single or double occupancy. Each room has color TV, air conditioning, refrigerators, shared bathrooms, and daily housekeeping service. All guests are also entitled to use the Health and Wellness Center, which includes a heated swimming pool, weight room, and Cardiovascular and Strength Training Center. Room rates start at about $75.

Hotels

02 Brownstone Boutique Hotel

102 W. 118th St., between Adam Clayton Powell Blvd. and Malcolm X/Lenox. (212) 662-4223. www.102brownstone.com. Bus—M2, M7, M102. Subway—B, C, 2, 3 to 116th St.

What is commonly called "downtown luxury" is quickly being associated with such elegant Harlem inns as the 102 Brownstone Boutique Hotel. Each room in this beautifully renovated brownstone is impeccably decorated from floor to ceiling. There are studio apartments complete with fully equipped kitchens and bathrooms with Jacuzzi tubs and showers, or private suites with private bathroom with shower as well as microwave and mini-refrigerator. All accommodations are air-conditioned and feature complimentary direct-dial telephones with private voicemail, high-speed Internet access, cable television with DVD player, radio/CD player, iron and ironing board, and hair dryer. Generally room rates range from $100 to $250, but ask about the special stimulus rates.

Aloft Harlem Hotel

2300 Frederick Douglass Blvd. at 124th St. 877-GO-Aloft. www.starwoodhotels.com/alofthotels. Bus—M2, M3, M10, M60, M100, M101, BX15. Subway—A, B, C, D to 125th St.

The first hotel opened in Harlem in forty years, Aloft Harlem, a vision of W Hotels and part of the Starwood family, ushers in a fresh and timely hotel experience at a better price point. It is bold and new, featuring a loft-inspired design, surrounded by urban energy, and conveniently located steps from the legendary Apollo Theater, near **Columbia University**, to transportation to the theater district in midtown Manhattan, and to New York's major airports. The 124-room hotel features ultra comfortable signature king- and queen-sized beds, oversized spa shower, custom amenities by Bliss® Spa, and more. Plug-and-play connectivity stations in the rooms allow you to charge all your electronics and links to the 42-inch LCD TV to maximize work and play. The public lobby spaces allow you to meet and mingle with friends at the hotel's bar, play pool, purchase grab-and-go sweet, savory, or healthy snacks at the 24/7 pantry, and stay connected with complimentary hotel-wired and wireless Internet access. For information about rates, visit the Web site or call.

DINING AND LIVE ENTERTAINMENT

Chez Lucienne

308 Malcolm X/Lenox, between 125th and 126th Sts. (212) 289-5555. www.chezlucienne.com. Cuisine: French. Lunch, Dinner, Brunch. $$$. Sun–Thu 11:30am–11pm, Fri and Sat 11:30am–12am. All major credit cards. Bus—M2, M7, M60, M100, M101, M102, BX15. Subway—2, 3 to 125th St.

It's like Rive Gauche in the heart of Harlem: Chez Lucienne, Harlem's first French bistro. This inviting eatery was opened in early 2009 by owners **Jerome Bougherdani** and chef **Matthew Tivy**, who both worked at Daniel, a noted Upper East Side French restaurant. Add to the mix executive chef **Thomas Obaton**, who cooked with master chef Guy Savoy in Paris, and you have a body of experience and talent here that delivers a memorable dining experience. Bistro classics such as chicken fricassee, salade nicoise, and a foie gras terrine are some of the favorite picks on a menu of traditional French dishes, an extensive wine list, exotic cocktails, and scrumptious desserts. The reasonably priced prix-fixe lunch special is one of the best bargains in Harlem. The sixty-seat eatery, with comfortable and inviting décor that includes powder blue banquettes, also offers outdoor dining during late spring, summer, and early fall. The friendly and professional service, authentic French music wafting in the background, and quality food at affordable prices makes this place a winner. Check out their live entertainment on Wednesday, Saturday, and Sunday. Because of its popularity, advance reservations are recommended.

Dining

Africa Kiné Restaurant

256 W. 116th St., between Frederick Douglass and Adam Clayton Powell Blvds. (212) 666-9400. www.africakine.com. Cuisine: West African, Senegalese. Lunch, Dinner. $$. Daily 12:30pm–2am. All major credit cards. Bus—M2, M3, M7, M10, M102, M116. Subway—B, C, 2, 3 to 116th St.

Africa Kiné, the first and largest African restaurant established in Harlem, is now one of the best among them. A popular hangout for the African and Afro-centric community, this restaurant was opened in 1995 by Senegalese businessman **Samba Niang** and his wife and chef, **Kiné Mar**. Traditional Senegalese dishes are the specialty here and favorites dishes include Thiebou Djeun (Senegal's national dish of fish, root vegetables, and broken jasmine rice), Dibi Couscous (grilled lamb and couscous), Yassa Poulet (lemon marinated chicken and onions), and Lamb Mafé (lamb stewed in a peppery peanut sauce). If your palate appreciates spicy food, Africa Kiné is made to order for you!

Amy Ruth's Restaurant

113 W. 116th St., between Adam Clayton Powell Blvd. and Malcolm X/Lenox. (212) 280-8779. www.amyruthsharlem.com. Cuisine: Southern, Soul Food. Breakfast, Lunch, Dinner. $$$. Mon 11:30am–11pm, Tue–Thu 8:30am–11pm, Fri 8:30am–5:30am, Sat 7:30am–5:30am, Sun 7:30am–11pm. All major credit cards. Bus—M2, M7, M102, M116. Subway—2, 3 to 116th St.

Amy Ruth's, named after first owner **Carl Redding**'s grandmother, revived the legendary chicken and waffles in Harlem when it opened in 1998. The combination was created in 1938 and made popular at **Well's Supper Club** to satisfy club-hopping customers who were ambivalent about what to order because they were too late for dinner and too early for breakfast. This eatery has a vast waffle menu that includes not only fried chicken, which some say is the best in Harlem, but smothered chicken, fried catfish or fried whiting, skirt steak, bacon and sausage, and an assortment of fresh fruit toppings available for breakfast, lunch, and dinner. There is also a full menu of traditional Southern soul food dishes, named after prominent local and national personalities, elected officials, and ministers who frequent the place.

Café Veg

2291 Adam Clayton Powell Blvd., between 134th and 135th Sts. (212) 491-3223. Cuisine: Vegetarian, Vegan, Smoothies/Juice Bar. Breakfast, Lunch, Dinner. $$. Mon–Sat 11am–10pm, Sun 11am–8pm. All major credit cards. Bus—M2, M7, M10, M102, BX33. Subway—B, C, 2, 3 to 135th St.

Café Veg offers pure organic cuisine. The all-vegan and organic menu offerings include items that range from roti to homemade soups and salads to full entrees. Some of the favorite entrees include tasty Southern staples like barbecued chicken, baked mac and cheese, mustard greens, and candied yams. The juice bar is also a winner.

Charles' Country Pan Fried Chicken

2839 Frederick Douglass Blvd., at 151st St. (212) 281-1800. Cuisine: Soul Food. Lunch, Dinner. $$. Mon–Thu 11am–11pm, Fri and Sat 11am–1am, Sun 11am–8pm. Cash only. Bus—M2, M10. Subway—3 to 148th St.

Fortunately, the famous Charles' Southern Style Kitchen has reopened as Charles' Country Pan Fried Chicken. The previous restaurant closed suddenly in 2008 and thereby created a void in Harlem for authentic soul food. Owner **Charles Gabriel** fries the best chicken in New York. Enjoy the house specialty—crusty and greaseless fried chicken—combined with everything else on the steam table, at the restaurant's all-you-can-eat buffet for $10.99 at lunch (before 4pm), and $13.99 at dinner and on weekends. Try the baked chicken, which is almost as good as the fried, finger-licking barbecued ribs, collard greens seasoned with smoked turkey, sweet and buttery candied yams, and crusty-topped mac and cheese that you should wash down with a glass of Southern sweet tea or lemonade that is refilled regularly (unheard of in New York!). If you still have room, don't miss the creamy banana pudding.

Cheesesteak Factory

2496 Adam Clayton Powell Blvd., at 145th St. (212) 690-1111. Cuisine: Cheesesteaks, salads, chicken wings. Lunch, Dinner. $. Sun–Thu 11am–2am, Fri and Sat 11am–4am. All major credit cards. Bus—M7, M10, M102, M103. Subway—3 to 145th St.

The Cheesesteak Factory is a chain that grew out of the original New York–based Cheesesteak restaurant best known for cheesesteaks (made popular in Philadelphia) and freshly baked bread. The eatery offers more than just meat and cheese on a roll—sandwiches, breakfast, lo-carb platters, wraps, salads, Angus burgers, ribs, and even wings and other appetizers.

Doc's Harlem Restaurant

1902 Adam Clayton Powell Blvd., between 115th and 116th Sts. (212) 531-8770. www.docsharlemrestaurant.com. Cuisine: Soul Food. Lunch, Dinner. $$. Mon 11am–7pm, Tue and Wed, 11am–9pm, Thu–Sat 11am–12am, Sun 11am–5pm. All major credit cards. Bus—M2, M3, M7, M10, M102. Subway—B, C, 2, 3 to 116th St.

The original owner of Amy Ruth's, Carl Redding, has opened a new place: Doc's. The take-out only restaurant specializes in chicken, ribs, and fried fish, with soul food sides like collard greens, candied yams, and mac and cheese. If you can't handle the cholesterol-heaped fried and barbecue-sauced selections, there's a "Harlem Health" menu, featuring salads and steamed vegetables.

El Nuevo Caribe In Harlem Restaurant & Grill

2133 Adam Clayton Powell Blvd., between 126th and 127th Sts. (212) 663-1006. Cuisine: Dominican. Breakfast, Lunch, Dinner. $. Daily 7am–11pm. V, MC. Bus—M2, M7, M10, M60, M100, M101, BX15. Subway—A, B, C, D to 125th St.

Traditional Dominican food (influenced by Spanish, African, and Indian cultures) is served here, primarily cafeteria style from steam tables. There is roast pork, steak and onions, fried and stewed chicken, seafood, beans and rice, sweet fried plantain and steamed green plantain, tostones or fried green plantain, and a Dominican favorite, mofongo (fried plantain and pork rind, mashed with garlic), just to name a few. El Nuevo Caribe carries succulent rotisserie chickens served up whole, half, or quartered at very reasonable prices. There is a great lunch special for $6.

Fishers of Men II

121 W. 125th St., between Adam Clayton Powell Blvd. and Malcolm X/Lenox. (212) 678-4268. Cuisine: Seafood. Lunch, Dinner. $. Mon–Sat 10am–10pm. Cash only. Bus—M2, M3, M7, M10, M60, M100, M101, M102, BX15. Subway—A, B, C, D, 2, 3 to 125th St.

This restaurant sells good fried seafood. The specialty is fried whiting, and there is a fish-and-chips lunch special for $5. For about a dollar less you can forgo the fries and get the same number of fish fillets. The portions are large—fillets are stacked high between two pieces of white bread. There is also the option of ordering your whiting with grits, which is a typical Southern breakfast meal that is served here all day.

Food for Life Supreme

108 W. 116ᵗʰ St., between Adam Clayton Powell Blvd. and Malcolm X/Lenox. (212) 222-7707. www.foodforlifesupreme.com. Cuisine: Fish, Veggies, Salads. Breakfast, Lunch, Dinner. $$. Tue and Wed 9am–8pm, Thu and Fri 9am–10pm, Sat 9am–11pm, Sun 9am–7pm. All major credit cards. Bus—M2, M7, M102, M116. Subway—2, 3 to 116ᵗʰ St.

Food For Life Supreme is a small chain with five restaurants based around a book of the same name, which promotes healthy, positive eating experiences. You won't find meat on the menu, but they do have fish (whiting or salmon) and dairy such as cheese and sour cream. Dishes on the menu have imaginative names, though the cuisine is basic new-American fare with a soul food twist. Some of the favorites at the 116ᵗʰ Street site are Cheddar Carrot Fries (carrots topped with cheddar cheese, sour cream, scallions, and smoked chunks of salmon) and the Bella Burger (a grilled portabella mushroom with veggies served on a bun). Wrap It Up is a fried whiting and veggie wrap, and the East of the Mississippi is a typical fried whiting sandwich on wheat bread.

Harlem Bar-B-Q

2367 Frederick Douglass Blvd., at 127ᵗʰ St. (212) 222-1922. Cuisine: Barbecue, Chicken, Ribs, Burgers, Sandwiches. Lunch, Dinner. $$. Daily 11am–12am. All major credit cards. Bus—M2, M3, M10, M60, M100, M101, BX15. Subway—A, B, C, D to 125ᵗʰ St.

One of Harlem's newest restaurant additions, Harlem Bar-B-Q opened in the summer of 2009. It is conveniently located two blocks away from the Apollo, Magic Johnson's Theater, and **Hue-Man Bookstore**. Portions are generous and prices reasonable. Customers are already praising the barbecue sauce.

Harlem Wing & Waffle

2394 Adam Clayton Powell Blvd., between 139ᵗʰ and 140ᵗʰ Sts. (212) 281-1446. www. harlemwingandwaffle.com. Cuisine: Chicken, Waffles. Breakfast, Lunch, Dinner. $. Mon–Thu 9:30am–10pm, Fri and Sat 9:30am–2am, Sun 9:30am–8pm. Cash only. Bus—M2, M10, M102. Subway—B, C, 2, 3 to 135ᵗʰ St.

This restaurant offers just what its name conveys—wings and waffles. The menu features several types of wings: Buffalo, Sweet and Sour, Barbecue, Jerk, Teriyaki, and more. Hands down, they have the best recipe for waffles. A meal is not complete if you haven't tried one of the restaurant's own line of sodas; choose from uptown orange, vanilla cream, black cherry, grape, and root beer.

Il Caffe Latte

189 Malcolm X/Lenox, between 119ᵗʰ and 120ᵗʰ Sts. (212) 222-2241. www.ilcaffelatte.com. Cuisine: Gourmet Coffee, Bakery Goods, Pasta, Sandwiches, Salads. Breakfast, Lunch, Dinner, Brunch. $$. Daily 8am–9pm. V, MC. Bus—M2, M7, M102. Subway—2, 3 to 116ᵗʰ St.

HARLEM WING & WAFFLE

This café opened in early 2009 adding yet another neighborhood gathering spot for the residents of the Mount Morris Park area. The atmosphere is laid-back, warm, and inviting, and the service is quick and courteous. This is the only eatery in central Harlem that serves up lox and bagels, which is one of New York's signature menu items. In a move that will please lactose-intolerant and diabetic diners, the café offers soy milk muffins and low-sugar and low-fat baked goods, in addition to traditional versions. They have a nice blend of pastas, burgers, sandwiches, salads, and pastries, and even serve beer and wine. This café has free Wi-Fi access.

Jacob's Restaurant Soul Food & Salad Bar

373 Malcolm X/Lenox, between 128th and 129th St. (212) 866-3663. www.jacobrestaurant. com. Cuisine: Soul Food, Salad Bar. Lunch, Dinner. $. Daily 10am–10pm. Cash only. Bus—M2, M7, M102. Subway—2, 3 to 125th St.

2695 Frederick Douglass Blvd., at 143rd St. (212) 283-3663. Bus—M2, M10. Subway—A, B, C, D, 3 to 145th St.

Jacob's, a buffet-style restaurant, opened in the spring of 2009. The restaurant offers a diverse selection of Southern, Caribbean, and West African dishes, along with an impressive array of fresh fruits and salad greens. The food is priced by the pound ($5.99 hot or mixed and $4.99 cold).

La Perle Noire Café and Bakery

420 Malcolm X/Lenox, at 131st St. (212) 234-1777. www.laperlenoirebakery.com. Cuisine: Café, Bakery. Breakfast, Lunch. $. Mon–Fri 7:30am–7pm, Sat 8am–6pm, Sun 9am–6pm. V, MC, Dis. Bus—M2, M7, M102. Subway—B, C, 2, 3 to 135th St.

A welcome addition to the neighborhood, La Perle Noire is a coffeehouse–cum–light fare restaurant that fills a void for this kind of dining in the stretch between 126th and 132nd Streets and Malcolm X/Lenox. There is good coffee, pastries, the *New York Times* for purchase, and access to free Wi-Fi here. Oh yes, they serve beer and wine, too.

Lee Lee's Baked Goods

283 W. 118th St., between Frederick Douglass Blvd. and St. Nicholas Ave. (917) 493-6633. Cuisine: Baked Goods. $. Mon–Sat 8:30am–7pm, Sun 9:30am–4pm. Cash only. Bus—M2, M3, M7, M10, M116. Subway—B, C to 116th St.

Rugelach (miniature strudels), a traditional Jewish pastry, can be found at Lee Lee's. **Alvin Lee**, the owner and baker, has scripted the slogan "Rugelach by a Brother" on his window. It seems that just about everyone who has tried his rugelach thinks highly of it, and even the *New York Times* cited him as "the last commercial baker in New York producing traditional butter-dough rugelach." You may want to get there close to opening as these sweet treats are generally gone in less than a half-hour after the morning's batch leaves the oven. Also at Lee Lee's: honey-nut pound cake, cinnamon Danish, cheesecake, pineapple upside-down cake Caribbean style, and even a chicken soup that reportedly draws on the baker's Caribbean roots.

Make My Cake

121 St. Nicholas Ave., at 116th St. (212) 932-0833. www.makemycake.com. Cuisine: Baked Goods. $$. Mon–Thu 7:30am–8pm, Fri 7:30am–9pm, Sat 9am–9pm, Sun 9am–7pm. V, MC, Dis. Bus—M2, M3, M7, M10, M102, M116. Subway—B, C, 2, 3 to 116th St.

2380 Adam Clayton Powell Blvd., at 139th St. (212) 234-2344. Mon 10am–5pm, Tue–Fri 7am–7:30pm, Sat 10am–7:30pm, Sun 10am–8pm. Bus—M2, M7, M102. Subway—2, 3 to 135th St.

At Make My Cake you will find the best baked goods in the traditional down-home Southern style. Known for its award-winning red velvet cake voted the best in New York by the *New York Times*, the bakery sells a variety of cakes, including sour cream pound cake, coconut pineapple cake, and chocolate layer cake. Favorite pies are sweet potato and pecan, while favorite cobblers are the peach and apple. The 116th St. store, which has more space to eat in, has an inviting décor and features free Wi-Fi access.

Manna's Soul Food and Salad Bar

70 W. 125th St., between Malcolm X/Lenox and Fifth Ave. (212) 828-1230. www. mannasrestaurants.com. Cuisine: Soul Food. Lunch, Dinner. $. Mon–Sat 11am–9pm, Sun 11am–8pm. Cash only. Bus—M3, M7, M10, M60, M100, M101, M102, BX15. Subway—2, 3, Metro North to 125th St.

486 Malcolm X/Lenox Ave., at 134th St. (212) 234-4488. Bus—M2, M7, M102, BX33. Subway—2, 3 to 135th St.

2353 Frederick Douglass Blvd., at 126th St. (212) 749-9084. Bus—M3, M7, M10, M60, M100, M101, M102, BX15. Subway—A, B, C, D to 125th St.

This soul food and salad bar buffet opened its doors in 1984 in central Harlem when there were very few restaurant options. Now an uptown institution, Manna's can be found in five locations in Harlem and Brooklyn. You'll find a double bank of regularly replenished steam-table provisions, including fried and baked chicken, oxtail stew, barbecued ribs and chicken, candied yams, collard greens, steamed cabbage, simmered pinto beans cooked with smoked turkey parts, crusted-over mac and cheese, stewed okra and tomatoes, and banana pudding and peach cobbler. There is also a generous salad and fresh fruit bar. Prices range from $4.49 a pound to $5.49 a pound. If you are feeling adventurous, order the chitlins, an African American delicacy of pig intestines that are carefully cleaned and simmered in vinegar, garlic, onion, and other spices for hours to make them tender.

Miss Maude's Spoonbread Too

547 Lenox Ave., between 137th and 138th Sts. (212) 690-3100. www.spoonbreadinc. com/miss_mamies.htm. Cuisine: Southern, Soul Food. Lunch, Dinner. $$$. Mon–Thu 12pm–10pm, Fri and Sat 12pm–11pm, Sun 11am–9:30pm. V, MC, Dis. Bus—M2, M7, M102, BX33. Subway—2, 3 to 135th St.

Miss Maude's (the owner's aunt) is the sister restaurant to Miss Mamie's (the owner's mother) which is located in West Harlem. It was opened by former Wilhelmina model, cookbook author **Norma Jean Darden**, who also runs a successful catering business. The restaurant serves comfort food based on family recipes from Ms. Darden's popular cookbook, *Spoonbread and Strawberry Wine*, which

she co-authored with her sister Carole. It's Southern down-home cooking here. Meals begin with a basket of hot corn bread and are served Southern style with your choice of sides, like homemade candied yams, collard greens, or mac and cheese. The *New York Post* says, "On its own or smothered in gravy, Spoonbread has the best fried chicken in NYC!" Or you might want to try Uncle CL's Short Ribs of Beef (falling off the bone). And make sure to leave room for pie á la mode or an Uncle John–inspired chocolate or butterscotch ice cream sundae.

MISS MAUDE'S SPOONBREAD TOO

Native

161 Lenox Ave., at 118th St. (212) 665-2525. www.harlemnativenyc.com. Cuisine: French-Moroccan, Caribbean, American. Lunch, Dinner, Brunch. $$$. Sun–Thu 11:30am–11pm, Fri and Sat 11am–12am. V, MC, AmEx. Bus—M2, M7, M10, M116. Subway—2, 3 to 116th St.

When it opened in 2001, Native brought healthy grilled pleasures to Harlem, such as a spicy Atlantic salmon in soy ginger sauce and lightly grilled lemon chicken salad. French/Caribbean/ Asian-flavored entrées like linguini with chicken in chipotle cream, steak au poivre, and basil curry chicken served with spicy curry sauce over coconut rice round out the eclectic menu, where the "lightly fried" calamari appetizer constitutes the greasiest dish. For vegetarians, there are selections such as black beans and red rice accompanied with garlic sautéed spinach and sweet plantain. The prix-fixe Saturday and Sunday brunch is a real bargain. It is a delight to sit outside on summer nights to enjoy a cool mixed drink or wine selected from Native's full cocktail and wine menu.

Pascal's Eatery

2 W. 129th St., at Fifth Ave. (212) 860-7777. Cuisine: Sandwiches, Salads, Burgers. Breakfast, Lunch, Dinner. $. Daily 7am–11pm. V, MC, AmEx. Bus—M1, M7, M102. Subway—2, 3 to 125th St.

Even though Pascal's Eatery's signage has a cool retro look, the almost clinical interior gives it away as really a super deli of sorts with a bright, shiny, and ample interior. This new addition to Central Harlem is a great place to have a burger or a quick bite to eat. There is indoor and outdoor seating.

Patisserie Des Ambassades

2200 Frederick Douglass Blvd., between 118th and 119th Sts. (212) 666-0078. www. patisseriedesambassades.com. Cuisine: French, Senegalese, Baked Goods. Breakfast, Lunch, Dinner, Brunch. $$. Mon–Thu 7am–2am, Fri 7am–3am, Sat and Sun 8am–3am. All major credit cards. Bus—M2, M3, M10. Subway—B, C to 116th St.

Craving that croissant you had on your trip to Paris? This Franco-Senegalese bakery and restaurant comes close—crusty on the outside and buttery soft inside. Enjoy it with a cappuccino for pure pleasure.

There is a lunch special for $7, but the winners are the $10 Senegalese specials noted on the chalkboard outside. They are only served at lunchtime, and you had better get there before 1pm because they sell out quickly. One of the favorites is Thiebou Djeun (Senegal's national dish of fish, root veggies, and broken jasmine rice). Some of the dinner winners are the grilled whole Tilapia fish topped with sautéed onions Senegalese style, and the garlic tiger shrimp that are served with a spicy tomato-based onion sauce.

Pee Dee Steak House II

50 W. 125th St., between Malcolm X/Lenox and Fifth Ave. (212) 996-1081. Cuisine: Steak, Barbecued Ribs and Chicken. Lunch, Dinner. $$$. Sun–Thu 11am–11pm, Sat and Sun 11am–12am. All major credit cards. Bus—M2, M7, M60, M100, M101, M102, BX15. Subway—2, 3, Metro North to 125th St.

Steaks, barbecued ribs and chicken, and burgers on an open-flame grill cooked to order, and that's not all; there's fish, shrimp, and snow crabs. Served cafeteria style, each entree comes with a choice of baked potato or rice, salad made with iceberg lettuce or coleslaw, and garlic bread. The 8-ounce sirloin steak lunch special is a bargain at $7.99!

Society Café

2104 Frederick Douglass Blvd., at 114th St. (212) 222-3323. www.societycoffee.com. Cuisine: Coffeehouse. Breakfast, Lunch, Dinner, Brunch. $$. Mon 12pm–10pm, Tue–Thu 9am–10pm, Sat 9am–12am, Sun 9am–9pm. All major credit cards. Bus—M2, M3, M7, M10, M116. Subway—B, C to 116th St.

Known locally for its fair-trade coffee blends and creative brunch menu, this modest South-Harlem café, which is four blocks from Central Park, functions as a communal living room for the neighborhood. Residents seem to congregate at Society—especially for Saturday and Sunday brunch. There is also wine and beer on the menu, and free Wi-Fi access every day except Saturday and Sunday during brunch.

Strictly Roots

2058 Adam Clayton Powell Blvd., at 122nd St. (212) 864-8699. Cuisine: Vegetarian, Vegan. Breakfast, Lunch, Dinner. $$. Mon–Sat 10am–11pm, Sun 12pm–9pm. V, MC. Bus—M2, M7, M10, M102. Subway—A, B, C, D, 2, 3 to 125th St.

Strictly Roots, which carries its philosophy on its facade, "We serve nothing that crawls, walks, swims or flies," opened more than a decade ago as a dietary alternative to Harlem's traditional cholesterol- and fat-heavy soul food. Decorated in Rastafarian colors of red, yellow, green, and black, this laid-back cafeteria-style eatery features a daily changing vegan buffet. Portions are doled out by a friendly server from steam tables, so arrive early for the freshest fare, or opt for a grilled-to-order veggie burger. Standouts include fried tofu balls stuffed with herbs and onions, black-eyed pea balls, a faux-chicken curry, collard greens, and tasty yams. The restaurant is also known for its free poetry nights.

Tonnie's Minis

264 Malcolm X/Lenox, between 123rd and 124th Sts. (212) 831-5292. www.
tonniesminis.com. Cuisine: Baked Goods. $$. Mon–Fri 7:30am–9pm, Sat 9am–9pm,
Sun 10am–7pm. All major credit cards. Bus—M7, M60, M100, M101, M102, BX15. Subway—2,
3 to 125th St.

Tonnie's Minis opened in the Mount Morris Park Historic District with a full menu of delicious cupcakes that are prepared to order as you watch. If you are not certain about what you want, the staff will prepare a sample one-and-a-half-inch cake shot that you can just pop into your mouth. Of course, you can purchase the shots by the dozen, which make for quite a novel addition to a dinner party. In addition to cupcakes, Tonnie's serves up assorted cakes, cookies, brownies, and beverages such as cappuccino, latte, espresso, and teas. Tonnie's Minis became the top destination for cupcakes after opening in the West Village in 2006. Already the cupcake haven has become a Harlem hangout for those with a sweet tooth. The "Carrot Dream" and "Death by Chocolate" cupcakes are signature cupcakes, but the "Red Velvet" is gaining as the hands-down favorite in Harlem.

Tropical Grill and Restaurant

2145 Adam Clayton Powell Blvd., between 127th and 128th Sts. (212) 531-0233.
Cuisine: Dominican. Breakfast, Lunch, Dinner. $. Mon–Sat 7am–10pm, Sun 11am–8pm.
V, MC. Bus—M2, M7, M10, M60, M100, M101, BX15. Subway—A, B, C, D to 125th St.

Step inside Tropical Grill and be pleasingly overwhelmed by the smells of homemade Dominican food rising from the steam table. Folks line up at lunchtime to get one of the cut-price combos. A winner is the $6 spice-rubbed rotisserie quarter chicken on a mound of yellow rice with either black or red beans, with salad and beverage. Other similarly priced specials include pepper steak, stewed beef, mofongo (fried plantain and pork rind, mashed with garlic), and baked ribs. For two dollars more you get grilled shrimp or kingfish. You can eat in or take out.

Zoma

2084 Frederick Douglass Blvd., at 113th St. (212) 662-0620. www.zomanyc.com.
Cuisine: Ethiopian. Dinner. $$. Mon–Fri 5pm–11pm, Sat and Sun 12pm–11pm. Cash
only. Bus—M2, M3, M7, M10, M116 Subway—B, C to 116th St.

Zoma, the city's most elegant Ethiopian eatery, prepares and serves its dishes with a nouvelle cuisine flair. For example, the well-spiced azifa salad (lentils flecked through with onions and chilies) is served on leaves of endive and not injera (a thin, spongy, flat teff grain-based bread that is used to scoop up and wrap food) as it is served elsewhere. The kitchen manages to avoid buttery overkill with vegetarian and meat dishes. The best way to sample Zoma's offerings is by ordering combination platters, available in meat and vegetarian choices. Zoma's injera bread is moist and greaseless, which makes it excellent for soaking up every drop. Gomen (ginger-laced collard greens), shiro wett (a berbere-coated fusion of chickpeas and lentils), kik aletcha (a savory purée of split peas), and doro wett (a spicy stew of tender chicken topped with a hard-boiled egg) are the hands-down favorites.

Live Entertainment

Bill's Place
148 W. 133rd St., between Adam Clayton Powell Blvd. and Malcolm X/Lenox. (212) 281-0777. www.billsaxton.com/billsplace.html. Fri: two sets, 10pm and 12am. $15 per person. Cash only. Bus—M2, M3, M7, M10, M102, BX33. Subway—B, C, 2, 3 to 135th St.

Harlem native and legendary saxophonist and bandleader **Bill Saxton**, who has appeared and/ or recorded with **Roy Haynes**, **Jackie McLean**, **Clark Terry**, **Nancy Wilson**, the Duke Ellington Orchestra, the **Count Basie Orchestra**, and **Tito Puente**, to name a few, launched his own jazz parlor—"Bill's Place"—in 2006. Located on the garden level of Saxton's vintage brownstone townhouse, the jazz club opening also rejuvenated an historical jazz landmark which was a popular speakeasy during Prohibition. The whole block of 133rd Street between Seventh Ave. (Adam Clayton Powell Blvd.) and Lenox Ave. was called **"Swing Street"** by Harlem locals, and the clubs on the block were the after-hours hangouts for the cultural and musical icons of the Harlem Renaissance. **Tillie Fripp** made No. 148 popular when she opened her restaurant on the garden level. She served up slammin' ham and eggs and her menu was augmented with a top-notch jazz lineup, including a young Billie Holiday, who sang there briefly. Bill's Place is continuing the purist legacy of serious straight-ahead jazz with guest musicians playing beside Saxton and those who are fortunate enough to be invited to sit in. Alcohol is not served here, so bring your own bottle, but most of all come to enjoy some of the best jazz in town.

Minton's Playhouse
206 W. 118th St., between St. Nicholas Ave. and Adam Clayton Powell Blvd. (212) 864-8346. www.mintonsuptown.com. Daily 4pm–4am. Sun–Thu: No cover charge, two-drink minimum, showtimes 9pm, 10:30pm and 12am. Fri and Sat: $10 cover charge, two-drink minimum, showtimes 10pm, 11:30pm and 1am. Cash only. Bus—M2, M3, M7, M10, M102, M116. Subway—B, C, 2, 3 to 116th St.

MINTON'S PLAYHOUSE

Located on the first floor of the former **Hotel Cecil** with its colorful neon sign outside, Minton's Playhouse was opened by tenor saxophonist **Henry Minton** in 1938 and became widely known as the place where bebop was created during the late-night jam sessions of **Thelonious Monk**, **Kenny Clarke**, **Charlie Christian**, Charlie Parker, and **Dizzy Gillespie**, who were the nucleus of the house band early on. This was the place in the forties and fifties where established and aspiring jazz musicians came after hours to compete with the musicians in Minton's house band during Monday night "cutting sessions" and to hone their skills in the new modern jazz format if they were lucky enough to sit in on other nights. After a thirty-two-year hiatus, a restored Minton's reopened in 2006 where patrons can enjoy live jazz every night. Check the Web or call for the schedule. Temporarily closed.

New Amsterdam Music Association (NAMA)

107 W. 130th St., between Adam Clayton Powell Blvd. and Malcolm X/Lenox. (212) 234-2973. Mon 7:30pm–11:30pm. Cash only. Bus—M2, M3, M7, M10, M102. Subway—A, B, C, D, 2, 3 to 125th St.

All are welcome to the nation's oldest Black musical association's open-mike jam session on Monday nights, featuring the NAMA band. NAMA dates back more than a hundred years when, by law, musicians had to be members of a union in order to perform in New York City. NAMA represented minority musicians not admitted into the white-only union. Its storied history includes some of the biggest names in jazz, including founding member James Reese Europe (who led the legendary **Harlem Hellfighters Orchestra** and is credited with introducing jazz to Europe during WWI). Jelly Roll Morton, Fletcher Henderson, Eubie Blake, **Sonny Greer, Zutty Singleton, Dicky Wells, Count Basie**, and others are among NAMA's famed alumni. Located on the garden level of the same brownstone it has owned since 1922, NAMA sponsors other activities to help pass jazz into the hands of the next generation of players in Harlem.

Dining and Live Entertainment

American Legion Post #398

248 W. 132nd St., between Frederick Douglass and Adam Clayton Powell Blvds. (212) 283-9701. Cuisine: Soul Food. Dinner. $$. Wed–Sun 7pm–12am. Cash only. Bus—M2, M3, M7, M10, M102. Subway—B, C, 2, 3 to 135th St.

Colonel Charles Young Post #398 is an historically Black American Legion Post in Harlem. Named for Colonel **Charles Young**, who was honored posthumously by Congress in 2001 as one of the Buffalo Soldiers' most distinguished heroes, the Post hosts the best-kept secret for jazz entertainment. Located in the lower level of a brownstone townhouse, the Legion's lineup includes jazz and a fish fry on Wednesdays, jazz on Thursdays, R&B oldies but goodies on Fridays, Harlem-style karaoke and R&B on Saturdays, and one of the best jam sessions in New York City on Sundays. There is usually a $10 soul food meal prepared in the back kitchen and drinks are cheap. Rather than a club, a visit to the Legion is like stumbling upon an old-style house party.

Billie's Black

271 W. 119th St., between Frederick Douglass Blvd. and St. Nicholas Ave. (212) 280-2248. www.billiesblack.com. Cuisine: Southern, Soul Food. Lunch, Dinner, Brunch. $$$. Tue–Thu 12pm–12am, Fri and Sat 12pm–4am, Sun 12pm–8pm. All major credit cards. Bus—M2, M7, M10, M102. Subway—B, C, 2, 3 to 116th St.

Billie's Black, named after owner **Adriane Ferguson's** mother, offers soul food with an elegant and creative twist. Catfish fingers on the appetizer menu, are so good that they are a meal unto themselves. You will also find an array of exotic mixed drinks on the menu, but the regulars swear by the mojitos. There is always something happening at Billie's, like karaoke every Tuesday (no cover), Funny Friday comedy where seasoned and up-and-coming comics get their jokes on (cover $10 in advance and $15 at the door), live jazz and R&B ($10 cover), and spoken word ($5 cover)—just check the Web site calendar. Billie's So Damn Happy Hour features $5 well drinks, beers, and appetizers from 5pm to 9pm.

L enox Lounge

288 Lenox Ave., between 124th and 125th Sts. (212) 427-0253. www.lenoxlounge.com/jazz.html. Cuisine: Soul Food. Dinner. $$$$. Daily 12pm–4am. Fri and Sat: cover charge $20 and $16 drink minimum per set, showtimes 9pm, 10:30pm, and 12am. Sun: cover charge $10 and $16 drink minimum per set, showtimes 7:30pm, 9pm, 10:30pm, and 12am. All major credit cards. Bus—M2, M7, M102. Subway—2, 3 to 125th St.

The world-famous Lenox Lounge opened its doors as a jazz club in the Harlem community in 1939. After eight months of restoration work, the legendary night spot reopened in 2001, reestablishing its distinction as the sole surviving Art Deco club interior in New York City. The Lounge was known in the 1940s for its famous **Zebra Room**, so named because of the zebra wall covering, which provided a venue for spectacular jazz organ performances. Billie Holiday frequently sat in with musicians and her favorite table is still there—the first one after you walk through the swinging doors. **Benny Powell, Dinah Washington, Dakota Staton, Ruth Brown**, and the **Ink Spots** have graced the stage of the Zebra Room. Today, local jazz legends like **Hank Johnson** and **Carrie Jackson** pack the house on the weekends. Monday night regular **Patience Higgins** and the **Sugar Hill Jazz Quartet** officiate over the jam session that also fills the rear and front rooms. Enjoy blues and R&B on Thursday night (no cover, two-drink minimum). The Lounge also has a small and competent kitchen that serves up good soul food dishes.

L ondel's Supper Club

2620 Frederick Douglass Blvd., between 139th and 140th Sts. (212) 234-6114. www.londelsrestaurant.com. Cuisine: Soul Food. Lunch, Dinner, Brunch. $$$. Tue–Sat 11:30am–11pm, Sun 11:30am–5pm, Fri and Sat: Live Jazz/R&B, two sets 8pm and 10pm with $5 cover charge per person. All major credit cards. Bus—M2, M3, M10. Subway—B, C to 135th St.

Londel's Supper Club, on the western edge of historic Striver's Row, is best known for its all-you-can-eat Sunday gospel brunch buffet. The brunch is also a good choice for those who want a little sampling of everything on the primarily upscale soul food menu. Signature dishes at Londel's include pan-seared salmon, honey barbecued baby back ribs, sautéed shrimp, chicken and waffles, and center-cut pork chops. Favorite desserts include sweet potato pie, bread pudding with rum and caramel sauce, and peach cobbler. Also, martini lovers rejoice—the daily happy hour features over twelve variations. Live jazz on the weekend makes this establishment a favorite hangout for Harlemites as well as for visitors.

Melba's Restaurant

300 W. 114th St., at Frederick Douglass Blvd. (212) 864-7777. www.melbasrestaurant.com. Cuisine: American. Dinner, Brunch. $$$. Mon–Sat 5pm–11pm, Sun 5pm–10pm, Brunch Sat and Sun 10am–3pm. All major credit cards. Bus—M2, M3, M7, M10, M116. Subway—B, C to 116th St.

It seems that talent runs in families, and the culinary gift was not lost on **Melba Wilson**, who spent over a decade building a following at Sylvia's, her aunt **Sylvia Wood**'s popular restaurant. Melba's is an intimate and elegantly designed restaurant that concentrates on serving up American "comfort" food like wine-braised short ribs over cheese grits, and the famous Harlem dish of Southern fried chicken and eggnog waffles with strawberry butter. Many of the entrées are soul-food centered, but there is lighter fare like the entrée salads and the grilled vegetable Napoleon (portobello mushrooms with squash and melted goat cheese). Every Tuesday there is live entertainment, and daily you can enjoy great cocktails like the slammin' mojitos.

MoBay Uptown Restaurant

17 W. 125th St., between Malcolm X/Lenox and Fifth Ave. (212) 876-9300. www. mobayrestaurant.com. Cuisine: Caribbean, Soul Food. Lunch, Dinner, Brunch. $$$$. Mon–Wed 11am–10pm, Thu 11am–11pm, Fri and Sat 11am–1am, Sun 11am–10pm. Live entertainment 9pm until closing Thu, Fri, and Sat, with a $5 cover charge per person. Sun Brunch 11am–4pm. All major credit cards. Bus—M2, M7, M60, M100, M101, M102, BX15. Subway—2, 3, Metro North to 125th St.

MoBay's offers a fusion of Cajun, Caribbean, Asian, and Southern-influenced cuisine and live entertainment (Wed–Sun) consisting of jazz, reggae, contemporary African music, and gospel during Sunday brunch. A must-try is the escovitch, which was featured on Bobby Flay's *Throwdown* on the Food Network. The barbecued ribs are also one of the standouts on the menu, as well as the St. Louis–style, dry-rubbed and slow-smoked with mesquite ribs. Here, you can enjoy a good meal, well-poured drinks, and great live music in an upscale but casually elegant setting.

Moca Restaurant and Lounge

2210 Frederick Douglass Blvd., at 119th St. (212) 665-8081. www.mocalounge.com. Cuisine: American. Lunch, Dinner, Brunch. $$$. Mon and Tue 5pm–2am, Wed and Thu 11am–2am, Fri and Sat 11am–4am, Sun 11am–2am. All major credit cards. Bus—M2, M3, M10. Subway—B, C to 116th St.

Moca is the gathering place for the young urban professional. Sporting an eclectically comfortable décor, this bar/lounge specializes in mixing up several varieties of flavored martinis for the amazingly low price of $5. While there is no live music entertainment here, there is racy and ribald erotic poetry reading— Red Room Erotica—held every Tuesday at 9pm. Sponsored by the Hottest Poets, it's like a poetry slam where wannabe and emerging poets come out to share their work. Also notable is Martini Monday which features outrageous comedy. Friday and Saturday a live DJ spins the latest hip-hop and R&B sounds for those who want to dance the night away. The menu features familiar food like Buffalo wings, beef and turkey burger sliders, sweet potato fries, pastas, salads, and an array of omelets during Sunday brunch from 11am–4pm.

Mojo

1855 St. Nicholas Ave., at 119th St., (212) 280-1924. www.mojo-harlem.com.
Cuisine: Middle Eastern, Mediterranean. Dinner, Brunch. $$$. Tue–Sat 6pm–12am,
Sun 11am–10pm. All major credit cards. Bus—M2, M3, M7, M10, M102. Subway—B, C, 2, 3 to
116th St.

Already this recently opened restaurant and bar has gained popularity among the smart set of Harlem and points beyond. Opened in early 2009, this stylishly designed restaurant offers a sophisticated menu of continental dishes with creative soul food spins—like the appetizer of grits with shitake mushrooms. A standout item on the menu is the perfectly seasoned and cooked-to-perfection lamb chops with crisp fries. There is a Sunday brunch from 11am–3pm, and a cute outdoor seating area of overstuffed divans and such. On Tuesday and Thursday nights jazz is featured.

MOJO

Nectar Wine Bar

2235 Frederick Douglass Blvd., at 121st St. (212) 866-9463. www.nectarwinenyc.com.
Cuisine: Cheeses, Hummus, Charcuterie. $$$. Daily 4pm–1am. All major credit cards.
Bus—M2, M3, M10. Subway—A, B, C, D to 125th St.

Nectar, the first wine bar in Harlem, was created with a downtown look and sensibility in mind for an uptown clientele who have been craving a good wine bar. It has been crowded since it opened in April of 2008, offering a nice cross-section of wines from a forty-selection list, including eleven champagne and sparkling wines from its sister shop, Harlem Vintage, located next door. A minimal menu of fine cheeses, charcuterie, hummus, paninis, and El Ray Venezuelan chocolates to complement the sweeter wines accent the wines rather than distract from them. The soothing modern design of a white sleek bar, asymmetrical sailcloth panels covering the walls and ceilings, a gray concrete floor, and a burgundy-toned rear wall where wine is stored horizontally, makes this bar look like no other in Harlem. The average cost of a glass of wine is $10. Live jazz on Mondays.

Ristorante Settepani

196 Malcolm X/Lenox, at 120th St. (917) 492-4806. www.settepani.com. Cuisine:
Italian – Lunch, Dinner, Brunch $$$. Tue–Fri 11am–11pm, Sat and Sun 10am–11pm. All
major credit cards. Bus—M2, M7, M102. Subway—2, 3 to 116th and 125th Sts.

Settepani, which opened as a gourmet bakery and later added light fare menu items, has been a gathering place for Mount Morris residents and visitors since 2000. In 2010 the establishment went through a renovation and reopened with a menu of Italian entrees such as mussels braised in orange sauce and black olives, trout cooked in parchment paper, and tuna marinated in olive oil and oregano, just to name a few. There is an extensive dessert menu, a complete wine list, and eight draft beers. The menu changes with the seasons and special menus are highlighted throughout the year. Also, special pre- and post-theatre menus are available. On Sunday, live music is featured that is curated by the restaurant's resident jazz musician Craig S. Harris. There is outdoor dining during warm weather. Deliveries have been added, and Settepani will continue providing full catering services for private functions off- and on-site in its new designed space.

Shrine Bar and Restaurant

2271 Adam Clayton Powell Blvd., between 133rd and 134th Sts. (212) 690-7807. www. shrinenyc.com/index.php. Cuisine: Mediterranean, African, American. Dinner, Brunch. $$. Daily 4pm–4am, Sun Brunch 10am–4pm. AmEx. Bus—M2, M7, M10, M102, BX33. Subway—B, C, 2, 3 to 135th St.

Named for the Lagos, Nigeria, musical enclave of the Fela Kuti clan, the Shrine is the newest center of alternative live World Music—Afro-Cuban, Brazilian, African, jazz, etc. The interior design features a great low-budget reproduction of the Afrobeat master and plenty of bargain-bin LP covers that reach back to the music heard in communities of color all over the country decades ago. Shows are often free, and if not there is a minimal music charge of $5. When there's no live music there's a DJ spinning. In addition there is comedy, poetry, theater, film, karaoke, and more. The bar offers a nice selection of cocktails with fancy Third World names attached to them and a restaurant brunch and dinner menu that include omelets and egg dishes, sandwiches, salads, vegetarian dishes and grilled meats, chicken, and fish entrees with sides of fries, couscous, plantain, and rice.

Sylvia's Restaurant

238 Lenox Ave., between 126th and 127th Sts. (212) 996-0660. www.sylviasrestaurant. com. Cuisine: Southern, Soul Food. Breakfast, Lunch, Dinner, Brunch. $$$. Mon–Sat 8am–10:30pm, Sun 11am–8pm. All major credit cards. Bus—M2, M7, M10, M60, M100, M101, BX15. Subway—2, 3 to 125th St.

Without a doubt, Sylvia's Restaurant is the most famous of Harlem's eateries! What started as a small luncheonette with counter service and a couple of tables when opened in 1962, has blossomed into a thriving family-run business enterprise that includes an expanded restaurant, a full catering hall and catering business, a nationwide line of Sylvia food products, two best-selling cookbooks, and a real estate firm. Even though local folks find it difficult to navigate because of the scores of tourists who are booked for lunch and dinner, they still enjoy breakfast here, and on any given morning, the movers and shakers of Harlem politics and business can be seen conducting business over thick old-fashioned grits, eggs, sausage and biscuits, and many other down-home breakfast dishes that helped establish the restaurant's fame. To this day, there are many who swear the fried chicken is the best in Harlem. Owner Sylvia Woods still comes around and greets visitors at dinnertime and will pose for photos, too. There is a lively gospel brunch on Sundays from 12:30pm–4pm.

Uptown Grand

2110 Adam Clayton Powell Blvd., at 126th St. (212) 280-2110. www.gospeluptown. com. Cuisine: Healthful Soul Fusion. Lunch, Dinner, Brunch. $$$$. Mon–Thu 11:30am–12pm, Fri 11:30am–1am, Sat 10:30–1am, Sun 10:30am–12pm. All major credit cards. Bus—M2, M3, M7, M10, M60, M100, M101, M102, BX33. Subway—A, B, C, D, 2, 3 to 125th St.

Uptown Grand is Harlem's most ambitious new restaurant to open in 2009. With 12,000 square feet of entertainment space, Uptown Grand's aim is to offer a unique dining experience and live inspirational entertainment seven days a week. The largest restaurant in Harlem, it seats 225 diners and can accommodate 500 people in the reception area. The handsomely designed space of wood, stainless steel, and exposed brick walls is accented by colorful abstract artwork. A sizable stage, supported by a broadcast-quality sound stage, dominates one side of the room and a bar the other side. An array of music acts which include R&B, soul, hip-hop, world music, Latin, cool jazz, and gospel are booked. Brunch is served on Saturday and Sunday with live entertainment from 11am to 4pm. Already *Mama I Want To Sing* creator/producer Vy Higginsen's musical production, *Let The Music Play Gospel*, is performed every Saturday at 2pm during Gospel Uptown's prix-fixe brunch. Leading the culinary team is the classically trained chef **Kenneth Collins**, previously executive chef at Ida Mae's Kitchen-n-Lounge in Chelsea. He calls his cooking style "multi-ethnic nouvelle," or Euro/Asian-inflected Southern comfort food.

Bars & Lounges

6 7 Orange Street

2082 Frederick Douglass Blvd., between 112th and 113th St. (212) 662-2030. www.67orangestreet.com. Cuisine: Eclectic Bar Food, Raw Bar. $$$. Mon–Tues 6pm–12am, Wed–Thu 6pm–2am, Fri–Sat 6pm–4am, Sun 6pm–12am. All major credit cards. Bus—M2, M3, M7, M10, M116. Subway—B, C to 110th St.

You won't find the usual suspects—mojitos and cosmos—on the menu at 67 Orange, which is an upscale cocktail lounge that takes its name from the final address of the African American-owned Almack's Dance Hall that flourished in the early 1800s in notorious Five Points. Instead, you will find $13 libations that combine luxury spirits from all ends of the globe with homemade liquor infusions of natural fruits, herbs, and spices. A must-try is *Madame Almack*—a cocktail made of Bak's Bison Grass Vodka, fresh mint, Cynar Artichoke Aperitif, and champagne. The food menu is just as atypical, with light fare offerings such as orange-roasted duck leg with cinnamon mashed potatoes and a daily selection of market-fresh shellfish. Owner **Karl Franz Williams**, who also owns Society Café, has outfitted the cozy vintage space with purple velvet curtains, distressed mirrors, filament light bulbs, and rotating fine art on the brick walls.

Paris Blues—Lounge/Bar

2021 Adam Clayton Powell Blvd., at 121st St. (212) 864-9110. Cocktail Lounge. $. Mon–Sat 11am–4am, Sun 12pm–3am. All major credit cards. Bus—M2, M7, M10, M102. Subway—A, B, C, D, 2, 3 to 125th St.

This neighborhood bar is an institution to Harlem locals. Although there is an outdoor seating area in the front of the bar, no one uses it. However, inside it is warm and inviting, with a wood-grain bar top and swivel bar stools. Music is provided by a jukebox that features a good selection of R&B tunes. You can get a good stiff traditional drink—not a lot of fancy nouveau mixed drinks here.

PJ's Bar and Lounge

2256 Adam Clayton Powell Blvd., between 132nd and 133rd Sts. (212) 862-1511. Cocktail Lounge. $$. Mon–Sat 1pm–4am. All major credit cards. Bus—M2, M7, M10, M102. Subway—2, 3 to 135th St.

This is an authentically Harlem bar where friendly Harlemites hang out. You are assured a well-poured drink compliments of bartender Tom Martin, who often prepares a mixed-drink special for customers. There is a spacious bar counter, and the R&B and hip-hop music, á la the jukebox, brings people off the stools and onto the dance floor.

SHOPPING

Apparel

American Appeal
250 W. 125th St., between Frederick Douglass and Adam Clayton Powell Blvds. (212) 678-5020. www.americanappeal.us. Mon–Thu 10am–7:30pm, Fri and Sat 10am–8pm, Sun 10am–6pm. All major credit cards. Bus—M2, M3, M7, M10, M60, M100, M101, M102, BX15. Subway—A, B, C, D, 2, 3 to 125th St.

Hip and stylish clothes for young adults.

Apollo Signature
215 W. 125th St., between Frederick Douglass and Adam Clayton Powell Blvds. (212) 961-1500. Mon–Sat 11am–8pm, Sun 12pm–6pm. All major credit cards. Bus—M2, M3, M7, M10, M60, M100, M101, M102, BX15. Subway—A, B, C, D, 2, 3 to 125th St.

Fine Italian fashion by the hottest designers including Prada, Fendi, Dolce & Gabbana, and Versace, shoes, jeans, suits, and accessories for men and women.

Ashley Stewart Flagship Store
216 W. 125th St., between Frederick Douglass and Adam Clayton Powell Blvds. (212) 531-0800. www.ashleystewart.com. Mon–Sat 10am–7pm, Sun 11am–6pm. All major credit cards. Bus—M2, M3, M7, M10, M60, M100, M101, M102, BX15. Subway—A, B, C, D, 2, 3 to 125th St.

Ashley Stewart – Renaissance Plaza
49 W. 116th St., between Malcolm X/Lenox and Fifth Ave. (917) 492-3693. Bus—M7, M102, M116. Subway—2, 3 to 116th St.

Fashionable clothes and accessories for plus-sized women.

Aysa Boutique
2310 Adam Clayton Powell Blvd., between 135th and 136th Sts. (212) 234-6050. www.aysaboutique.com. Mon and Tue 11am–7pm, Fri and Sat 11am–8pm, Sun 11am–4pm. All major credit cards. Bus—M2, M7, M10, M102, BX33. Subway—B, C, 2, 3 to 135th St.

Stylish evening and special occasion clothes, shoes, jewelry, and handbags for women. Plus sizes carried here.

B. Oyama
2330 Adam Clayton Powell Blvd., at 137th St. (212) 234-5128. www.boyamanyc.com. Mon 3pm–7pm, Tue–Sat 12pm–7pm. All major credit cards. Bus—M2, M7, M10, M102, BX33. Subway—B, C, 2, 3 to 135th St.

Luxury apparel for men and women including tailored suits, shirts, and accessories.

B.O.R.N. Vintage Boutique
52 W. 125th St., between Malcolm X/Lenox and Fifth Ave. (212) 722-3706. Mon–Sat 11am–7pm, Sun by appointment. All major credit cards. Bus—M1, M2, M7, M60, M100, M101, M102, BX15. Subway—2, 3, Metro North to 125th St.

Upscale consignment boutique with a fabulous collection of clothes and accessories.

B.O.R.N. VINTAGE BOUTIQUE

Ballers Denim Boutique
252 W. 125th St., between Frederick Douglass and Adam Clayton Powell Blvds. (212) 665-7230. Mon–
Sat 10am–7:30pm, Sun 11am–6:30pm. All major credit cards. Bus—M2, M3, M7, M10, M60, M100, M101,
M102, BX15. Subway—A, B, C, D, 2, 3 to 125th St.

Name-brand jeans, sneakers, T-shirts, and accessories for men and women.

Bebenoir
2164 Frederick Douglass Blvd., between 116th and 117th Sts. (212) 828-5775. www.bebenoir.com. Mon
2pm–9pm, Tue–Fri 1pm–9pm, Sat 12pm–9pm, Sun 12pm–7pm. All major credit cards. Bus—M2, M3,
M7, M10, M116. Subway—B, C to 116th St.

Fashionable, bold, and exotic shirts, jeans, jackets, and accessories for men and women.

Dr. Jay's
162 W. 125th St., between Adam Clayton Powell Blvd. and Malcolm X/Lenox. (212) 316-0057. www.
drjays.com. Mon–Thu 9:30am–7pm, Fri and Sat 9:30am–8pm, Sun 10am–7pm. All major credit cards.
Bus—M2, M3, M7, M10, M60, M100, M101, M102, BX15. Subway—A, B, C, D, 2, 3 to 125th St.

Trendy brand-name clothes, sneakers, sportswear, and accessories for men. Also, sneakers for women
and kids can be found here.

Fino
118 W. 125th St., between Adam Clayton Powell Blvd. and Malcolm X/Lenox. (646) 698-1407. www.
portabellastores.com. Mon–Fri 9:30am–8pm, Sat 9:30am–8:30pm, Sun 10am–7pm. All major credit
cards. Bus—M2, M3, M7, M10, M60, M100, M101, M102, BX15. Subway—A, B, C, D, 2, 3 to 125th St.

Fine menswear clothing store with designer suits, outerwear, shirts, shoes, accessories, and more.

Generation
30 W. 125th St., between Malcolm X/Lenox and Fifth Ave. (212) 369-8510. Mon–Thu 10am–7:30pm, Fri
and Sat 10am 8pm, Sun10:30am–6:30pm. V, MC. Bus—M1, M2, M7, M60, M100, M101, M102, BX15.
Subway—2, 3, Metro North to 125th St.

Name-brand sneakers and clothes for men.

H & M
125 W. 125th St., between Adam Clayton Powell Blvd. and Malcolm X/Lenox. (212) 665-8300. www.
hm.com. Mon–Sat 10am–8pm, Sun 11am–8pm. V, MC, Dis. Bus—M2, M3, M7, M10, M60, M100, M101,
M102, BX15. Subway—A, B, C, D, 2, 3 to 125th St.

Fashionable clothing store that operates 1,800 stores spread over thirty-four markets and specializes in
apparel and accessories for women, men, teenagers, and children at the best prices.

Harlem NYC
256 W. 125th St., between Frederick Douglass and Adam Clayton Powell Blvds. (212) 665-7795. Mon–
Wed 9:30am–7:15pm, Thu–Sat 9:30am–7:45pm, Sun 10am–7pm. All major credit cards. Bus—M2, M3,
M7, M10, M60, M100, M101, M102, BX15. Subway—A, B, C, D, 2, 3 to 125th St.

Brand-name clothes, sneakers, shoes, accessories, and more for men, women, and children. Also, there
is a nice "big and tall" department.

HATS BY BUNN

Harlem's Heaven Hat Boutique
2538 Adam Clayton Powell Blvd., at 147th St. (212) 491-7706. www.harlemsheaven.com. Tue–Sat 12pm–6pm. All major credit cards. Bus—M2, M3, M7, M10, M102, BX19. Subway—A, B, C, D, 3 to 145th St.

Hats for all occasions are at this boutique.

Hats by Bunn
2283 Adam Clayton Powell Blvd., between 134th and 135th Sts. (212) 694-3590. www.hatsbybunn.com. Mon–Sat 11am–7pm. All major credit cards. Bus—M2, M7, M10, M102, BX33. Subway—B, C, 2, 3 to 135th St.

Designer and custom-made waxed-straw and flat-top felt hats for men and women. Designer Bunn, who hails from Trinidad, sponsors a summer and winter fashion show that includes cutting-edge African American designer apparel, as well as hats. Call for dates.

Jimmy Jazz
132 W. 125th St., between Adam Clayton Powell Blvd. and Malcolm X/Lenox. (212) 665-4198, www.jimmyjazz.com. Mon–Thu 9:30am–7:30pm, Fri and Sat 9:30am–8pm, Sun 11am–6pm. All major credit cards. Bus—M2, M3, M7, M10, M60, M100, M101, M102, BX15. Subway—A, B, C, D, 2, 3 to 125th St.

239 W. 125th St., between Frederick Douglass and Adam Clayton Powell Blvds. (212) 663-2827. Mon–Thu 9:30am–7:30pm, Fri and Sat 9:30am–8pm, Sun 11am–6:30pm.

Stylish brand-name clothes, sneakers, and accessories for men, women, and children.

K & G Fashion Superstore
2321 Frederick Douglass Blvd., between 124th and 125th Sts. (212) 222-2389. www.kgstores.com. Mon–Fri 9:30am–9pm, Sat 9:30am–9pm, Sun 11am–7pm. All major credit cards. Bus—M2, M3, M7, M10, M60, M100, M101, M102, BX15. Subway—A, B, C, D, 2, 3 to 125th St.

Discounted brand-name clothes and accessories for men, women, and children.

Lane Bryant
222 W. 125th St., between Frederick Douglass and Adam Clayton Powell Blvds. (212) 678-0546. www.lanebryant.com. Mon–Sat 10am–8pm, Sun 10am–7pm. All major credit cards. Bus—M2, M3, M7, M10, M60, M100, M101, M102, BX15. Subway—A, B, C, D, 2, 3 to 125th St.

Fashionable clothes and accessories for plus-sized women.

Lazarus
264 W. 125th St., between Frederick Douglass and Adam Clayton Powell Blvds. (212) 222-6023. Mon–Thu 9am–7pm, Fri and Sat 9am–7:30pm, Sun 10am–6pm. All major credit cards. Bus—M2, M3, M7, M10, M60, M100, M101, M102, BX15. Subway—A, B, C, D, 2, 3 to 125th St.

Affordably priced children's clothes, accessories, toys, and furniture.

Leather
116 W. 125th St., between Adam Clayton Powell and Malcolm X/Lenox. (212) 865-0257. Mon–Sat 10am–7:30pm, Sun 11am–7pm. V, MC. Bus—M2, M3, M7, M10, M60, M100, M101, M102, BX15. Subway—A, B, C, D, 2, 3 to 125th St.

Leather jackets and clothes for men, women, and children.

Modell's
300 W. 125th St., between St. Nicholas Ave. and Frederick Douglass Blvd. (212) 280-9100. www.modells. com. Mon–Sat 9am–9pm, Sun 10am–8pm. All major credit cards. Bus—M2, M3, M7, M10, M60, M100, M101, M102, BX15. Subway—A, B, C, D, 2, 3 to 125th St.

Sporting goods, sporting apparel, menswear, women's wear, and brand-name athletic footwear.

Montgomery
2312 Adam Clayton Powell Blvd., between 135th and 136th Sts. (646) 260-14486. Tue–Sat 11am–6:30pm. V, MC. Bus—M2, M7, M10, M102, BX33. Subway—B, C, 2, 3 to 135th St.

Designer **Montgomery Harris** moved her SoHo boutique to Harlem, where she continues to showcase her latest designs, signature pieces from her private collection, and her popular Jolinda &

Family memorabilia. She creates beautiful one-of-a-kind outfits, using only hard-to-come-by prints that are often fifty to a hundred years old. Many celebrities and models wear her garments, such as Iman, Sting, Diana Ross, Brandy, and Oprah. She has also won peer accolades: the Vidal Sassoon Award for Style 1995 and the Absolut Vodka Style Award in 1999.

My Kids
6 W. 125th St., between Malcolm X/Lenox and Fifth Ave. (212) 828-3888. Mon–Sat 9:30am–7:30pm, Sun 11am–6pm. All major credit cards. Bus—M1, M2, M7, M60, M100, M101, M102, BX15. Subway—2, 3, Metro North to 125th St.

Brand-name clothing and accessories for kids.

MY KIDS

N HARLEM NEW YORK

N Harlem New York
171 Malcolm X/Lenox, between 117th and 118th Sts. (212) 961-9100. www.nharlemnewyork.com. Tue–Fri 11am–8pm, Sat 12pm–7pm. All major credit cards. Bus—M2, M7, M102, M116. Subway—2, 3 to 116th St.

N is renowned for its well-edited assortment of clothing, shoes, and accessories. It features fashion-forward menswear and women's wear collections from local and international designers.

Old Navy
300 W. 125th St., between St. Nicholas Ave. and Frederick Douglass Blvd. (212) 531-1544. www.oldnavy. gap.com. Mon–Sat 9:30am–9pm, Sun 10am–8pm. All major credit cards. Bus—M2, M3, M7, M10, M60, M100, M101, M102, BX15. Subway—A, B, C, D, 2, 3 to 125th St.

Men's, women's, and children's apparel and accessories. This store also carries maternity clothes.

Olympic Town

114 W. 125th St., between Adam Clayton Powell Blvd. and Malcolm/Lenox. (212) 678-0450, Mon–Sat 9:30am–7:30pm, Sun 11am–6pm. All major credit cards. Bus—M2, M3, M7, M10, M60, M100, M101, M102, BX15. Subway—A, B, C, D, 2, 3 to 125th St.

Stylish brand-name clothes, sneakers, and accessories for men and women.

Porta Bella

253 W. 125th St., between Frederick Douglass and Adam Clayton Powell Blvds. (212) 663-6375. www.portabellastores.com. Mon–Thu 9:30am–8pm, Fri and Sat 9:30am–8:30pm, Sun 10am–7:30pm. V, MC. Bus—M2, M3, M7, M10, M60, M100, M101, M102, BX15. Subway—A, B, C, D, 2, 3 to 125th St.

Fine menswear clothing store with designer suits, outerwear, shirts, shoes, accessories, and more.

S & D Underground

136 W. 125th St., between Adam Clayton Powell Blvd. and Malcolm X/Lenox. (212) 222-1577. www.jimmyjazz.com. Mon–Thu 9:30am–7:30pm, Fri and Sat 9:30am–8pm, Sun 11am–6:30pm. All major credit cards. Bus—M2, M3, M7, M10, M60, M100, M101, M102, BX15. Subway—A, B, C, D, 2, 3 to 125th St.

Stylish brand-name clothes, sneakers, and accessories for men, women, and kids.

The Children's Place

248 W. 125th St., between Frederick Douglass and Adam Clayton Powell Blvds. (212) 866-9616. www.childrensplace.com. Mon–Sat 9am–8pm, Sun 10am–6pm. All major credit cards. Bus—M2, M3, M7, M10, M60, M100, M101, M102, BX15. Subway—A, B, C, D, 2, 3 to 125th St.

Clothing and accessories at unbelievable prices for girls and boys sizes 0–14.

The Scarf Lady

408 Malcolm X/Lenox, between 130th and 131st Sts. (646) 228-5036. Mon-Fri 12pm-7pm, Sat 11am-8pm, Sun 11am-6pm. All major credit cards. Bus—M7, M102. Subway—2, 3 to 125th or 135th Sts.

The nicest selection of unique scarves, hats, jewelry, accessories and gift items in Harlem.

Books

HUE-MAN BOOKSTORE

Hue-Man Bookstore

2319 Frederick Douglass Blvd., between 124th and 125th Sts. (212) 665-7400. www.huemanbookstore.com. Mon–Sat 10am–8pm, Sun 11am–7pm. All major credit cards. Bus—M2, M3, M7, M10, M60, M100, M101, M102, BX15. Subway—A, B, C, D, 2, 3 to 125th St.

Hue-Man Bookstore, which has an in-house café, hosts wonderful book signings and children's events.

Cosmetics/Salons/Spas

Carol's Daughter Flagship Store

24 W. 125th St., between Malcolm X/Lenox and Fifth Ave. (212) 828-6757. www.carolsdaughter.com. Mon–Sat 10am–8pm, Sun 11am–6pm. All major credit cards. Bus—M1, M2, M7, M60, M100, M101, M102, BX15. Subway—2, 3, Metro North to 125th St.

All-natural hair, body, cosmetic, and fragrance products with a hand and foot day spa.

MAKARI

MAC
202 W. 125th St., between Frederick Douglass and Adam Clayton Powell Blvds. (212) 665-0676. www.maccosmetics. com. Mon–Thu 11am–8pm, Fri and Sat 10am–8pm, Sun 12pm–6pm. All major credit cards. Bus—M2, M3, M7, M10, M60, M100, M101, M102, BX15. Subway—A, B, C, D, 2, 3 to 125th St.

Makeup, skin care products, nail care, and accessories.

Makari
52 W. 125th St., between Malcolm X/Lenox and Fifth Ave. (212) 348-7464. www.makari.com. Daily 10am–6:15pm. All major credit cards. Bus—M1, M2, M7, M10, M60, M100, M101, M102, BX15. Subway—2, 3, Metro North to 125th St.

High-end skin care and cosmetics line especially suited for dark-skinned men and women.

SADE SKINCARE

Sade Skincare
2046 Adam Clayton Powell Blvd., between 122nd and 123rd Sts. (212) 749-4533. www.sadeskincare.com. Wed–Sun 11am–7pm. All major credit cards. Bus—M2, M7, M10, M102. Subway—A, B, C, D, 2, 3 to 125th St.

Traditional herbal skincare therapy and cosmetics that are handmade in Africa, as well as spa services including organic herbal facials and facial peels, waxing, massage services, and hot stone therapy.

Scents of Nature
321 Lenox Ave., at 126th St. (212) 222-2773. www.scentsofnatures.com. Mon–Sat 10am–8pm. All major credit cards. Bus—M2, M3, M7, M10, M60, M100, M101, M102, BX15. Subway—A, B, C, D, 2, 3 to 125th St.

Fragrance oils, essential oils, lotions, incense, candles, accessories, and more, wholesale and retail. They also have their own brand of cosmetics and skincare, as well as QEI + Paris.

Turning Heads Salon & Day Spa
218 Lenox Avenue, at 121st St. (212) 828-4600. www.turningheadsdayspa.com. Mon 12pm–5pm, Tue–Fri 10am–7pm, Sat 9am–5pm, Sun 12pm–4pm. All major credit cards. Bus—M2, M7, M102. Subway—2, 3 to 125th St.

A full-service day spa and beauty salon specializing in natural hair care including locks, lock extensions, and braids. Other salon services include color, cuts, weaves, relaxers, press and curl, and barbering. Day spa services include facials, massage services, hot stone therapy, waxing, and spa manicures and pedicures.

Discount Stores

Conway
101 W. 116th St., at Malcolm X/Lenox. (212) 865-8783. Mon–Sat 9:30am–7:45pm, Sun 10:45–6:45pm. All major credit cards. Bus—M2, M7, M102, M116. Subway—2, 3 to 116th St.

Discount store with clothes, household items, and more. Great place to get clothes for children and teenagers. Bargains galore!

Marshall's
125 W. 125th St., between Adam Clayton Powell and Malcolm X/Lenox. (212) 866-3963. www.marshall-sonline.com. Mon–Sat 9:30am–9pm, Sun 11am–7pm. All major credit cards. Bus—M2, M3, M7, M10, M60, M100, M101, M102, BX15. Subway—A, B, C, D, 2, 3 to 125th St.

Discount department store with a plus-sized women's and "big and tall" men's section. Home goods also are sold here.

Fabric Stores

Kaarta Imports and Exports
121 W. 125th St., between Adam Clayton Powell Blvd. and Malcolm X/Lenox. (212) 866-5190. Mon–Sat 9am–8:30pm, Sun 1pm–8pm. All major credit cards. Bus—M2, M7, M60, M100, M101, M102, BX15. Subway—A, B, C, D, 2, 3 to 125th St.

Large selection of wholesale and retail African fabrics, clothes, accessories, and more. On-site tailoring is also available.

Welcometoharlemhiddentreasures.com
This online store has a large selection of African cotton fabrics and mudcloth, wholesale and retail. They also have a large selection of wax prints, batik, silk, lace, brocade, and more. Just email them at orders@welcometoharlem.com and they will find that perfect piece of fabric for you. They ship worldwide.

Yara African Fabrics
2 W. 125th St., between Malcolm X/Lenox and Fifth Ave. (212) 289-3842. Mon–Sat 10am–7:30pm, Sun 1pm–6:30pm. All major credit cards. Bus—M1, M7, M60, M100, M101, M102, BX15. Subway—2, 3 to 125th St.

Large selection of wholesale and retail African fabrics, clothes, accessories, and more. On-site tailoring is also available.

Flea Markets & Thrift Stores

Goodwill Harlem Store
2196 Fifth Ave., between 134th and 135rd Sts. (212) 862-0020. Mon–Sat 10am–8pm, Sun 10am–7pm. All major credit cards. Bus—M1, M7, M102, BX33. Subway—2, 3 to 135th St.

One of the most well-known thrift stores in the country, this Goodwill store features gently used and often brand-new home goods, furniture, accessories, and clothing for men, women, and children.

Harlem Community Flea Market
Salvation Army, 540 Malcolm X/Lenox, between 137th and 138th Sts. Sat 10am–6pm. Bus—M2, M7, M102, BX33. Subway—2, 3 to 135th St.

Indoor/outdoor market.

Malcolm Shabazz Harlem Market
52 W. 116th St., between Malcolm X/Lenox and Fifth Ave. (212) 987-8131. Daily 10am–8pm. Bus—M2, M7, M102, M116. Subway—2, 3 to 116th St.

The Malcolm Shabazz Harlem Market has a large selection of carved wooden figurines, African fabrics, jewelry, African-style clothes for men, women, and children, and more.

Food

Best Yet Market of Harlem
2187 Frederick Douglass Blvd. between 118th and 119th Sts. (212) 377-2300. www.bestyetmarket.com. Mon–Sun 7am–10pm. All major credit cards. Bus—M2, M3, M10. Subway—B, C to 116th St.

New gourmet supermarket with a large produce department, including organic produce, as well as prepared foods, an olive bar, and much more. Supermarket includes a top floor café, with free Wi-Fi, that serves up fresh-squeezed juices, smoothies, artisanal coffees, and teas. Space contains comfortable seating and tables that can be used to enjoy deli sandwiches and paninis that can be purchased on the floor below.

Karrot Health Food Store
304 W. 117th St., between Manhattan Ave. and Frederick Douglass Blvd. (212) 870-0290. Mon–Sat 8am–8pm, Sun 9am–7pm. V, MC, Bus—M2, M3, M7, M10, M116. Subway—B, C to 116th St.

Organic produce, groceries, frozen foods, and juice bar.

Pathmark Supermarket
300 W. 145th St., between Bradhurst Ave. and Frederick Douglass Blvd. (212) 281-3158. www.pathmark. com. 24 hours. All major credit cards. Bus—M2, M3, M10, BX19. Subway—A, B, C, D to 145th St.

Supermarket with underground parking that is free for one hour when grocery receipt is shown.

Watkins Health Foods
46 W. 125th St., between Malcolm X/Lenox and Fifth Ave. (212) 831-2955. Mon–Sat 9am–8pm, Sun 11am–6pm. All major credit cards. Bus—M2, M7, M60, M100, M101, M102, BX15. Subway—2, 3, Metro North to 125th St.

66 W. 116th St., between Malcolm X/Lenox and Fifth Ave. (212) 369-5032. Mon–Sat 9am–8pm, Sun 11am–6pm. All major credit cards. Bus—M2, M7, M102, M116. Subway—2, 3 to 116th St.

Health food store providing sugar-free snacks, dry goods, organic produce, natural hair and skin care products, vegetarian groceries, and juice bar.

Home Furnishings

Paramount
124 W. 125th St., between Adam Clayton Powell Blvd. and Malcolm/Lenox. (212) 678-6800. Mon–Sat 9:30am–7:30pm, Sun 11am–6pm. All major credit cards. Bus—M2, M7, M60, M100, M101, M102, BX15. Subway—A, B, C, D, 2, 3 to 125th St.

Housewares, linens, drapes, bedspreads, and more.

Swing
1960 Adam Clayton Powell Blvd., at 118th St. (212) 222-5802. www.swing-nyc.com. Wed–Fri 12pm–8pm, Sat 11am–7pm and Sun 10am–6pm. Bus—M2, M7, M10, M102. Subway—B, C, 2, 3 to 116th St.

Swing is a concept shop that embodies the meaning of swing music and dance made popular during the Harlem Renaissance. The store serves as the metaphor for where melody, balance, and harmony converge. Owner **Helena Greene**, a New York native who returned after having lived and traveled extensively around the world, opened Swing to share what she'd experienced in her travels. You can find reasonably priced gift items that come from all corners of the world, or that "just right" decorative item for your home at Swing. A fashion designer by trade, Greene's couture touch is evident throughout the store that features collectibles, accessories, eclectic apparel, and trendy home goods. It's a store that reflects the verve of a neighborhood well on the upswing.

Recreation

Harlem Lanes
2110-2118 Adam Clayton Powell Blvd., 3rd and 4th Flrs., between 125th and 126th Sts. (212) 678-BOWL. www.harlemlanes.com. Mon–Wed 11am–9pm, Thu 11am–11pm, Fri and Sat 11am–2am, Sun 11am–9pm. All major credit cards. Bus—M2, M3, M7, M10, M60, M100, M101, M102, BX15. Subway—A, B, C, D, 2, 3 to 125th St.

State-of-the-art bowling lanes. Happy Hour from 5pm to 8pm features $3 cocktails, beer, and wine, and 25-cent jumbo Buffalo wings dipped in sauce of choice.

ModSquad Cycles
2199 Frederick Douglass Blvd., between 114th and 115th Sts. (212) 865-5051. www.modsquadcycles.com. Mon–Fri 11am–7pm, Sat 11am–6pm, Sun 12pm–5pm. All major credit cards. Bus—M3, M7, M10, M116. Subway—B, C to 116th St.

Bike rentals.

Sneakers/Shoes

Aerosoles
200 W. 125th St., between Frederick Douglass and Adam Clayton Powell Blvds. (212) 865-5221. www.aerosoles.com. Mon–Fri 9:30am–8pm, Sat 10am–8pm, Sun 11am–7pm. All major credit cards. Bus—M2, M3, M7, M10, M60, M100, M101, M102, BX15. Subway—A, B, C, D, 2, 3 to 125th St.

ATMOS

Women's fashionable footwear at affordable prices.

Atmos
203 W. 125th St., between Frederick Douglass and Adam Clayton Powell Blvds. (212) 666-2242. Mon–Sat 11am–8pm, Sun 12pm–7pm. V, MC, AmEx. Bus—M2, M3, M7, M10, M60, M100, M101, M102, BX15. Subway—A, B, C, D, 2, 3 to 125th St.

Features exclusive Jordan products including the Air Jordan IX retro x Skull Candy "For the Love of the Game" pack.

House of Hoops
268 W. 125th St., between Frederick Douglass and Adam Clayton Powell Blvds. (212) 316-1667. www.footlocker.com. Mon–Sat 10am–8pm, Sun 10am–7pm. All major credit cards. Bus—M2, M3, M7, M10, M60, M100, M101, M102, BX15. Subway—A, B, C, D, 2, 3 to 125th St.

All Nike Basketball, Air Jordan, Converse, and Sport Culture products. For the hardcore collector, every three weeks House of Hoops receives exclusive limited-edition sneakers.

Nine West Outlet
228 St. Nicholas Ave., between 124th and 125th Sts. (212) 665-1022. www.ninewest.com. Mon–Sat 10am–7pm, Sun 11am–6pm. All major credit cards. Bus—M2, M3, M7, M10, M60, M100, M101, M102, BX15. Subway—A, B, C, D, 2, 3 to 125th St.

GRANDMA'S PLACE

Discounted women's shoes, sandals, boots, handbags, and accessories.

Payless
208 W. 125th St., between Frederick Douglass and Adam Clayton Powell Blvds. (212) 662-3582. www.payless.com. Mon–Sat 9am–8pm, Sun 10am–8pm. All major credit cards. Bus—M2, M3, M7, M10, M60, M100, M101, M102, BX15. Subway—A, B, C, D, 2, 3 to 125th St.

Fashionable footwear and accessories for women, men, and children at great prices.

Toys

Grandma's Place
84 W. 120th St., between Malcolm X/Lenox and Mt. Morris Park West. (212) 360-6776. www.grandmasplaceinharlem.com. Tue–Sat 11am–8pm, Sun 12pm–6:30pm, V, MC, AmEx. Bus—M2, M7, M102. Subway—2, 3 to 116th St.

Treasure trove of games, dolls, toys, and books for kids.

Wine/Liquor

Harlem Vintage
2235 Frederick Douglass Blvd., at 121st St. (212) 866-9463. www.harlemvintage.com. Mon–Thu 11am–9pm, Fri and Sat 11am–10pm, Sun 1pm–9pm. All major credit cards. Bus—M2, M3, M10. Subway—A, B, C, D to 125th St.

Nice selection of wines from South Africa and spirits in a warm and inviting setting. Free wine tasting on Sat 4pm–7pm.

Lenox Wines
381 Lenox Ave., at 129th St. (212) 410-9463. www.lenoxwinestore.com. Mon–Sat 11am–10pm, Sun 1pm–9pm. All major credit cards. Bus—M2, M3, M7, M102. Subway—A, B, C, D, 2, 3 to 125th St.

Lenox Wines carries a unique and distinct selection of wines from South Africa and South America. Free wine tasting Thu and Sat 7pm–9pm.

The Winery
257 W. 116th St., (212) 222-4866. www.thewineryonline.com. Sun–Fri 1pm–9pm, Sat 12pm–9pm. All major credit cards. Bus—M2, M3, M7, M10, M116. Subway—B, C, 2, 3 to 116th St.

Wine shop focusing on small-production boutique wines from both the new and old worlds. Free wine tasting Fri 6pm–8pm.

SIGNIFICANT FAITH-BASED INSTITUTIONS
AND BURIAL GROUNDS

Mother A. M. E. Zion Church
140-7 W. 137th St., between Adam Clayton Powell Blvd. and Malcolm X/Lenox. (212) 234-1544. Bus—M2, M7, M102, BX33. Subway—B, C, 2, 3 to 135th St.

MOTHER A. M. E. ZION CHURCH

The first Black church to be founded in New York State, Mother A. M. E. Zion Church is known as the **"Freedom Church"** for the central role it played in the Underground Railroad providing sanctuary for escaped slaves. Among the escaped slaves the church hid was Frederick Douglass, an icon in American history who became a noted abolitionist, orator, and statesman. Douglass, abolitionists **Sojourner Truth**, **Harriet Tubman**, and millionaire **Madam C. J. Walker** were famous congregants of the church. It was established in lower Manhattan in 1796 when a group of about a hundred worshipers, tired of sitting in the Negro pews and wanting to worship as equals, were led by **James Varick** to a rented building on Cross Street to worship separately. By 1820 they voted to leave the white Methodist Episcopal Church because it would not ordain Black bishops. Varick became the first A. M. E. Zion bishop. As African Americans moved uptown, Mother A. M. E. Zion relocated to Harlem in 1914 and moved into a grand edifice in 1925 that was designed by **George W. Foster Jr.**, the first African American architect registered in New Jersey. The neo-Gothic stone church received landmark designation in 1993. The pastor in 1936 who believed in taking the church to the streets to the people, the **Rev. Benjamin Robeson**, was the brother of actor, singer, and activist **Paul Robeson**, who often attended church services and spoke out against discrimination. The **Rev. Gregory Robeson Smith**, grandson of Benjamin Robeson, is the current pastor of the church.

Abyssinian Baptist Church
132 Odell Clark Place (Formerly 138th St.), between Adam Clayton Powell Blvd. and Malcolm X/Lenox. (212) 862-7474. www.abyssinian.org. Bus—M2, M7, M102, BX33. Subway—B, C, 2, 3 to 135th St.

ABYSSINIAN BAPTIST CHURCH

Though Harlem has been home to the Abyssinian Baptist Church for over eighty years, the church has been in existence since 1808. Founded by a group of African Americans and Ethiopian merchants who were unwilling to accept the racially segregated seating of the First Baptist Church of New York City, Abyssinian (the ancient name for Ethiopia) has evolved from its early beginnings in lower Manhattan in a small wooden structure on Worth Street into an imposing neo-Gothic complex in Harlem that was designed by the Philadelphia-based firm of **Charles W. Bolton & Son**, 1922–23, which was known for its Protestant church design. The church was designated a landmark in 1993. The **Rev. Adam Clayton Powell Sr.**, a social activist who was instrumental in the move to Harlem and the building of the church in 1923, turned the church over to his son,

Adam Clayton Powell Jr., in 1937, who continued his father's dynamic and charismatic leadership until 1971. During this time he was elected to the City Council in 1941 and was the first Black person from New York elected to Congress in 1944; he served until 1972. Today Abyssinian, under the guidance of the **Rev. Dr. Calvin O. Butts**, is a social justice and economic development leader in Harlem. Through its not-for-profit development corporation, the church has helped transform Central Harlem into the community that we know today.

E benezer Gospel Tabernacle Church
225 Lenox, at 121ˢᵗ St. (212) 222-0470. Bus—M2, M7, M60, M100, M101, M102, BX15. Subway—2, 3 to 125ᵗʰ St.

EBENEZER GOSPEL TABERNACLE CHURCH

This Gothic Revival church, which was designed by **Charles Atwood** and constructed in 1889–91 for the **Lenox Avenue Unitarian Church**, was the third Unitarian Church built in New York City and the only one located north of 34ᵗʰ Street. In 1919 the building was sold to a congregation of orthodox Jewish immigrants from Eastern Europe who established the **Congregation and Chebra Ukadisha B'nai Israel Mikalwarie** (Holy Sons of Israel from Kalwarie, Lithuania). In 1942 the building was sold to Ebenezer when Harlem had transitioned into an African American community. The church was one of the first to participate in the New York Landmarks Conservancy's Upper Manhattan Historic Preservation Fund, which financed the restoration of the slate roof, new copper-cladding on the dormers, and new terra-cotta tiles on the tower. Unfortunately. this work covered the stained glass with a visible star of David on the second story gable on the 121ˢᵗ Street side of the building.

E phesus Seventh Day Adventist Church
101 W. 123ʳᵈ St., at Malcolm X/Lenox. (212) 662-5536. www.ephesus.org. Bus—M2, M7, M60, M100, M101, M102, BX15. Subway—2, 3 to 125ᵗʰ St.

EPHESUS SEVENTH DAY ADVENTIST CHURCH

Ephesus Seventh Day Adventist Church has the distinction of being both an architectural and a cultural landmark because it is where, in 1968, the **Boys Choir of Harlem** was formed. The church's origin is steeped in early Americana history because it grew out of **The Reformed Low Dutch Church of Harlem**, which was organized in 1660 shortly after the founding of **Nieuw Haarlem** by the Dutch in 1658. This history is shared with the **Elmendorf Reformed Church** (see East Harlem), which remained in East Harlem when the church separated after the building on Lenox Avenue was constructed as the **Second Collegiate Church of Harlem** to serve the wealthier families living in the neighborhood. A fine example of late Victorian Gothic Revival architecture, this structure—which is faced in yellow Ohio sandstone, sports an imposing steeple, and features corbels of carved monsters and cherubs that flank the central entrance—was designed and constructed between 1885–1887 by **John Rochester Thomas**. The Church Hall, now the Youth Chapel, was erected at the rear of the building between 1894 and 1895. Architect Thomas is best known for the design of the Hall of Records/Surrogate's Court on Chambers Street. As the white population ebbed, the building was leased to the Ephesus Seventh Day Adventist congregation which purchased the building in 1939. Ephesus was established through a merger of New York's two oldest Black Adventist congregations. In 1969 the church interior was completely destroyed by fire. The renovation took eight years to complete. More recently, the crockett which was damaged in the fire was added to the steeple and decades of grime was steam cleaned from the façade.

First Corinthian Baptist Church

1912 Adam Clayton Powell Blvd., at 116th St. (212) 864-5976. www.fcbc.com. Bus—M2, M7, M10, M102, M116. Subway—2, 3, B, C to 116th St.

The building that is home to First Corinthian Baptist Church was designated a landmark in 1994 because, in addition to its architectural significance, it represents the transition of movie theaters in America to luxurious palaces. Built in 1912–13 as the **Regent Theater**, this building was one of the earliest movie palaces in America designed by **Thomas W. Lamb**, an architect who designed over 300 movie theatres in the world and who became internationally noted for his fantasy design. He also designed the **Audubon Ballroom** in **Washington Heights**, which was the site where Malcolm X was assassinated, and the West Harlem **Hamilton Palace**, which is now a store. The Regent's Italian Renaissance–inspired facade of glazed, polychromatic terra-cotta is loosely modeled after the Doges' Palace of Venice and definitely commands the attention of anyone in close proximity. The Regent was managed by then up-and-coming impresario **S. L. "Roxy" Rothafel**, who first made his name in the theatre world at the Regent. In 1932 he realized his greatest achievement when he opened the world-renowned Radio City Music Hall and later introduced the equally famous Rockettes Chorus Line. The Regent Theater, which seats 1,800, was saved in 1964 when it was purchased by First Corinthian, which has retained the spectacular Spanish-Moorish designed auditorium.

Masjid Malcolm Shabazz

102 W. 116th St., at Malcolm X/Lenox. (212) 662-2200. Bus—M2, M7, M102, M116. Subway—2, 3 to 116th St.

Masjid Malcolm Shabazz is the center of Muslim life in Harlem. Originally built as the **Lenox Casino** in 1905, by 1912 it was among one of the first porno movie theaters in New York. The building was opened as a mosque in 1957, and was led by Malcolm X until 1964. It was known as **Temple No. 7**. The original building was dynamited after Malcolm X's assassination in 1965. From this tragic event, the new masjid was born. Architect **Sabbath Brown** redesigned the building, which reopened in 1969, to resemble a traditional Middle Eastern-style masjid, with arches and the aluminum dome, once topped by a golden crescent. The masjid, which ended its affiliation with the Nation of Islam, was named in honor of **El Hajj Malik Shabazz** (Malcolm X) and follows the orthodox teachings of the Sunni Muslims. Now under the leadership of **Imam El Hajji Izak-El Mu'eed Pasha**, the masjid is a powerful presence in Harlem, sponsoring numerous housing development projects and operating the business incubator, Malcolm Shabazz Market, which has drawn many tourists into its casbah-like environment selling imported items from West Africa, made-to-order Afro-centric apparel, and, among other things, Harlem-themed T-shirts.

Mount Morris Ascension Presbyterian Church
15 Mt. Morris Park West, at 122nd St. (212) 666-8200. Bus—M1, M2, M7, M60, M100, M101, M102, BX15. Subway—2, 3 to 125th St.

MOUNT MORRIS ASCENSION PRESBYTERIAN CHURCH

Built as the **Harlem Presbyterian Church** in 1905, Mount Morris Ascension Presbyterian Church is Harlem's last Romanesque Revival church structure. Designed by **Thomas H. Poole**, who was a specialist in the design of Roman Catholic buildings, this eclectic structure is clad in rough granite with vertical bands of gold Roman brick. The squared-off roofline hides a tall copper dome (one of just three in New York) that is only fully visible from a distance. With a history dating back to 1844, Harlem Presbyterian Church merged in 1915 with the **New York Presbyterian Church**, which moved as a result of the increase in the African American population in the neighborhood surrounding its church on Seventh Avenue and 128th Street. The united congregation left the Mount Morris area in the 1930s for the same reason. The Presbytery of New York left the church vacant until in 1942, the **Rev. Arthur Eugene Adair** was invited to organize an African American congregation. In 1943 he opened the doors of the church to the community and, with the able assistance of his wife, **Dr. Thelma Davidson Adair**, began operating vital outreach services for families and children. The Community Life Center was organized in 1944 to provide day-care services, and a Head Start early learning program was organized in 1965.

Mount Nebo Baptist Church
1883 Adam Clayton Powell Blvd., between 114th and 115th Sts. (212) 866-7880. www.mountneboh.org. Bus—M2, M7, M10, M102. Subway—B, C, 2, 3 to 116th St.

The building that Mount Nebo Baptist Church now occupies was built in 1908 for **Temple Ansche Chesed**. This synagogue was designed by **Edward Shire**, who created a Jewish house of worship that resembles a church like those built in early eighteenth-century London, with a neo-Classical porch behind six tall columns supporting a pediment with a Decalogue representing the tablets of the Ten Commandments. The cornerstone displays the dual dates of 1908 and 5668, on the Hebrew calendar. The first Christian church to occupy the building in the mid-twentieth century once Temple Ansche Chesed moved to the Upper West Side was **Our Lady of the Miraculous Medal**, a Roman Catholic Church that served a Spanish congregation. Its presence is felt inside the sanctuary around the tall arched windows which are adorned with elaborate hand-painted yellow-and-blue tiles with floral patterns, cherubs, and medallions of saints and patrons such as Our Lady of High Grace, Our Lady of the Angels, and St. Catherine Labouré. Mount Nebo Baptist Church, which was organized in 1937, purchased the building in 1979 and occupied it in 1980. Famed for its choir that belts out powerful gospel music, the church was home to famed R&B singer **Freddie Jackson**, a native Harlemite who got his musical start as a gospel singer.

Mount Olivet Baptist Church

201 Lenox Ave., at 120th St. (212) 666-6890. Bus—M2, M7, M102. Subway—2, 3 to 116th St.

MT. OLIVET BAPTIST CHURCH INTERIOR

The majestic Mount Olivet Baptist Church appears as if it could be something out of imperial Rome, and actually it was modeled after the then recently excavated **Second Temple** in Jerusalem, which was built in the Roman Classical style during Roman occupation. This building was designed by **Arnold Brunner** for **Temple Israel**, which was the first Jewish congregation incorporated in Harlem as **Hand-In-Hand** in 1873. A German-Jewish architect who studied at L'Ecole des Beaux-Arts in Paris and the first Jewish architect registered in the state of New York, Brunner was a pioneer in the design of Classical revival synagogues, for which Temple Israel set the precedent when it was completed in 1907. The Stars of David are nestled in leafy capitals of the building's four Corinthian columns and are also embedded in the window casements. Temple Israel, unlike some of the other Harlem synagogues, catered to affluent Western European Jews like **Myron Sulzberger** (father of retired *New York Times* publisher Arthur Ochs Sulzberger, Sr.) and **Louis Blumstein**, whose department store on 125th Street bore his name. Temple Israel was acquired in 1925 by Mount Olivet, which organized in 1876 and had been located in mid-Manhattan prior to moving uptown. The church has a rich history of activism, including assisting the Underground Railroad and helping to organize the YMCA in Harlem. In addition to operating a weekly food pantry, it is used as a speaking platform for important international dignitaries such as Zimbabwean **President Robert Mugabe**, Venezuelan **President Hugo Chavez**, and Nation of Islam leader **Honorable Minister Louis Farrakhan**. The church's proud congregation has left the sanctuary pretty much intact. The marble pediment and columns of the ark were left in place, but its gold doors now open to a baptismal pool rather than to the Torah scrolls.

Muhammad Mosque No. 7

106-8 W. 127th St., between Adam Clayton Powell Blvd. and Malcolm X/Lenox. (212) 865-1200. www.mosque7.org. Bus—M2, M7, M102. Subway—2, 3 to 125th St.

Muhammad Mosque No. 7 is the official New York headquarters of the Nation of Islam, which was founded by the **Honorable Elijah Muhammad** and is now headed by the Honorable Minister Louis Farrakhan. Since its founding in the 1930s, the Nation of Islam teachings stress Black self-reliance and self-determination. Mosque No. 7 was established by the late Malcolm X in the 1950s, who presided over it until his split with the Nation in 1964. The building in which the mosque held its services was bombed and destroyed in 1965, after which the Nation of Islam moved to its present location and continued meeting under the teachings of Elijah Muhammad. Today Mosque No. 7 is led by **Student Minister Abdul Hafeez Muhammad**. Services are open to the public on Sunday 10am, Wednesday 8pm, and for Jum'mah Prayer on Friday at 1:15pm.

Salem United Methodist Church

211 W. 129th St., at Adam Clayton Powell Blvd. (212) 678-2700. Bus—M2, M7, M10, M102. Subway—A, B, C, D, 2, 3 to 125th St.

SALEM UNITED METHODIST CHURCH

Built in 1887 as the **West Harlem Methodist Episcopal Church**, this imposing and handsome red-brick Romanesque Revival–style structure housed the largest Protestant church auditorium and membership until **Riverside Church** was built. This building was designed by John Rochester Thomas, who also designed the structure that now houses Ephesus Seventh Day Adventist Church. Salem United Methodist Church was founded in 1881 as a mission of **St. Mark's Methodist Episcopal Church**. The mission first met in a storefront on St. Nicholas Avenue and later in six brownstones that were renovated to create a chapel and meeting room. By the early 1920s the membership had swelled to 600 under the able leadership of the **Rev. Frederick A. Cullen**, adopted father of Harlem Renaissance poet **Countee Cullen**. In 1923, Salem purchased the imposing **Calvary Methodist Episcopal Church**, and by the mid 1920s the church membership had grown to 2,500. Salem has been home to many of Harlem's cultural and intellectual elite, including singer **Marian Anderson**. As early as the late 1920s the church offered its membership instruction in French, Latin, typewriting, shorthand, and math. It could boast that it had five large choirs and a full orchestra, as well as a highly competitive youth athletic club including a notable amateur boxing program. Today the church opens its doors to accommodate important events such as lectures, symposiums, and concerts.

St. Aloysius Roman Catholic Church

209 W. 132nd St., between Frederick Douglass and Adam Clayton Powell Blvds. (212) 234-2848. Bus—M7, M10, M102. Subway—B, C, 2, 3 to 135th St.

ST. ALOYSIUS ROMAN CATHOLIC CHURCH

One of New York's most distinctive Catholic church designs, St. Aloysius Roman Catholic Church was designated a landmark in 2007. Originally organized in 1899 for a growing German, Italian, and Irish immigrant community, St. Aloysius' present building was completed in 1904. Designed by **William W. Renwick**, nephew of noted architect **James Renwick, Jr.**, the handsome building's design is based on Italian Gothic prototypes, which at the time was an unusual style for New York City. Considered one of W. W. Renwick's most important commissions, the intricate facade consists of alternating bands of red-brick, celadon-colored glazed brick, glazed "granitex" (which has the color and texture of gray granite), and terra-cotta with cobalt-blue accents. The design also features four sculptural reliefs depicting the Holy Family, the head of Christ, and angels, set on densely glazed cobalt-blue backgrounds. St. Aloysius is a very early example in New York City of the use of polychromatic architectural ceramic. By 1935, in response to the changed demographics of Harlem, St. Aloysius became a mission church for the conversion of African Americans to Catholicism. In 1947, the parish again became independent. Noted congregants include **Rev. Joseph E. Price**, first African-American permanent deacon of the Archdiocese of New York; **Monsignor Owen J. Scanlon**, an assistant pastor and, later, pastor from 1969 to 1979; U.S.

Congressman **Charles B. Rangel**, also an alumnus of St. Aloysius School; and composer and musician **Daniel Coakley**.

St. Martin's Episcopal Church
230 Malcolm X/ Lenox, at 122nd St. (212) 534-4531. Bus—M2, M7, M60, M100, M101, M102. Subway—A, B, C, D, 2, 3 to 125th St.

This fine Romanesque Revival–style church was originally built for the **Holy Trinity Episcopal Church** between 1887–89. The church was designed by **William Potter**, brother of **Henry Codman Potter**, a well-known Episcopalian bishop who was responsible for spearheading the construction of the Cathedral Church of St. John the Divine. Holy Trinity was built from rough red granite with brownstone trim and was designated a landmark in 1966. Since 1928 the church has been known as St. Martin's Episcopal Church and was one of a number of new congregations established by Caribbean immigrants. During the 1930s rector **Rev. John Johnson, Sr.**, was one of the most influential and politically active leaders in the Black community. Johnson actively supported the "Don't Buy Where You Can't Work" campaign that urged African American shoppers to boycott businesses on 125th Street that did not hire Black employees. He also worked to integrate major league baseball. A Harlem treasure is the forty-two carillons that were installed at St. Martin's in 1939. They are the second largest set of carillons in New York City and are second only to the ones at Riverside Church. A fund was established to which the working class congregation donated their hard-earned money to commission the bells from the Netherlands. **Queen Juliana** of the Netherlands came to see the bells in 1952, thronged by more than 7,000 Harlem well-wishers. A small theater with stage that was used by Harlem-based thespians still exists in the parish house that is attached to the church, and was recently renovated to serve as the home theater for the Forces of Nature Dance Theatre. At one time the church operated the largest credit union in Harlem.

St. Philip's Episcopal Church
204 W. 134th St., between Adam Clayton Powell and Frederick Douglass Blvds. (212) 862-4940. www.stphilipsharlem.dioceseny.org. Bus—M2, M10, BX33. Subway—B, C to 135th St.

Founded in 1809 as the **Free African Church of St. Philip's**, in 1818 St. Philip's Episcopal Church became the first African American Episcopal parish in New York City. The church was initially located in lower Manhattan and as the African American population shifted further north, St. Phillip's moved with them until its final move to Harlem in 1910. The church building was designated a landmark in 1993. Vertner Tandy, the first African American architect registered in the State of New York, and George W. Foster, Jr., who was one of two Black architects registered in New Jersey in 1908, designed the church. The neo-Gothic style church stands out on W. 134th Street with its majestic Roman brick and terra-cotta facade. At the same time the land for the church was purchased, the church rector, the **Rev. Hutchens Bishop**, who appeared to be white, was also able to purchase a block of ten tenement buildings on 135th Street between Lenox and Adam Clayton Powell Blvd. during a time when white landlords would not sell to Blacks. Most of the Black families that moved into the building after whites were evicted were parishioners of St. Phillip's. This marked the first time that Blacks moved west of Lenox Avenue. St. Phillip's has a tradition of social activism beginning with the **Rev. Peter Williams, Jr.**, a leading abolitionist who was the first African American Episcopalian minister in the United States and the first rector of the church. Under his leadership the church played a major role in the debate about slavery and injustice against Blacks. Over the years St. Philip's has retained its position as one of the most influential of Harlem's churches and operates many outreach programs that are a stabilizing force for Harlem.

CHURCHES WITH GOSPEL SERVICES

Abyssinian Baptist Church
132 Odell Clark Place, (formerly 138th St.), between Adam Clayton Powell Blvd. and Malcolm X/Lenox. Bus—M2, M7, M10, M102, BX33. Subway—B, C, 2, 3 to 135th St. Sunday, 9am and 11am.

Beulah Baptist Church
125 W. 130th St., between Adam Clayton Powell Blvd. and Malcolm X/Lenox. Bus—M2, M7, M10, M102. Subway—2, 3 to 125th St. First Sunday of each month, 11am.

Canaan Baptist Church of Christ
132 W. 116th St., between Adam Clayton Powell Blvd. and Malcolm X/Lenox. Bus—M2, M3, M7, M10, M102, M116. Subway—B, C, 2, 3 to 116th St. Sunday, 8am and 11am.

First Corinthian Baptist Church
1912 Adam Clayton Powell Blvd., at 116th St. Bus—M2, M3, M7, M10, M102, M116. Subway—B, C, 2, 3 to 116th St. Sunday, 8am, and 10:45am.

First Ebenezer Baptist Church
2457 Frederick Douglass Blvd., between 131st and 132nd Sts. Bus—M2, M3, M10. Subway—B, C to 135th St. Sunday, 11am.

Friendship Baptist Church
144 W. 131st St., between Adam Clayton Powell Blvd. and Malcolm X/Lenox. Bus—M2, M7, M102. Subway—B, C, 2, 3 to 135th St. Sunday, 11am.

Greater Hood Memorial AME Zion Church
160 W. 146th St., between Adam Clayton Powell Blvd. and Malcolm X/Lenox. Bus—M1, M2, M7, M102, BX19. Subway—3 to 145th St. First and fourth Sunday of each month, 11am. Thursday, 7pm: Hip-Hop Gospel Choir.

LaGree Baptist Church
362 W. 125th St., between Morningside and Manhattan Aves. Bus—M2, M3, M10, M60, M100, M101, BX15. Subway—A, B, C, D to 125th St. Sunday, 11am.

Memorial Baptist Church
Bishop Preston R. Washington Sr. Place, 141 W. 115th St., between St. Nicholas Ave. and Malcolm X/Lenox. Bus—M2, M3, M7, M10, M102, M116. Subway—B, C, 2, 3 to 116th St. Sunday, 10:45am.

Mother A. M. E. Zion Church
146 W. 137th St., between Adam Clayton Powell Blvd. and Malcolm X/Lenox. Bus—M2, M7, M10, M102, BX33. Subway—B, C, 2, 3 to 135th St. Sunday, 11am.

Mount Nebo Baptist Church
77 Saint Nicholas Ave., at 114th St. Bus—M2, M7, M10, M102, M116. Subway—B, C, 2, 3 to 116th St. Sunday, 11:45am.

Second Canaan Baptist Church
10 Malcolm X/Lenox, at 110th St. Bus—M2, M3, M4. Subway—2,3 to 110th St. Sunday, 11am.

United House of Prayer for All People
2320 Frederick Douglass Blvd., between 124th and 125th Sts. Bus—M2, M3, M10, M60, M100, M101, BX15. Subway—A, B, C, D to 125th St. Tuesday 8pm and Sunday 11am.

PARKS

Jackie Robinson Park
Bus—M3, M10, BX33. Subway—A, B, C, D to 145th St.

Jackie Robinson Park is located in a ten-block area between 145th and 155th Streets and between Edgecombe and Bradhurst Avenues, and is 12.8 acres in size. It opened as **Colonial Park** in 1911. In 1978 the park was renamed Jackie Robinson (1919–1972) to honor the first Black Major League Baseball player. The park was one of ten city parks to receive a pool in 1936. The recreation center, which opened the same year, contains a two-story bath house that boasts Romanesque Revival–inspired details including recessed bays, a parapet with a cast-stone balustrade, and large round towers that rise above the roof line of the building. On April 10, 2007, the interior of the Jackie Robinson Pool and Recreation Center was designated a landmark. It contains a swimming pool, bath house, bandshell, and dance floor. A bronze portrait bust of Jackie Robinson, by **Inge Hardison**, is mounted on the wall of the entryway of the recreation center.

Facilities: Gymnasium, physical fitness center that includes cardiovascular equipment and weight room, library, computer resource center, Olympic-sized pool, two baseball diamonds, basketball courts, volleyball courts, two playgrounds (one with a water play area), and bandshell.

GARAGES

144 W Garage
310 W. 144th St., between Bradhurst Ave. and Frederick Douglass Blvd. 24 Hrs/Indoor/Valet/Credit and Cash.

270 W. 126th St. Parking
270 W. 126th St., between Frederick Douglass and Adam Clayton Powell Blvds. 24 Hrs/Outdoor/ Valet/ Cash-Only.

Deb Parking
300 W. 135th St., between St. Nicholas Ave. and Frederick Douglass Blvd. 24 Hrs/Indoor/ Valet/Cash-Only.

Impark Parking
120 W. 126th St., between Adam Clayton Powell Blvd. and Malcolm X/Lenox. 24 Hrs/Indoor/Self-Park/ Credit and Cash.

Imperial Parking
71 W. 116th St., between Malcolm X/Lenox and Fifth Ave. 24 Hrs/Indoor/Valet/Cash-Only.

Imperial/145 Bradhurst Garage
320 W. 146th St., between Bradhurst Ave. and Frederick Douglass Blvd. 24 Hrs/Indoor/Valet/Cash-Only.

J and L Parking, Inc.
280 W. 155th St., between Harlem River Dr. and Frederick Douglass Blvd., 24 Hrs/Outdoor/Valet/ Cash-Only.

506 Malcolm X/Lenox, at 137th St. 24 Hrs/Outdoor/Valet/Credit and Cash.

MPG Lardon 575
310 W. 145th St., between Bradhurst Ave. and Frederick Douglass Blvd. 24 Hrs/Indoor/ Valet/Cash-Only.

Park–It Magic Parking
225 St. Nicholas Ave., at 121st St., 24 Hrs/Indoor/Valet/Credit and Cash.

Quik Park Garage
40 W. 116th St., Entrance on 115th St., between Malcolm X/Lenox and Fifth Ave. 24 Hrs/Indoor/Valet/ Credit and Cash.

Solo Parking
316 W. 118th St., between Manhattan Ave. and Frederick Douglass Blvd. 24 Hrs/Indoor/ Valet/Cash-Only.

SERVICE STATIONS

BP Service Station
2040 Frederick Douglass Blvd., at 110th St.

Getty Service Station
119 W. 145th St., between Adam Clayton Powell Blvd. and Malcolm X/Lenox.

Mobil Service Stations
150 W. 145th St., between Adam Clayton Powell Blvd. and Malcolm X/Lenox.

800 St. Nicholas Ave., between 151st and 152nd Sts.

Shell Service Stations
117 Morningside Ave., at 124th St.

232 W. 145th St., between Frederick Douglass and Adam Clayton Powell Blvds.

LIBRARIES/INTERNET/WI-FI

Libraries with Free Internet

115th St. Branch
203 W. 115th St., between Adam Clayton Powell Blvd. and Malcolm X/Lenox. (212) 666-9393. Mon, Tue and Thu 11am–7pm, Wed 11am–6pm, Fri 11am–5pm, Sat 10am–5pm.

Countee Cullen Branch
104 W. 136th St., between Adam Clayton Powell Blvd. and Malcolm X/Lenox. (212) 491-2070. Mon–Fri 10am–8pm, Fri and Sat 10am–5pm.

Harlem Branch
9 W. 124th St., between Malcolm X/Lenox and Fifth Ave. (212) 348-5620. Mon and Wed 11am–6pm, Tue and Thu 11am–7pm, Fri 11am–5pm, Sat 10am–5pm.

Macomb's Bridge Branch
2650 Adam Clayton Powell Blvd., between 152nd and 153rd Sts. (212) 281-4900. Mon and Wed 11am–6pm, Tue and Thu 11am–7pm, Fri 12pm–5pm, Sat 10am–5pm.

Schomburg Center for Research in Black Culture
515 Malcolm X/Lenox, at 135th St. (212) 491-2200. Mon–Wed 12pm–8pm, Thu–Fri 11am–6pm, Sat 10am–5pm.

Wi-Fi

Starbucks
(Free Wi-Fi available for existing T-Mobile subscribers, AT&T DSL subscribers and AT&T mobile devices that are Wi-Fi enabled. You also can purchase two consecutive hours of Wi-Fi access for $3.99.)

77-83 W. 125th St., between Malcolm X/Lenox and Fifth Ave. Mon–Fri 5:30am–11pm, Sat 6am–12am, Sun 6am–11pm.

201 W. 125th St., between Frederick Douglass and Adam Clayton Powell Blvds. Mon–Thu 6am–11pm, Fri and Sat 6am–12am, Sun 6am–11pm.

301 W. 145th St., at Bradhurst Ave. Sun–Fri 6am–11pm, Sat 6am–11pm.

2195 Frederick Douglass Blvd., at 118th St. Mon–Thu 6am–11pm, Fri and Sat 6am–11pm, Sun 7am–10pm.

POSTAL SERVICES

FedEx Office Print & Ship Center
207 W. 125th St., between Frederick Douglass and Adam Clayton Powell Blvds. (212) 531-0150. Mon–Fri 7:30am–9pm, Sat 10am–6pm, Sun 12pm–6pm.

U.S. Postal Service/College Station
217 W. 140th St., between Frederick Douglass and Adam Clayton Powell Blvds. (212) 283-2235. Mon–Fri 8am–5pm, Sat 8am–4pm.

U.S. Postal Service/Hamilton Grange Annex Station
99 Macombs Pl., at 154th St. (212) 368-9849. Mon–Fri 8am–5pm, Sat 8am–4pm.

U.S. Postal Service/Manhattanville Station
365 W. 125th St., between Morningside and St. Nicholas Aves. (212) 662-1540. Mon–Fri 8am–7pm, Sat 8am–4pm.

U.S. Postal Service/Morningside Station
232 W. 116th St., between Frederick Douglass and Adam Clayton Powell Blvds. (212) 864-3158. Mon–Fri 8:30am–5pm, Sat 9am–4pm.

UPS Store #4163
55 W. 116th St., between Malcolm X/Lenox and Fifth Ave. (212) 878-8800. Mon–Fri 8:30am–7:30pm, Sat 10am–6pm.

UPS Store #5017
2216 Frederick Douglass Blvd., between 119th and 120th Sts. (212) 865-9601. Mon–Fri 8am–8pm, Sat 10am–6pm.

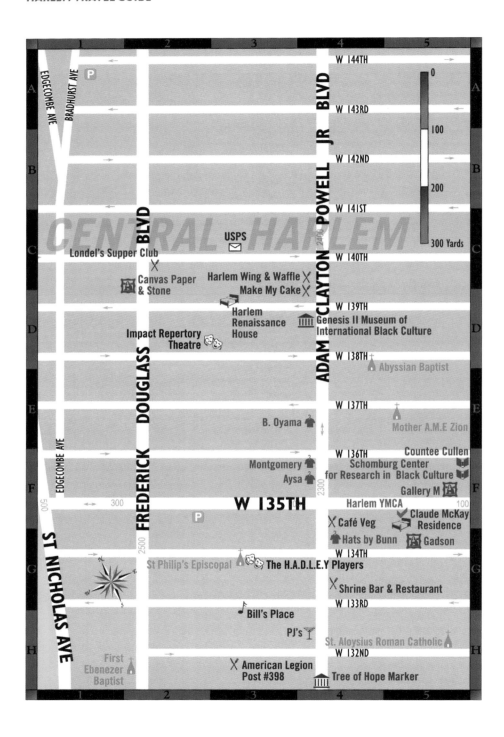

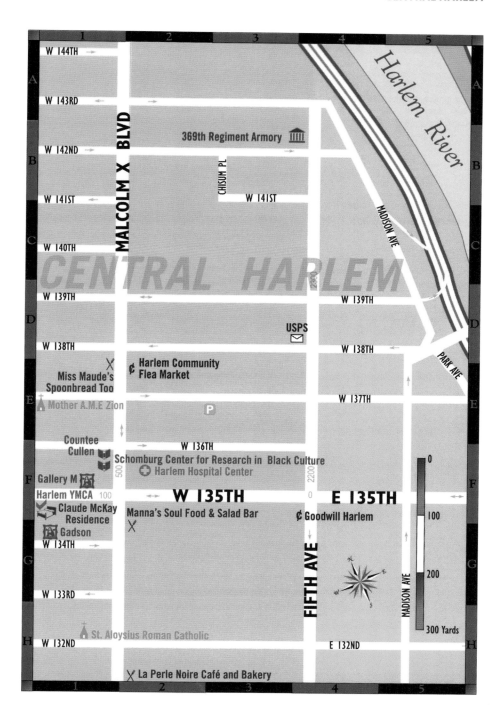

Central Harlem Map A1

Charles' Country Pan Fried Chicken, D2
Cheesesteak Factory, H4
Getty, H5
Greater Hood Memorial AME Zion, G4
Harlem Heaven Boutique, F4
Jackie Robinson Park, F1
Macomb's Bridge Branch NYPL, C4
Mobil, H5
Pathmark Supermarket, H2
Shell, H3
Starbucks, H2
USPS, B3

Central Harlem Map A2

Abyssinian Baptist, D4
American Legion Post #398, H3
Aysa, F4
B. Oyama, E4
Bill's Place, H3
Cafe Veg, F4
Canvas Paper & Stone, C2
Claude McKay Residence, F5
Countee Cullen Branch NYPL, F5
First Ebenezer Baptist, H2
Gadson, G5
Gallery M, F5
Genesis II Museum of International Black
    Culture, D4
Harlem Renaissance House, D3
Harlem Wing & Waffle, C4
Harlem YMCA, F5
Hats by Bunn, G4

Impact Repertory Theatre, D2
Londel's Supper Club, C2
Make My Cake, D4
Montgomery, F4
Mother A.M.E. Zion, E5
PJ's, H4
Schomburg Center for Research in Black
    Culture, F5
Shrine Bar & Restaurant, G4
St. Aloysius Roman Catholic, H5
St Philip's Episcopal, G3
The H.A.D.L.E.Y Players, G3
Tree of Hope Marker, H4
USPS, C3

Central Harlem Map A3

369th Regiment Armory, B3
Claude McKay Residence, F1
Countee Cullen Branch NYPL, F1
Gadson, G1
Gallery M, F1
Goodwill Harlem, F4
Harlem Community Flea Market, E2
Harlem Hospital Center, F2
Harlem YMCA, F1
La Perle Noire Cafe and Bakery, H2
Manna's Soul Food & Salad Bar, G2
Miss Maude's Spoonbread Too, E1
Mother A.M.E Zion, E1
Schomburg Center for Research in Black
    Culture, F1
St. Aloysius Roman Catholic, H1
USPS, D4

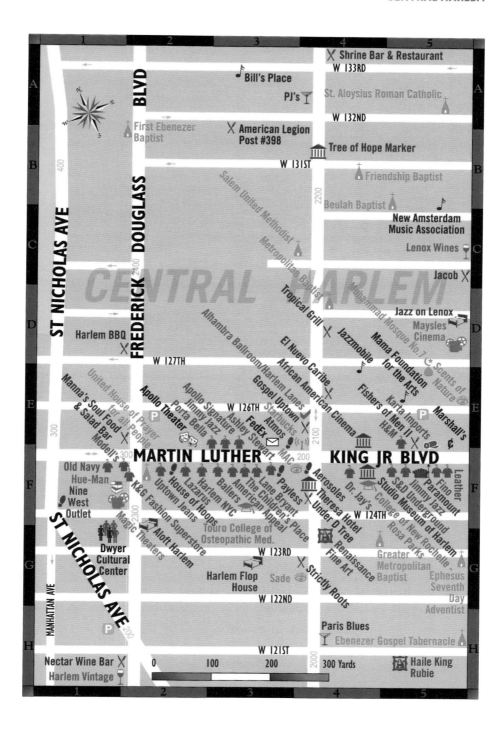

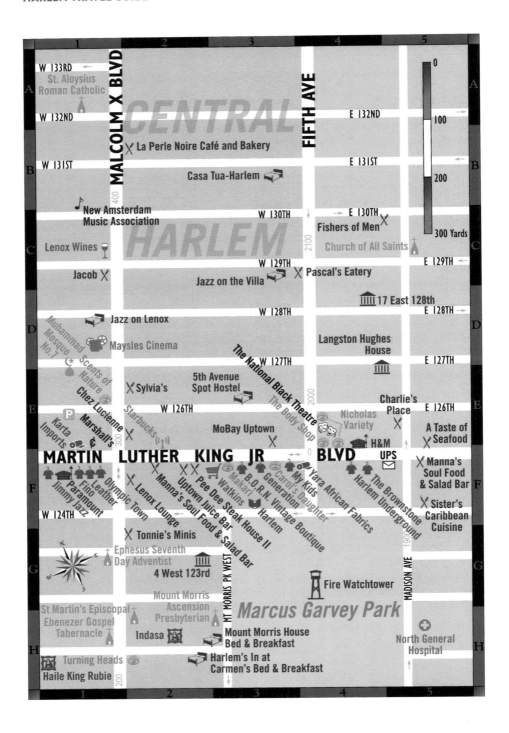

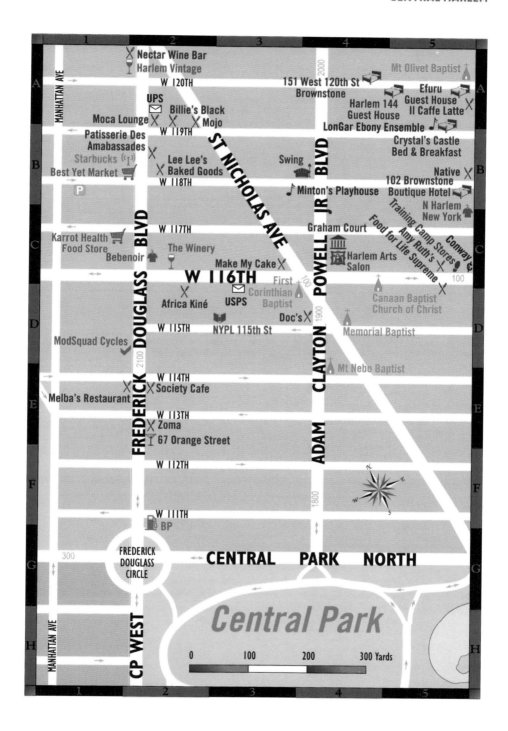

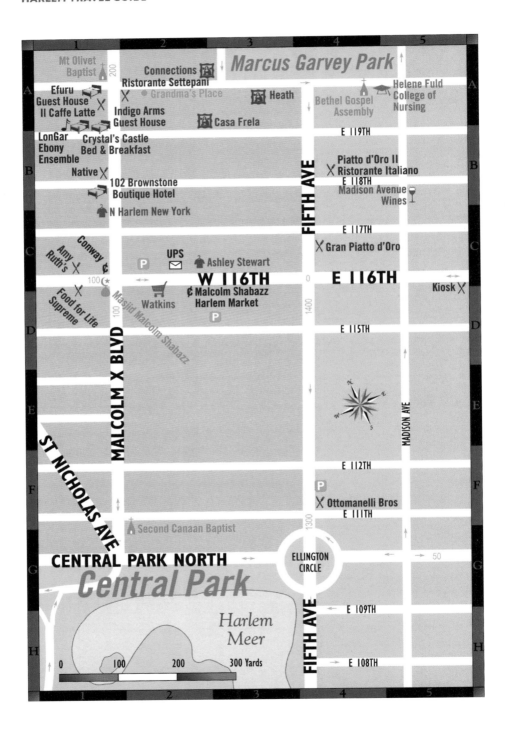

Mt Olivet Baptist

Marcus Garvey Park

Connections
Ristorante Settepani

Efuru
Guest House
Il Caffe Latte

Grandma's Place

Heath

Helene Fuld
College of
Nursing

Bethel Gospel
Assembly

Indigo Arms
Guest House

Casa Frela

E 119TH

LonGar
Ebony
Ensemble

Crystal's Castle
Bed & Breakfast

FIFTH AVE

Piatto d'Oro II
Ristorante Italiano

E 118TH

Native

102 Brownstone
Boutique Hotel

Madison Avenue
Wines

N Harlem New York

E 117TH

Conway

Amy
Ruth's

UPS

Gran Piatto d'Oro

P

Ashley Stewart

Food for Life
Supreme

100

W 116TH

0

E 116TH

Kiosk

Masjid Malcolm Shabazz

Watkins

Malcolm Shabazz
Harlem Market

1400

P

MALCOLM X BLVD

E 115TH

ST NICHOLAS AVE

MADISON AVE

E 112TH

P

1300

Ottomanelli Bros
E 111TH

Second Canaan Baptist

CENTRAL PARK NORTH

ELLINGTON
CIRCLE

50

Central Park

FIFTH AVE

E 109TH

Harlem
Meer

0   100   200   300 Yards

E 108TH

Central Harlem Map B1

Aerosoles, F4
African American Cinema, E4
Alhambra Ballroom/Harlem Lanes,E4
Aloft Harlem, G2
American Appeal, F3
American Legion Post #398, B3
Apollo Signature, E3
Apollo Theater, E2
Ashley Stewart, F3
Atmos, E3
Ballers, F3
Beulah Baptist, B5
Bill's Place, A3
College of New Rochelle - Rosa Parks, F4
Dr. Jay's, F4
Dwyer Cultural Center, G1
Ebenezer Gospel Tabernacle, H4
El Nuevo Caribe, E4
Ephesus Seventh Day Adventist, G5
FedEx, E3
Fino, F5
First Ebenezer Baptist, B2
Fishers of Men II, E5
Friendship Baptist, B4
Uptown Grand, E4
Greater Metropolitan Baptist, G4
H&M, E5
Haile King Rubie, H5
Harlem BBQ, D1
Harlem Flop House, G3
Harlem NYC, F2
Harlem Vintage, H1
House of Hoops, F2
Hue-Man, F1
Jacob, C5
Jazz on Lenox, D5
Jazzmobile, D4
Jimmy Jazz, E3
Jimmy Jazz, F5
K&G Fashion Superstore, F2
Karta Imports, E5
Lane Bryant, F3
Lazarus, F2
Leather,   F5
Lenox Wines, C5
MAC, F3
Magic Theaters, F1
Mama Foundation for the Arts, E5
Manna's Soul Food & Salad Bar, E2
Marshall's, E5
Maysles Cinema, D5
Metropolitan Baptist, D4

Modell's, F1
Muhammad Mosque No.7, D5
Nectar Wine Bar, H1
New Amsterdam Music Association, C5
Nine West Outlet, F1
Old Navy, F1
Paramount, F5
Paris Blues, H4
Payless, F3
PJ's, A4
Porta Bella, E3
Renaissance Fine Art, G4
S&D Underground, F5
Sade, G4
Salem United Methodist, C3
Scents of Nature, E5
Shrine Bar & Restaurant, A4
St. Aloysius Roman Catholic, A5
Starbucks, E4
Strictly Roots, G4
Studio Museum in Harlem, F4
The Children's Place, F3
Theresa Hotel, F4
Touro College of Osteopathic Med., F3
Tree of Hope Marker, B4
Tropical Grill, D4
United House of Prayer for all People, E2

Central Harlem Map B2

5th Avenue Spot Hostel, E3
4 West 123rd, G2
17 East 128th, D4
A Taste of Seafood, E5
B.O.R.N. Vintage Boutique, F3
Carol's Daughter, F3
Casa Tua-Harlem, B3
Charlie's Place, E5
Chez Lucienne, E1
Church of All Saints, C5
Ebenezer Gospel Tabernacle, H1
Ephesus Seventh Day Adventist, G1
Fino, F1
Fire Watchtower, G4
Fishers of Men, C5
Generation, F3
H&M, E4
Haile King Rubie, H1
Harlem Branch NYPL, F3
Harlem's In at Carmen's Bed & Breakfast, H2
Harlem Underground, F4
Indasa, H2
Jacob's, C1

Central Harlem Map B3

Central Harlem Map B4

WEST HARLEM

THE CITY COLLEGE OF NEW YORK – SHEPARD HALL

INTRODUCTION

West Harlem generally stretches from 110th to 155th Streets between the west side of St. Nicholas Avenue to the east and the Hudson River to the west. Unlike Central and East Harlem, West Harlem is comprised of three distinct neighborhoods: **Morningside Heights**, **Manhattanville**, and **Hamilton Heights**.

Morningside Heights

Morningside Heights is chiefly known as the home of institutions such as Columbia University, the Cathedral Church of Saint John the Divine, Riverside Church, and **St. Luke's Hospital**. It is bounded by 110th Street to the south, 125th Street to the north, Riverside Drive to the west, and Manhattan Avenue to the east. Broadway, the main thoroughfare, winds through all three neighborhoods. Through the years the neighborhood has been referred to as the "**Academic Acropolis**," the "**Acropolis of New York**," "**Bloomingdale Village**," "**White Harlem**," or "**South Harlem**" (SoHa).

CATHEDRAL CHURCH OF SAINT JOHN THE DEVINE

Historically, on September 16, 1776, the **Battle of Harlem Heights** was fought in Morningside Heights, with the most intense fighting occurring in a sloping wheat field that is now the location of **Barnard College**. Use of the name "Morningside Heights" for the neighborhood arose in the late nineteenth century as a replacement for "Bloomingdale Village," which was associated with the **Bloomingdale Asylum** that once occupied what is now the main campus of Columbia University. Following Columbia's move to the neighborhood from midtown in the 1890s, residential and institutional development accelerated.

Many of the apartment buildings and row houses were built for New York's prosperous middle class, but by the mid-twentieth century the increasing prevalence of Single Room Occupancy (S.R.O.) hotels and their attendant socioeconomic problems prompted Columbia to purchase much of the neighborhood's real estate, leading to accusations of forced eviction and gentrification. This process reached its apotheosis in 1968, when protests erupted in both the neighborhood and on Columbia's campus over the university's proposal to build a gym in **Morningside Park**. Allegations were hurled that the park's proposed separate entrance for Harlem residents on the lower level of the park was segregated, and that public park space

MORNINGSIDE PARK

was being annexed by a wealthy private institution. The university was eventually forced to abandon the plan, though it has still expanded its presence in the neighborhood markedly over the last few decades. Recently, the university has been seeking to expand significantly in nearby Manhattanville.

The label "Academic Acropolis" has been used to describe the area, since it's on one of the highest natural points in Manhattan and contains numerous academic institutions. Much of the neighborhood is the campus of Columbia University, and the university also owns a large amount of the non-campus real estate. Other educational institutions in the neighborhood are described below under Educational Institutions. **NASA's Goddard Institute for Space Studies** is also located in the neighborhood, directly above **Tom's Restaurant** (made famous by the popular television show *Seinfeld*).

GRANT'S TOMB

Non-academic landmarks in Morningside Heights include the Cathedral Church of Saint John the Divine, Grant's Tomb Riverside Church, **The Interchurch Center** (a.k.a., "**The God Box**," where most of the major Christian denominations' administrative offices are headquartered), **International House**, and St. Luke's Hospital. In addition to Tom's Restaurant, the West End Bar (now **Havana Central at the West End**) is another famous local restaurant, one which served especially as a meeting place for writers of the **Beat Generation** in the 1940s and 1950s.

Comedian **George Carlin** grew up on W. 121st Street in Morningside Heights. He has a comedy piece called "White Harlem," which appears on his *Occupation: Foole* album. While writing a master's thesis on William Blake at Columbia University, Trappist monk and author **Thomas**

Merton attended **Corpus Christi Catholic Church** on W. 121st St., where he formally converted to Catholicism. **George Gershwin** began composing his *Rhapsody in Blue* while living on 110th Street in Morningside Heights. Singer/composer **Fiona Apple** grew up in **Morningside Gardens**, an experimental co-op project built in 1957 between 123rd and LaSalle Streets, and Broadway and Amsterdam Avenues. Morningside Gardens was the result of **Robert Moses'** Morningside-Manhattanville urban renewal plan, and was successful in the sense that it combined the middle-income Gardens with the NYCHA **General Grant Houses** to the east and north of it, and maintained a commercial strip along Amsterdam Avenue. Many professional African Americans moved to Morningside Gardens to maintain roots with the Black community of Central Harlem. Among those were **Thurgood Marshall**, first Black justice named to the Supreme Court; award-winning science fiction writer **Samuel Delany**; **Edward R. Dudley**, New York judge and former Manhattan Borough President (1961–1964), whose career took him from civil rights advocacy to an ambassadorship in Liberia; and **Bettie Esther Parham**, the first Black retail store owner on 125th Street in 1940, who made a substantial fortune selling hair care products and cosmetics domestically and in Africa through her National Beauty Supply Company.

HARLEM SUNRISE

Manhattanville

Manhattanville is bordered on the south by Morningside Heights, on the west by the Hudson River, on the east by Central Harlem, and on the north by Hamilton Heights. Manhattanville was incorporated as a village in 1806. The village soon boasted a commercial waterfront, stables, warehouses, icehouses, and factories. A rail station and ferry terminal in the 1800s, and then the IRT subway station in the early 1900s, helped spur industrial growth, and commerce and transportation converged in a thriving waterfront. Dairies and meatpacking industries, including **Sheffield Farms** (today's **Prentis Hall**) and the **McDermott-Bunger Dairy**, moved into the area. Automobile manufacturers established operations in the 1920s, and the **Studebaker and Warren Nash Service Center** buildings still stand. As the neighborhood's residential population grew, colleges and institutions like Columbia University established themselves in the area. The stock market crash of 1929 and the Great Depression signaled the end of strong commercial growth in Manhattanville. Trucking replaced water and rail transportation, leaving Manhattanville's waterfront access no longer advantageous to manufacturers. As industries—and the jobs they created—left the area, Manhattanville lost its industrial base in the decades that followed.

Manhattanville's development parallels the development of St. Mary's Episcopal Church, which established the first free school (1824, later P.S. 43) and the first pew-free Episcopal church in New York City (1831). The village's original streets were laid out by **Jacob Schieffelin**, who founded the drug firm of **Schieffelin and Company**. He also donated the plot of land on which St. Mary's stands. Schieffelin built a country house at 144th Street, overlooking the Hudson River, and further east on land which he had sold to his friend, **Alexander Hamilton**, stood **Hamilton Grange**. Hamilton's widow was a pew holder in the first St. Mary's church, and a son served on the Vestry. Since it opened its doors, St. Mary's has been concerned about the spiritual needs of the mostly poor residents of Manhattanville, and that concern continues today. During the hard times that followed the cholera panic of 1857, Rector **Dr. Rev. Thomas McClure Peters** instituted a public works project which consisted of breaking stone for the macadam used in the first street paving in Manhattanville, some of which survives today under the viaduct. The church currently is a social justice advocate and operates numerous programs, including youth outreach and an HIV/AIDS health-care organization, and organizes the community around environmental justice issues as well as Columbia University's proposed expansion.

Later, noteworthy population changes occurred around the mid-nineteenth century with the influx of mostly Catholic Irish (who established the **Church of the Annunciation** in 1854) and Germans (who established **St. Joseph's Roman Catholic Church** in 1860). After the Civil War, the

IRT SUBWAY VIADUCT

Jewish immigrant population established the **Old Broadway Synagogue**, in 1911. Other prominent nineteenth-century Manhattanville institutions include the **Academy of Convent of the Sacred Heart** (later called **Manhattanville College** and **Manhattan College**).

The principal landmarks in Manhattanville are the elevated section of the IRT Broadway–Seventh Avenue Line and the elevated Riverside Drive viaduct. The **IRT subway viaduct** has an arch spanning 168 feet and rising 55 feet above the street. Several businesses have opened under the viaduct, including **Fairway Market** (a major neighborhood boon, providing fresh produce and a wide variety

of groceries), which opened on W. 131st Street in 1995, the **Hudson River Café** at W. 133rd Street, and a thriving restaurant row at W. 135th (see Restaurants section). The neighborhood also contains the landmark **Claremont Theater**, which was the first movie house built specifically to show films. Manhattanville's most prominent resident was industrialist **Daniel F. Tiemann** (1805–1899), owner of the Manhattanville-headquartered **D. F. Tiemann & Company Color Works**, which was the first manufacturer of ready-mixed paints in 1852. Tiemann was also Mayor of New York City, 1858–1859. The major event during his administration was the laying of the Atlantic telegraph cable. The six-story **Tiemann Hall** apartment house was built on the site of the old Tiemann homestead in 1920. The street is now called **Tiemann Place**, which is located approximately at W. 124th Street between Broadway and Riverside Drive.

THE CITY COLLEGE OF NEW YORK – TOWNSEND HARRIS HALL

To the north, a 600-unit student dorm known as **The Towers** finished construction in June 2006 as an extension of The City College of New York on St. Nicholas Terrace. This is the first time that City College has housed students on the campus. The **West Harlem Piers Park** opened in 2009. Also, **Harlem Stage Gatehouse** opened at a former nineteenth-century water-pumping station at 135th Street and Amsterdam, which was renovated. Within the neighborhood is Manhattanville Houses, a 1,272-unit public housing project which opened in 1961. Designed in the international style by noted Swiss-born architect **William Lescaze**, the development was initially created to house middle-income residents.

Hamilton Heights/Sugar Hill

The greater area of Hamilton Heights/Sugar Hill generally is bounded by City College and St. Nicholas Avenue to the south, the Hudson River to the west, 155th Street to the north, and Edgecombe Avenue to the east. The community derives its name from Alexander Hamilton, whose estate and summer home, Hamilton Grange, still stands in the area. Beautiful brownstones and stately row houses sit behind the leafy trees on the eastern streets of Hamilton Heights, a multi-ethnic area and longtime home to a large Black professional class. The neighborhood is also blessed with first-class parkland, being the home of **Riverbank State Park**, around which **Riverside Park** winds its way to up to Washington Heights, and the historic **St. Nicholas Park**.

Today, Hispanics and Latinos make up the majority of the population in the area, followed by African Americans and West Indian immigrants. Its history spans a period of over 350 years and contains landmarks that date back to Colonial New York. During the **Revolutionary War**, temporary fortifications were built throughout Harlem Heights as far north as 160th Street. In 1791, the **Bloomingdale Road** was extended to meet the **Kingsbridge Road** at present-day W. 147th Street and St. Nicholas Avenue, giving easier access to the area and attracting residents who often created grand estates and country retreats, enticed by the cool breezes, panoramic views, and inexpensive land with rich soil.

The last remaining great house of this period is Hamilton Grange (1801–1802), the twelve-room country home of Alexander Hamilton, the nation's first Secretary of the Treasury. The house is now a museum operated by the National Park Service. Having recently been moved into St. Nicholas Park, the Grange will again be open to the public for touring daily.

HARLEM STAGE GATEHOUSE.

With the construction of the New York State-financed **Croton Water Aqueduct** in 1842, the area began to lose its rural character. The aqueduct ran along present-day Amsterdam Avenue, bringing water to the city through iron pipes placed inside masonry channels. The partially buried and covered-over aqueduct created a ten-foot-high high roadway that impeded drainage and obstructed views from the surrounding grand estates. New transportation links (the elevated railroad on Eighth Avenue with stations at 135th and 145th Streets opened in 1879, and the IRT subway line in 1904) spurred rapid urbanization. The large country estates were sold and divided into building lots for speculative development. **William H. De Forest**, one of the early developers, along with his son, **William De Forest, Jr.**, developed much of the land south of 145th Street. In the 1870s and 1880s, De Forest purchased the Grange and surrounding property in several transactions. He later donated the house to **St. Luke's Presbyterian Church** and arranged to have it moved to accommodate his development plans. The De Forests laid out streets and planned single-family houses. St. Nicholas Avenue and St. Nicholas Place attracted freestanding mansions, including one in a Romanesque Revival–style still standing at **10 St. Nicholas Place**, the grand home of **James A. Bailey**, the circus king and partner of **Phineas T. Barnum**.

By the early twentieth century, when affluent Black families began to move to the area, much of Hamilton Heights as it exists today had already been constructed. The row houses, built in a variety of styles such as Beaux Arts, Queen Anne, Dutch, and Romanesque Revival, and in a rich palette of colors and materials, are considered among New York City's most beautiful. Apartment buildings became more fashionable and the most comfortable were described as "French Flats." Early residents of these houses were middle-class, professional people and their families, either native-born or immigrants from

Germany, Ireland, and Italy. **Norman Rockwell**, America's great illustrator, lived from age three to seven with his parents at **789 St. Nicholas Avenue**. The opera house impresario **Oscar Hammerstein** lived at **333 Edgecombe Avenue**. **George Gershwin** wrote his first hit song "Swanee" at his residence at **520 W. 144th Street** in 1919.

EDGECOMBE AVENUE

In the 1920s the Harlem Renaissance was in full swing, and many of the new Black residents were artists, writers, musicians, government workers, and professionals. Part of the area became known as "**Sugar Hill**," indicating that the residents had money. At that time, the neighborhood's most elite addresses were **409** and **555 Edgecombe Avenue**. Important residents of 409 included singer **Julius Bledsoe**, the original Joe in *Showboat*; **William Braithwaite**, poet and novelist; **Eunice Carter**, one of New York State's first African American judges; **May Chinn**, a pioneering physician; Aaron Douglass, the great muralist; **W. E. B. DuBois**, founder of the **National Association for the Advancement of Colored** (NAACP) and editor of *Crisis*; **Walter White**, president and CEO of the NAACP whose apartment was so frequently the gathering place for New York's Black and white power brokers that 409 was called the "**White House**"; and Thurgood Marshall, the first African American Supreme Court Justice. Number 555 boasted actor and political activist Paul Robeson; activist couple **William L.** and **Louise Patterson**; legendary jazz pianist Count Basie; and

groundbreaking social psychologist **Dr. Kenneth Clark**. These people inspired children in the building, including quilt artist **Faith Ringgold**, jazz saxophonist **Sonny Rollins**, and child piano prodigy **Roy Eaton**, who became a trail-blazer in advertising.

In spite of the neighborhood's decline during the 1950s and 1960s, Hamilton Heights retained its remarkable beauty. In 1974, the New York City Landmarks Preservation Commission designated a significant portion of the neighborhood an historic district. After a long campaign, a much wider area was given protection by the landmark laws. In March 2000, the Landmarks Commission designated the **Hamilton**

WEST HARLEM BUILDINGS

Heights Historic District Extension, which includes the fine apartment houses along the east side of Amsterdam Avenue between W. 140th and W. 145th Streets. The **Hamilton Heights/Sugar Hill Historic District**, designated in 2000–2002, takes in the blocks between W. 145th and W. 155th Streets and stretches generally between Amsterdam and Convent Avenues to Edgecombe Avenue.

Some notable cultural institutions that add to the fabric of life in the area include **Dance Theatre of Harlem**, which was founded in 1968 by **Arthur Mitchell**, who was premier danseur with the New York City Ballet. He found a permanent home for the organization at 466 W. 152nd Street in 1971 in a renovated former garage which was further enlarged by **Hardy Holtzman Pfieffer Associates** in 1994. The **Harlem School of the Arts** at 645 St. Nicholas Avenue was founded by acclaimed soprano **Dorothy Maynor**, who was never given the opportunity to sing at New York's Metropolitan Opera but became the first African American to join its board of directors. She married the noted **Rev. Dr. Shelby Rooks**, pastor of St. James Presbyterian Church, where Ms. Maynor opened the school in the basement in 1964. Today it sits next to St. James in a 37,000-square-foot facility designed by **Ulrich Franzen & Associates** (1977). **The Children's Art Carnival** at 62 Hamilton Terrace was founded in 1969 by painter **Betty Blayton Taylor** as a Museum of Modern Art outreach program for children. It began operating independently in 1972.

LANDMARK DISTRICTS

Hamilton Heights Historic District and Extension

Boundaries: W. 140ᵗʰ Street between Convent and Amsterdam Avenues; 141ˢᵗ Street between St. Nicholas and Amsterdam Avenues; North from 142ⁿᵈ to 145ᵗʰ Streets between Hamilton Terrace and Amsterdam Avenue; 145ᵗʰ Street between St. Nicholas and Amsterdam Avenues.

WEST HARLEM STREETSCAPE

The Hamilton Heights Historic District was designated a landmark in 1974 and the extension in 2000. Another area distinctive for its streetscapes of fine row houses, apartment buildings, and churches, the land was once part of the estate of one of our nation's founding fathers, Alexander Hamilton. His summer house, Hamilton Grange, was recently moved from Convent Avenue to St. Nicholas Park. When the elevated rail line along Eighth Avenue opened in 1879 and the IRT line opened in 1904, speculative developers erected houses in a variety of styles, including Queen Anne, Beaux Arts, Gothic, Tudor, Dutch, and Romanesque Revival, in a rich palette of colors and materials. By the early twentieth century, much of Hamilton Heights as it exists today had been built. In addition to row houses which at one time were the only structures allowed to be built, the area includes interesting limestone-faced apartment houses which were erected after deed restrictions expired in 1911. Early residents of these row houses were middle-class, professional people, both native-born as well as immigrants from Germany, Ireland, and Italy. During the height of the Harlem Renaissance in the 1920s many affluent African Americans moved to Hamilton Heights and the area became known as Sugar Hill—*sugar* being the Black slang term for money and *hill* recognizing the geography of the area west of St. Nicholas Avenue. The celebrated musician/composer **Billy Strayhorn**, who collaborated with **Duke Ellington**, and jazz composer and performer **Mary Lou Williams** lived in the district, as well as numerous writers and civic leaders.

Hamilton Heights/Sugar Hill Historic District

Boundaries: North 145ᵗʰ Street to 146ᵗʰ Street between St. Nicholas and Convent Avenues; North 146ᵗʰ Street to 149ᵗʰ Street between Edgecombe and Amsterdam Avenues; 150ᵗʰ Street between Edgecombe and Convent Avenues.

This large district, which was designated a landmark in 2000 and 2001, has both architectural and cultural significance. This area is full of grand apartment buildings as well as row houses. The district was home to Abyssinian Baptist Church's dynamic pastor Adam Clayton Powell Sr., and celebrated authors Countee Cullen and **Zora Neale Hurston**, who resided at **435 Convent Avenue** at 149ᵗʰ Street, which was the first Black-owned cooperative building in Manhattan. Designed by **Neville & Bagge**, this six-story, twenty-nine-unit French Renaissance Revival–style building was completed in 1910. It features a facade of gorgeous buff Roman brick with terra-cotta trim and a rugged granite base.

WEST HARLEM STREETSCAPE

The apartments contain from six to nine rooms with ten-foot ceilings and fireplaces. The Queen Anne–inspired mansion designed by **Richard Rosentock** at **8 St. Nicholas Place** on the southeast corner of 150th Street was one of the earliest houses built in the area (1885). The Romanesque-inspired mansion built in 1895 for yeast manufacturer **Jacob P. Baiter, 6 St. Nicholas Place**, was designed by **Theodore G. Stein**. Both have been altered but contain design elements that still survive. Now used as a hotel, these two buildings were connected in a conversion to a psychiatric sanitarium in 1912. A row of fine houses were treated as block-long compositions containing materials and decorative features arranged to create an unusually coherent streetscape such as the Romanesque Revival grouping at **718–730 St. Nicholas Avenue**, which was designed by **Arthur Bates Jennings** and completed in 1889–90. Another group of neo-Renaissance houses at **757–775 St. Nicholas Avenue** were designed by **Frederick P. Dinkelberg** and completed in 1894–95. Dramatic in form and detailing, several Beaux Arts-style apartment buildings—Nos. **746 St. Nicholas Avenue** (built in 1901–02) and **772–778 St. Nicholas Avenue** (built in 1904–05)—were designed by **Henri Fouchaux**, who was the district's most prolific architect.

Hamilton Heights/Sugar Hill Northeast Historic District
Boundaries: 150th Street and St. Nicholas Place; St. Nicholas Place to Edgecombe Avenue between 151st to 154th Streets.

Nearly all the buildings in this district, which was designated a landmark in 2001, were constructed between 1905 and 1930, a period when developers began building medium-sized apartment buildings rather than single-family houses. Before the apartment building boom, several freestanding mansions were built in the late 1800s on St. Nicholas Place, including the majestic **Bailey House** located on the northeast corner of 150th Street. Built in 1888 for the "king of circus men"—James A. Bailey of Barnum and Bailey Circus fame—this extravagant building is faced in gray Indiana limestone with Flemish-inspired gables, a large tower and crocketed corner towerlettes reminiscent of a medieval castle. Designed by **Samuel B. Reed**, the building's biggest feature is the sixty-six windows made of mass-produced Belcher mosaic glass, which have the appearance of Tiffany-stained glass, but were made using a technique of arranging individual bits of colored glass on a gummed sheet of asbestos

BAILEY HOUSE

and holding them together with an alloy of molten mercury poured between the pieces. Of the apartment buildings in the area, perhaps the most famous is 409 Edgecombe Avenue, which was designed by **Schwartz & Gross**, completed in 1916–17, and individually designated a landmark in 1993. Home to Harlem's Black elite, *Ebony* magazine in 1947 commented that "bombing 409 would wipe out Negro leadership for the next twenty years." During the 1930s, 409 was home to the **Talented Tenth**, including

NAACP executive Walter White and his successor Roy Wilkens; author and scholar W. E. B. DuBois; Thurgood Marshall, who became the first African American Supreme Court Judge; singer Julius Bledsoe, who was the original Joe in Broadway's *Show Boat* and the first to sing "Ole Man River"; painter and muralist Aaron Douglass; and bandleader **Jimmie Lunceford**. Designed by **George Pelham** and completed in 1925–26 is **379–381 Edgecombe Avenue**, where Duke Ellington and family lived from 1929 to 1939.

Hamilton Heights/Sugar Hill Northwest Historic District

Boundaries: 150th Street at Convent Avenue; 150th Street at St. Nicholas Avenue; North from 151st to 153rd Streets between Amsterdam Avenue and St. Nicholas Place; North from 153rd to 155th Streets between Amsterdam and St. Nicholas Avenues.

WEST HARLEM STREETSCAPE

This area is the last of Harlem's neighborhoods to be designated a landmark, in 2002. During the last decades of the nineteenth century, speculative development transformed the blocks between 151st and 155th Streets. Among the earliest houses in the district are **411–423 W. 154th Street** and **883–887 St. Nicholas Avenue**, all designed by **James Stroud**. Built in 1883–84, these Queen Anne–styled brick houses stand out because they are uncharacteristically sited behind raised gardens, giving off a sense of suburban charm with urban style. Other houses in the area were built in historical styles, including neo-Grec, neo-Renaissance, and Beaux Arts. Henri Fouchaux designed one of the earliest apartment buildings erected in the district as one of his first commissions. The Queen Anne–inspired **468 W. 153rd Street** was built in 1886 as a companion to three row houses. A large number of classically inspired apartment houses were built over the next three decades, and architects of note include Neville & Bagge, Schwartz & Gross, and **John P. Leo**. Most of the new residents were African Americans and immigrants from the West Indies.

100

HISTORIC SITES NOT TO MISS

Hamilton Grange
St. Nicholas Park, at 141ˢᵗ St. (212) 283-5154. www.nps.gov/hagr. Bus—M3, M100, M101. Subway—A, B, C, D to 145ᵗʰ St.

ALEXANDER HAMILTON STATUE

West Harlem is the only community in the northeast that is home to two national memorials—Ulysses S. Grant National Memorial Park (see Riverside Park) and Alexander Hamilton's Hamilton Grange. The Grange, which was named for Hamilton's ancestral estate in Scotland, was his country home, designed by **John McComb Jr.**, and originally sat on Hamilton's 32-acre estate—the house was erected on what is now 143ʳᵈ Street. Hamilton was one of our American Founding Fathers and the first U. S. Secretary of the Treasury. The two-story Federal-style frame house was completed in 1802, just two years before his death in a duel with **Aaron Burr**, another Founding Father and the nation's third Vice President. The Grange was moved four blocks west on Convent Avenue in 1889. The original porches and other features were removed for the move. The staircase was removed and retrofitted to accommodate a makeshift entrance on the side of the house and the original grand Federal-style entrance was boarded up. To make room for the development of a row house community, the developer gave the Grange to **St. Luke's Episcopal Church**, which in 1885 erected its landmark church at 141ˢᵗ Street and Convent Avenue after moving uptown from Greenwich Village. The Grange was wedged between the church and an apartment building which obscured its original beauty. It was purchased by the American Scenic and Historic Preservation Society in 1924, opened to the public nine years later, and donated to the U.S. Department of the Interior in 1962. In 1960 the property was designated a National Historic Landmark and in 1967 it was designated a New York City landmark. It was moved inside St. Nicholas Park (still inside the boundaries of Hamilton's original estate) in 2008, which allows it to be returned to its former glory with the original porches, main entrance doorway, and main staircase. The Grange is currently under renovation and will be surrounded by new landscaping, a stone wall, and paths. When it reopens some time in 2010, the public will again be allowed to enjoy guided tours inside the national landmark.

Hamilton Theatre
3560–3568 Broadway, at 146ᵗʰ St. Bus—M4, M5, M100, M101, BX19. Subway—1 to 145ᵗʰ St.

The RKO Hamilton Theatre was one of the first movie theaters in New York to show "talking pictures" in the late 1920s. Built in 1913 as a vaudeville house for **B. S. Moss** and **Solomon Brill**, the Hamilton's developers, who were major builders and operators of vaudeville houses in the New York City area, the structure was designed by the great theater architect Thomas W. Lamb (see First Corinthian Baptist Church in the Significant Faith-Based Institutions section). Designated a landmark in 2000, the terra-cotta facade of this neo-Renaissance building is dominated by large, round arched windows with centered oculi. The upper stories feature cast-iron and terra-cotta details including caryatids, brackets, and Corinthian engaged columns. In 1928, the Hamilton was sold to the newly created RKO Pictures, Inc., which converted it to a movie house. Closed as a theater in 1958, it was afterward used as a sports

HAMILTON THEATRE

arena, a discotheque, and a church. The front of the house foyer spaces have been gutted and converted into today's retail use as the Hamilton Palace, which sells discounted housewares and clothing. Inside, the auditorium, which is no longer accessible from the building's front (you must go in a side door), is dusty but remarkably intact. Said architectural historian Michael Henry Adams, "It's a typical Thomas W. Lamb theater with a big saucer dome and decorative plaster work, and little loges, or balconies, flanking the proscenium arch. The loges have these cherubs all over them and there are masks of comedy and tragedy. It is one of those Harlem time capsules." Seating remains in the balcony but not downstairs, as it was used for storage. Some stage rigging remains.

Joseph Loth & Company Silk Ribbon Mill
1828 Amsterdam Ave., between 150th and 151st Sts. Bus—M4, M5, M100, M101. Subway—1 to 145th St.

A designated West Harlem landmark since 1993, the Joseph Loth and Company Silk Ribbon Mill stands out among American textile mill buildings due to its exceptional architectural character and unusual designs. Completed in 1886, this **Hugo Kafka**-designed building is unique for its original K-shaped layout, which permitted the construction of interior spaces uninterrupted by columns and walls and maximized the light entering the building. The hand of the architect, noted for his commercial and residential designs, is apparent in the carefully detailed facades that are organized with central and end pavilions, above which panels at the parapets identify the firm and its product. These facades are enlivened with rock-faced sandstone, ornamental pressed brick elements, and corbelled brick features. Built during an interim between periods of residential development, the mill (which produced silk ribbon marketed under the trademark "Fair and Square") was one of the few industries to locate in this area. Even though the building was altered and enlarged in 1904, it retained its distinctive K-plan and architectural character. The building now houses a variety of industrial and commercial tenants.

Nicholas C. and Agnes Benziger House
345 Edgecombe Ave., at 150th St. Bus—M3. Subway—A, B, C, D to 145th St.

NICHOLAS C. AND AGNES BENZIGER HOUSE

Very few freestanding mansions still exist in Manhattan. The Benziger House, which sits right behind the Bailey House (see Landmark Districts: Hamilton Heights/Sugar Hill Northeast Historic District) on a ridge overlooking the Harlem Plains, is a freestanding house that was designated a landmark in 1999. Built in 1891, the two-and-one-half-story house's most prominent feature is a flared mansard roof which projects out over the facade roughly three feet and incorporates a series of gabled dormers. Faced with ironspot tan, brown, and ochre bricks and trimmed with wood, brownstone, and granite, the structure was designed by **William Schickel**. The building's eclectic style incorporates mostly medieval forms inspired by central European sources. **Nicholas C. Benziger**, a Swiss émigré, was a successful publisher, manufacturer, and importer of books and articles used in Catholic worship. He also was an early auto enthusiast; thus, the house also had one of Harlem's first private garages, a rare amenity even today. In 1920 the house was converted into a hospital. After World War II, a nursery school occupied the building, and later it was used as a hotel. Since 1989, it has been owned by the Broadway Housing Development Fund Company, a nonprofit organization providing permanent housing for formerly homeless adults.

ur Lady of Lourdes Roman Catholic Church
467 W. 142nd St., between Amsterdam and Convent Aves. (212) 862-4380. Bus— M3, M100, M101, BX19. Subway—A, B, C, D to 145th St.

OUR LADY OF LOURDES ROMAN CATHOLIC CHURCH

Just to the west of Convent Avenue on W. 142nd Street stands the highly unusual Church of Our Lady of Lourdes, a Roman Catholic Church built in 1902–04. Receiving landmark designation in 1975, this church is an assemblage of pieces salvaged from three famous nineteenth-century structures and combined by **Cornelius O'Reilly** of the architectural firm **O'Reilly Brothers**. The main part of the facade was salvaged from Peter B. Wight's National Academy of Design, which stood on Park Avenue South at 24th Street from 1863 to 1900. Its "Ruskinian Gothic" style made it one of the most influential nineteenth-century buildings in New York. Inside, we see bits, including stained-glass windows, from the original east end of St. Patrick's Cathedral on Fifth Avenue. These became available when the Cathedral's Lady Chapel began to be built in 1901. The stone pedestals that flank the front steps come from department store magnate A. T. Stewart's Fifth Avenue and 34th Street mansion, designed by John Kellum and completed in 1869. It's not orthodox preservation, but there is something laudable about parts of superannuated buildings migrating to the then newest neighborhood uptown.

GALLERIES

Chashama Gallery
461 W. 126th St., between Amsterdam and Morningside Aves. www.chashama.org.
Bus—M60, M100, M101, M104, BX15, Subway—A, B, C, D, 1 to 125th St.

Chashama transforms empty storefronts and offices into spaces where art flourishes. The gallery holds monthly exhibits by community artists from Harlem and the Bronx.

Contemporary African Art Gallery
330 W. 108th St., #6, between Riverside Dr. and Broadway. (212) 749-8848. www.contempafricanart.com. Openings have specific hours and by appointment. Bus—M4, M60, M104, M116. Subway—1 to 110th St.

Located right at the edge of Harlem in a lovely brownstone townhouse, this gallery exclusively shows contemporary African fine art and represents over thirty artists from various regions in Africa. Exhibits are as diverse as the regions they come from and include sculpture, paintings, etchings, collages, and installations.

DiasporA-NoW, Inc.
80 St. Nicholas Pl., Ste. 1B, between 154th and 155th Sts. (212) 491-4652. www.diaspora-now.com. Bus—M2, BX6. Subway—A, C to 155th St.

DiasporA-NoW, Inc. is an online gallery with a mission to increase awareness of Caribbean culture through works of art. To this end, the gallery features a catalog of fine arts and crafts, and coordinates a continuing series of exhibitions and workshops, featuring primarily artists from Barbados and from the African Diaspora.

Essie Green Galleries
419A Convent Ave., at 148th St. (212) 368-9635. www.essiegreengalleries.com. Tue–Sat 10am–6pm. Bus—M100, M101. Subway—A, B, C, D to 145th St.

Located in a restored brownstone townhouse in the Sugar Hill Historic District, Essie Green Galleries' collection consists of works by the senior Black masters who include Romare Bearden, Charles Alston, Edward M. Banister, Allen Stringfellow, Sam Gilliam, Lois Mailou Jones, and Norman Lewis, to name a few.

Hamilton Landmark Galleries
467 W. 144th Street, between Amsterdam and Convent Aves. (212) 863-9209. Wed–Sat 11am–7pm. Bus—M100, M101, Subway—A, B, C, D to 145th St.

Situated in a beautiful brownstone built in 1886 in the Hamilton Heights Historic District, Hamilton Landmark Galleries is dedicated to the presentation of fine art and the development of contemporary artists. The gallery has presented the work of over seventy contemporary artists, many of whom have work featured in the permanent collections of the Smithsonian and the Brooklyn Museum. Past presentations have included the work of contemporary artists from the Americas, Africa, Asia, the Caribbean, and Europe. From time to time, Hamilton Landmark Galleries invites poets, playwrights, and musicians to present their material in its space.

Miriam & Ira D. Wallach Art Gallery

Columbia University Campus, Schermerhorn Hall, 8th Fl., at 116th St. and Broadway. (212) 854-7288. www.columbia.edu/cu/wallach/. Wed–Sat 1pm–5pm. Bus—M4, M60, M104, Subway—1 to 116th St.

The gallery mounts exhibitions and related programming that reflects Columbia University's diversity of interests and approaches to the arts.

Rio Gallery II

583 Riverside Dr., 7th Fl., at 135th St. (212) 568-2030. www.broadwayhousing.org. Mon–Thu 10am–4pm. Bus—M4, M5, M11, Subway—1 to 137th St.

Located on the penthouse level of Broadway Housing Communities' building, the gallery mounts exhibitions of works by Latin American and African emerging artists. The gallery also organizes programs that feature the works of poets, writers, musicians, dancers, and photographers.

Simmons Gallery

265 Edgecombe Ave., at 146th St. (212) 234-7454. www.simmonsgalleryny.com. Tue–Sat 11am–7pm and Sun 11am–4pm. Bus—M3, BX19. Subway—A, B, C, D to 145th St.

Simmons Gallery promotes and sells the work of emerging and mid-career artists of color. The gallery opened in 2001 and since that time has exhibited the work of over twenty artists.

Triple Candie

500 W. 148th St., at Amsterdam Ave., (212) 368-3333. www.triplecandie.org. Thu–Sun 1pm–6pm. Bus—M4, M5, M100, M101, BX19. Subway—1 to 145th St.

Triple Candie is a gallery that features alternative art, and when it opened in 2001 was the only location in Harlem, other than the Studio Museum in Harlem, for contemporary art. Triple Candie mounts cutting-edge and off-the-beaten-art-path exhibitions that include giving artists free rein to express themselves anonymously without the fear of a critic tearing them apart for experimenting, or curating an "unauthorized" exhibition that consists of reproductions and photocopies of a noted artist's work. What they do best at this gallery is deconstruct the high walls of so-called "serious" art and help the viewer to understand what they are seeing and the meaning behind it.

THEATERS AND CULTURAL INSTITUTIONS

H**arlem Stage Gatehouse**
150 Convent Ave., at 135th St. (212) 281-9240, ext. 19. www.harlemstage.org. Box Office Hours: 12pm–6pm and two hours prior to events. Bus—M4, M5, M11, M100, M101. Subway—A, B, C, D, to 125th, 1 to 137th St.

In October 2006, **Aaron Davis Hall** moved into its new home in the Gatehouse and became known as Harlem Stage. This breathtaking structure, designed by **Frederick S. Cook** in a Romanesque Revival style, was part of the Croton Aqueduct water system. In 1981, this extraordinary structure was designated a landmark and listed on the National Register of Historic Places.

Harlem Stage is recognized for its creation and development of new works by performing artists of color. Programs include: *Waterworks,* which supports the creation of significant new works and provides a forum for dialogue between artists and audiences; *Harlem Stage on Screen,* which supports the works of independent filmmakers; *Harlem Stride,* which offers a laboratory for musicians to explore historic and new trends in music, develop collaborative projects, participate in humanities activities with audiences, and present unique and exceptional music programs; *E-Moves,* an annual program where emerging choreographers showcase their work, which ranges from modern dance to contemporary ballet, hip-hop, and dance theater; *SundayWorks,* which is a free reading series for artists to present new works; *Harlem Stage Partners Program,* which supports co-presentations with significant artists and organizations; and *Fund for New Work,* which provides direct support to emerging artists through commissions, subsidized rehearsal space, and/or workshop presentations.

C**olumbia Stages—International Visions**
91 Claremont Ave., between 120th and 121st Sts. (212) 854-3408. www.columbiastages.org. Bus—M4, M5, M60, M104. Subway—1 to 116th St.

Columbia Stages is the producing arm of the Oscar Hammerstein II Center for Theatre Studies of Columbia University's School of the Arts. Here is where you will find the best emerging actors, directors, playwrights, and producers honing their skills beyond the theoretical while at the same time earning a Master of Fine Arts degree. All performances, which are affordably priced, are held at the **Riverside Theatre**, located inside the historic Riverside Church (120th St. at Claremont Ave.).

D**ance Theatre of Harlem**
466 W. 152nd St., between St. Nicholas and Amsterdam Aves. (212) 690-2800. www.dancetheatreofharlem.org. Bus—M3, M100, M101. Subway—A, B, C, D to 145th St. (front of train)

After the death of Dr. Martin Luther King Jr., in 1968, Arthur Mitchell, the first permanent African American male dancer with the New York City Ballet, was inspired to give ballet classes to local children in his community of Harlem. Mitchell and his teacher and mentor, **Karel Shook**, founded the Dance Theatre of Harlem (DTH) as a school of the allied arts and a professional ballet company.

Over the past forty years the theatre, world-renowned as a multicultural institution with students and dancers from the United States and abroad, has shattered the myth that Blacks could not perform classical ballet due to their physical build, or because ballet was foreign to Black culture. DTH serves as a living reminder that the arts belong to us all.

Treat yourself to the DTH Open House Series, which hosts affordably priced community performances by its students, the Dance Theatre of Harlem Ensemble, as well as special guest artists.

ARTISTIC DIRECTOR VIRGINIA JOHNSON AND EDDIE J. SHELLMAN IN *GISELLE*

Harlem Opera Theater
Convent Avenue Baptist Church. 425 W. 144th St., at Convent Ave. (212) 592-0780. www.harlemoperatheater.org. Bus—M3, M100, M101, BX15. Subway—A, B, C, D, to 145th St.

Founded in 2001 by **Gregory Hopkins**, internationally acclaimed tenor, conductor, organist, and pianist, the Harlem Opera Theater provides performance opportunities for professional and developing Harlem classical music artists. The organization has organized numerous concerts that feature opera, oratory concerts, and recitals that focus on Negro spirituals and varied forms of American music to cultivate and expand audience appreciation for opera and classical music. Most of the concerts focus on the works of African American composers.

Harlem School of the Arts
645 St. Nicholas Ave., between 141st and 145th Sts. (212) 926–4100. www.harlemschoolofthearts.org. Bus—M3, M4, M11, BX19. Subway—A, B, C, D to 145th St.

The Harlem School of the Arts, Inc. (HSA) is a not-for-profit arts institution that for more than forty years has served over 3,000 students annually in four core artistic disciplines: dance, music, theater, and the visual arts. The faculty is comprised of arts professionals who possess extensive performing and exhibition credentials, as well as expertise in motivating and encouraging students to challenge themselves and fully develop their talents. Through HSA's numerous partnerships and artists-in-residence, the school has also become a cultural destination in Harlem, presenting theatrical, music, and dance productions and visual arts exhibitions in its "G-Space Gallery."

Harlem Textile Works
1677 Amsterdam Ave., between 142nd and 143rd Sts. (212) 234-5257. www.harlemtextileworks.org. Bus—M4, M5, M100, M101. Subway—A, B, C, D, 1 to 145th St.

Located in historic Hamilton Heights, Harlem Textile Works is a design studio and training facility that grew out of the Children's Art Carnival in the early 1980s. They are dedicated to preserving the traditional art of textile design, while offering arts education, professional internships, and entrepreneurial experiences to youth and adults. Programs include workshops in screen printing, hand-generated and computer-aided fabric and textile design, professional mentoring, and internships in the fashion industry, textile design firms, and in communications.

Miller Theatre at Columbia University

2960 Broadway, at 116th St. (212) 854-1633. Box Office: (212) 854-7799. www.millertheater.com. Bus—M4, M5, M60, M104. Subway—1 to 116th St.

Founded in 1988, the Miller Theatre, located on the Columbia University campus, is a hidden treasure in Harlem. The theatre offers contemporary classical music, opera, dance, and film, and is dedicated to developing and presenting new work from world-class artists. Their free lunchtime concert series held at Philosophy Hall, also on Columbia's campus, is an inexpensive way to enjoy great classical music in New York.

Riverside Theatre

91 Claremont Ave., at 120th St. (212) 870-6784. www.theriversidechurchny.org/theatre. Daily 7am–10pm. Bus—M4, M5, M60, M104. Subway—1 to 116th St.

Riverside Theatre, founded in 1960, is conveniently located in the historic landmark Riverside Church. The theatre is well-known for exposing its audiences to arts from many cultures. There are as many as 120 annual performances, including original dance productions, film premieres, musicals, and plays, as well as the following series and festivals: the NuDance Festival, the New York Family Arts Festival, the Cultural Animators Series, and the African Diaspora Summer Film Festival.

The Children's Art Carnival

62 Hamilton Terrace, at 144th St. (212) 234-4093. www.childrensartcarnival.org. Bus—M100, M101, BX19. Subway—A, B, C, D, to 145th St.

The Children's Art Carnival is a not-for-profit organization dedicated to providing innovative art programs for young people, ages four through twenty-one. It was founded as a community outreach program of the Museum of Modern Art more than forty years ago and became independent in 1972. Today, this arts institution uses art as a youth development tool to build self-esteem, explore cultural heritage, develop critical thinking, cultivate artistic and leadership skills, and build a sense of community. A recognized leader in providing outstanding arts education, the Carnival operates after school and Saturday programs in Arts Education, Communication Arts Production and Entrepreneurial Training, and Community Outreach and Partnership programs.

The Classical Theatre of Harlem, Inc.

566 West 159th Street, #44, between Amsterdam Ave. and Broadway. (212) 564-9983. www.classicaltheatreofharlem.org.

Founded in 1999, the Classical Theatre of Harlem (CTH) has enriched the community of Harlem with more than forty productions that have earned it a loyal following. The company, which was recognized by the Drama League as "One of Eight Theatres in America to Watch," has a fresh and innovative approach to the classics—most noticeable in its nontraditional casting, original adaptations, and music and dance. Productions have included works by Anton Chekhov, Samuel Beckett, Langston Hughes, William Shakespeare, and August Wilson, among others. CTH also earned the Lucille Lortel Award for an Outstanding Body of Work, an OBIE Award for Artistic Excellence, and a Drama Desk Award for Artistic Excellence, to name a few. This theater is one of Harlem's true gems in every sense. Currently, CTH performs at Harlem Stage Gatehouse and Harlem School of the Arts located at 150 Convent Avenue at 135th St. CTH is slated to move into the historic **Victoria Theater** on 125th Street, several doors down from the Apollo Theater, once it is renovated.

EDUCATIONAL INSTITUTIONS

Bank Street College of Education
610 W. 112th St., between Broadway and Riverside Dr. (212) 875-4400. www.bankstreet.edu. Bus—M4, M5, M60, M104. Subway—1 to 110th St.

Bank Street College of Education was founded in 1916 as the Bureau of Educational Experiments. The founder, **Lucy Sprague Mitchell**, convinced that public schools were not serving children well, set out to discover the environments in which children grow and learn to their full potential, and to educate teachers and others to create these environments. From small beginnings as an experimental nursery school, Bank Street College grew over the years, and influenced the design and implementation of such national educational programs as Head Start and Follow Through. Today, Bank Street is a graduate school that offers a master's degree program in education, a school for children, and an early childhood day-care facility; operates a continuing education program that outreaches to various communities; and publishes innovative media materials for and about children.

Barnard College
3009 Broadway, between 116th and 120th Sts. (212) 854-5262. www.barnard.edu. Bus—M4, M5, M60, M104. Subway—1 to 116th St.

Founded in 1889 and one of the original **Seven Sisters**, Barnard is a women's liberal arts college. The college is named after **Frederick A. P. Barnard**, an American educator and mathematician who served as then-Columbia College's president from 1864 to 1889. The first Barnard class met in a rented brownstone at 343 Madison Avenue; there was a faculty of six and fourteen students in the School of Arts. Nine years later the college moved to its present location, a four-acre campus in Harlem. In 1900, the college was included in the educational system of Columbia University. One of Barnard College's most noted graduates is Zora Neale Hurston, a Harlem Renaissance writer.

Columbia University
2960 Broadway, at 116th St. (212) 854-1754. www.columbia.edu. Bus—M4, M5, M60, M104. Subway—1 to 116th St.

Columbia University is a private Ivy League university and is the oldest institution of higher education in New York State. The institution was established as King's College by the Church of England, receiving a royal charter in 1754 from **George II of Great Britain**. One of only two universities in the United States to have been founded by royal charter, it was the fifth established in the Thirteen Colonies and the only college established in the Province of New York. After numerous moves from its first location in lower Manhattan, Columbia moved to West Harlem in the 1890s. The uptown campus, which occupies six city blocks or thirty-two acres,

COLUMBIA UNIVERSITY LOW LIBRARY

was designed along Beaux-Arts principles by the famous McKim, Mead & White architectural firm. Many of the buildings have been designated landmarks and are listed on the National Register of Historic Places. A must-see is the **Low Library** which houses the visitor's center. Also of note, the Battle of Harlem Heights (1776) was fought on what is now the area between 116th and 117th Streets on Broadway. Columbia annually grants the Pulitzer Prizes. More Nobel Prize winners are affiliated with Columbia than with any other institution in the world. Notable alumni and affiliates include five Founding Fathers of the United States, four U.S. presidents (including Nobel Prize winner Barack Obama), nine justices of the Supreme Court, ninety-six Pulitzer Prize winners, and ninety -three Nobel Prize winners.

Manhattan School of Music
120 Claremont Ave., between 122nd and 123rd Sts. (212) 742-2802. www.msmnyc.edu. Bus—M4, M5, M60, M104. Subway—1 to 116th St.

The Manhattan School of Music, which is one of the world's leading music conservatories, was founded in 1917 as the Neighborhood Music School. It currently sits where Julliard School was first located. The school offers a wide range of degrees in jazz and classical music. You don't want to miss the free jazz and classical music concerts that are held year-round at the school. Two of its most noted alumni are **Max Roach** (American jazz percussionist, drummer, and composer) and **Herbie Hancock** (jazz pianist and composer).

New York Theological Seminary
475 Riverside Dr., Ste. 500, between 119th and 120th Sts. (212) 870-1211. www.nyts.edu. Bus—M4, M5, M60, M104. Subway—1 to 116th St.

Founded in 1900 by **Wilbert Webster White** as the **Bible Teacher's College** in Montclair, New Jersey, the New York Theological Seminary's mission was to be the leading school for theological education. In 1902, the seminary moved to New York City and was renamed the **Bible Teachers' Training School**. In 1967 the name was changed to New York Theological Seminary. The seminary currently offers three accredited degrees—Master of Professional Studies, Master of Divinity, and Doctor of Ministry—and a non-accredited Certificate in Christian ministry. The school trains its students for ministry in the real world. The administrative offices are located in the Interchurch Center on Riverside Drive and classrooms are located across the street in Riverside Church. The seminary also makes use of the Columbia University Library System, which includes the Burke Library at Union Theological Seminary.

Teachers College—Columbia University: Graduate School of Education
525 W. 120th St., between Broadway and Amsterdam Ave. (212) 678-3235. www. tc.columbia.edu. Bus—M4, M5, M60, M104. Subway—1 to 116th St.

In 1887 the New York School for the Training of Teachers was founded. In 1892 its name was changed to Teachers College and in 1894 it moved to its current location. From its modest beginnings as a school to prepare home economists and manual arts teachers for the children of the poor, the college affiliated with Columbia University in 1898, and went on to become the leading intellectual influence on the development of the American teaching profession. Under the terms of the agreement, Teachers College functions as Columbia's Graduate School of Education and confers all advanced degrees in education. One of the finest graduate schools of education in the country, the college, where anthropologist **Margaret Meade** taught for over twenty years, was a pioneer in the understanding that the home environment plays a major role in a child's ability to learn and develop. Notable graduates of this school include **Charles Alston**, an artist, teacher, and muralist who created numerous murals in Harlem under the WPA public arts program; and **Shirley Chisholm**, the first African American woman elected to Congress and to seek the Democratic nomination for U.S. president.

The City College of New York

Convent Ave., between W. 130th and 141st Sts. (212) 650-7000. www1.ccny.cuny.edu. Bus—M100, M101. Subway—A, B, C, D, to 145th St.

THE CITY COLLEGE OF NEW YORK – GREAT HALL

The City College (CCNY) of the City University of New York was founded in 1847 as the Free Academy of the City of New York, and was the first free public institution of higher education in the United States. CCNY moved to West Harlem in 1907 on 35 acres. Architect **George Post's** Collegiate Gothic-designed buildings, a popular style for Ivy League schools at the turn of the century, symbolized the fact that the education received by the poor immigrant student body was as good as if not better than most prestigious schools in the nation. Popularly known back in the day as the "Poor man's Harvard," City College today offers academic programs that lead to undergraduate degrees in liberal arts and the sciences, and graduate and post-graduate degrees in a number of disciplines. Many of the buildings on campus have obtained landmark status. A must-see is Shepard Hall and the magnificent Great Hall auditorium inside it. **Gen. Colin Powell**, former Secretary of State, is one of the distinguished graduates of the school. Other noted graduates include: **Herman Badillo** former Congressman and chairman of CUNY's Board of Trustees; writers **Walter Mosley**, whose bestselling novels about private eye Easy Rawlins have received Edgar and Golden Dagger Awards; **Oscar Hijuelos,** who won the 1990 Pulitzer Prize for his novel *The Mambo Kings Play Songs of Love*; and **Ernesto Quiñonez**, national best-selling author of *Bodega Dreams* and other titles.

The Jewish Theological Seminary

3080 Broadway, at 122nd St. (212) 678-8000. www.jtsa.edu. Bus—M4, M5, M60, M104. Subway—1 to 116th St.

The Jewish Theological Seminary was founded in 1886 and is the academic and spiritual center of Conservative Judaism, which was formed to preserve Jewish tradition, rather than reform or abandon it. In 1887 the seminary held its first class of ten students in the vestry of the Spanish-Portuguese Synagogue, New York City's oldest congregation. In 1930 the organization commissioned a new headquarters at 122nd Street and Broadway in a neo-Colonial style, with a tower at the corner. The architects were **Gehron, Ross and Alley**. The Seminary operates five schools: Albert A. List College of Jewish Studies, which is affiliated with Columbia University and offers joint/double bachelor's degree programs with both Columbia and Barnard College; the Graduate School; The William Davidson Graduate School of Jewish Education; H. L. Miller Cantorial School and College of Jewish Music; and the Rabbinical School.

Union Theological Seminary

3041 Broadway, at 121st St. (212) 662-7100. www.utsnyc.edu. Bus—M4, M5, M60, M104. Subway—1 to 116th St.

Founded in 1836 by the **Presbyterian Church**, Union Theological Seminary is the oldest nondenominational seminary in the nation. The school confers master's degrees of Arts, Divinity, and Sacred Theology; doctorates in Theology and Philosophy; and joint degree programs with Columbia University. Union appointed its first female president—**Dr. Serene Jones**—in 2008. In 1910 Union moved to its present location in Harlem. The brick and limestone English Gothic architecture, by **Allen and Collins**, includes the tower, which adapts features of the crossing tower of Durham Cathedral, one of the finest examples of Norman architecture and a UNESCO World Heritage Site. The Union building was added to the National Register of Historic Places in 1980. It is also home to the Burke Theological Library, the largest theological library in the Western Hemisphere. Due to declining enrollments, large sections of the campus are now on long-term lease to Columbia University. It also has an impressive list of past and present faculty, including **Dr. James Cone**, who is one of the founders of Black liberation theology.

ACCOMMODATIONS

Sugar Hill Harlem Inn

460 W. 141st St., between Amsterdam and Convent Aves. (212) 234-5432. www. sugarhillharleminn.com. Bus—M4, M5, M100, M101. Subway—A, B, C, D, 1 to 145th St.

Located in a beautifully restored Victorian townhouse built in 1906, the inn is proudly named after the landmark Sugar Hill district in Harlem, "the place to be" during the Harlem Renaissance. In fact, the rooms are named after famous African Americans and decorated in a style that represents individuals like **Lena Horne**, **Miles Davis**, Louis (Satchmo) Armstrong, and more. There are two rooms with private bathrooms, two studios with private bathrooms and kitchens, and one two-bedroom apartment with both private bathroom and kitchen. All rooms are equipped with TV, DVD player, cable, and AC, and come with iron, ironing board, and hair dryer. The inn also has a lovely function/reception space that can be rented for events and special occasions. Room rates range from $100 to $250, depending on the day of the week.

International House Guest Accommodations

500 Riverside Drive, at 122nd St. (212) 316-8436. www.ihouse-nyc.org. Bus—M4, M5, M60, M104. Subway—1 to 125th Street.

While the International House, located in the Columbia University area, is a residence for more than 700 foreign graduate students and interns, it offers hotel-like accommodations for alumni and visitors. There are seven guest rooms that can sleep two to three and contain private baths and two single beds, and room for a cot if there is a third person; and four guest suites that can sleep four to five and are equipped with living rooms that include either a sofa bed or a day bed, private baths, and either two twin beds, a king-sized bed, or a double bed. Each guest room and suite contain the following amenities: air-conditioning, in-room telephone service (all calls billed separately), color TV, small refrigerator, daily housekeeping service, hair dryer, and linens. Guests can also use the International House facilities and services that include the cafeteria, laundry room, coin-operated copy machine, a pub with dancing, vending machines, and an indoor basketball court, and participate in weekly social and cultural activities. Rates for guest rooms range from $130 to $165 a night, and the guest suites rate range is $145 to $180 based on occupancy.

St. Nicholas Inn

883 St. Nicholas Ave., between 154th and 155th Sts. (800) 941-1658. www.saintnicholasinn.com. Bus—M2, M3. Subway—A, C train to 155th St.

Located at the tip of Harlem overlooking the Bronx and Yankee Stadium, St. Nicholas Inn is tucked away in the Hamilton Heights/Sugar Hill Historic District. It includes five guest accommodations (two with private bathrooms) with single or double rooms, as well as a kitchen and lounge area. In-room amenities include air-conditioning, hair dryer, coffee/tea facilities, wireless Internet, radio, satellite/cable TV. Continental breakfast is available. Room rates range from $119 to $239, with a three-night minimum. Check for specials and seasonal rates. The inn cannot accommodate pets or small children.

The Landmark Guest Rooms

Union Theological Seminary. 3041 Broadway, at 121st St. (212) 280-1313. www.utsnyc.edu. Bus—M4, M5, M60, M104. Subway—1 to 125th St.

The Landmark Guest Rooms is conveniently situated near religious and educational institutions located in the Columbia University area. Landmark is actually located on the campus of Union Theological Seminary. There are three types of rooms available, including a single, which contains a twin bed; a twin, which contains two twin beds; and a double, which contains a full-sized bed. Each of its twenty-five air-conditioned guest rooms feature private baths, cable TV, wireless Internet access, iron, hair dryer, miniature refrigerator, daily housekeeping services, and 24-hour access and front-desk security. There is also free local telephone service. Rates start at $135 a night.

DINING AND LIVE ENTERTAINMENT

H udson River Café
697 W. 133rd St., at Twelfth Ave. (212) 491-9111. www.hudsonrivercafe.com. Cuisine: American, Seafood. Dinner, Brunch. $$$$. Mon–Sat Dinner 5pm–12am, Sat–Sun, Brunch 11am–4pm, Mon–Thu Bar 4pm–12am, Fri–Sat 4pm–4am. All major credit cards. Bus—M4, M100, M101, BX15. Subway—1 to 125th St. or 137th St.

Hudson River Café is the first of four trendy destination restaurants to open on the west side of Twelfth Avenue in a desolate area that once was home to a thriving meatpacking industry. Despite its name, the café, which opened in 2007, has no appreciable river view. Offering a fresh take on seafood and grill, with Latin and soulful overtones, the bi-level restaurant has both indoor and outdoor seating on two levels, with live jazz on Thursday, Friday, and Saturday nights and during Sunday brunch. The spot's real draw is the spacious front patio with its own covered bar that serves up some incredible mojitos and a knockout martini made from white cranberry juice, gin, and cucumber. Upstairs, under the vaulted ceiling, is a calmer dining setting ; the ground floor features another bar and a noisier atmosphere for dining. It sports a seafood-centric menu; favorite appetizers are coconut-crusted shrimp in a fiery Thai chili sauce, and arctic char ceviche. The pièce de résistance is the main course seafood paella or Max's Paella, named after co-owner **Max Piña**. One of the popular grilled items is the juicy churrasco steak that rivals any in Argentina. A $21 prix-fixe brunch allows unlimited bellinis and mimosas. The service is cordial and effective, from the valet parking attendants, to the greeting at the door, to the thanks and farewell at meal's end. Reservations are strongly recommended.

Dining

A rtopolis Expresso Cafe
1090 Amsterdam Ave., between 113th and 114th Sts. (212) 666-3744. www.artopolisespresso.com. Cuisine: Baked Goods, Crepes. $$. Daily 11am–11pm. All major credit cards. Bus—M4, M11, M60. Subway—1 to 110th St.

A sweet taste of Greece, Artopolis Expresso Café stands out as a bakery/café for its amazing pastries, breads, cakes, baklava, tarts, and pies. For lunch it offers tasty crepes, omelets, and salads that can be created with a variety of fresh ingredients and enjoyed in a great outdoor seating area. Not to be missed are the dessert crepes, yogurt parfaits, fresh fruit smoothies, and gelato, which its fans swear is the best. In addition to a variety of gourmet coffees including espresso, beer and wine are served. A strong fan base has developed that returns over and over, not only for the great desserts and food but also because of the fast and friendly service.

Boca Chica

1354 Amsterdam Ave., between 125th and 126th Sts. (212) 222-6660. Cuisine: Dominican. Breakfast, Lunch, Dinner. $$. Open 24 hours. All major credit cards. Bus— M4, M11, M60, M104, BX15. Subway—1 to 125th St.

This Dominican restaurant's specialties are seafood dishes that are easy on the pocketbook (most items do not exceed $10). The popular chofan, or black rice with seafood, is the Dominican version of the Haitian riz djon djon. There is an extensive menu, but some of the standouts include the fish fillet in coconut, which features two extremely fresh fillets surrounded by a creamy coconut sauce that is counterbalanced with peppers and spices, and the Chica Combo of shrimp and fish that includes a generous-sized fried fillet and three fried shrimp that are neither too greasy, nor too dry, nor over-battered, and the taste of which can be heightened with just a squeeze from a slice of lime that comes with the order.

Bus Stop Restaurant

3341 Broadway, at 135th St. (212) 690-2150. Cuisine: American, Spanish. Breakfast, Lunch, Dinner. $$. Daily 6am–11pm. Cash only. Bus—M4, M5, M11. Subway—1 to 137th St.

Bus Stop Restaurant is a diner that serves great American and Spanish food at very reasonable prices. The American breakfast is super and enhanced by café con leche, Spanish coffee made with scalded milk. Those who regularly visit this eating spot rave about the fries, which they say are crispy and the best outside France. Another winner is the Chicken Francaise with yellow rice. This tiny family-owned place excels at getting your order in front of you pronto.

Caridad Restaurant

3533 Broadway, between 144th and 145th Sts. (212) 862-4053. www.caridad145.com. Cuisine: Dominican, Italian. Breakfast, Lunch, Dinner. $$. Mon–Thu 7am–12am, Fri– Sun 7am–1am. All major credit cards. Bus—M4, M5, BX19. Subway—1 to 145th St.

Authentic Dominican cuisine can be found here. From their Spanish-style rotisserie chicken to their sandwiches, this restaurant serves up big portions for low prices, and the taste is wonderful. Several types of specials are offered, including the daily $6 luncheon special of a quarter-chicken, fried plantain, rice and beans, and a can of soda. The family special includes a whole rotisserie chicken, large white or yellow rice, medium container of beans, sweet plantains, and a two-liter bottle of soda for $13.95. Inside, the atmosphere is relaxing and the serving staff friendly.

Che Bella Pizza

1215 Amsterdam Ave., between 119th and 120th Sts. (212) 864-7300. www. chebellapizza.com. Cuisine: Pizza, Sandwiches. Lunch, Dinner. $$. Mon–Sat 11am– 10pm, Sun 11am–9pm. V, MC, AmEx. Bus—M4, M11, M60, M104. Subway—1 to 116th St.

This local pizza shop has an extensive menu of pizzas, sandwiches, hot dishes, and Greek specialties. However, it's the formidable panini sandwiches, fresh salads, fried calamari, and daily specials that keep the lines long. The $7.95 special grilled chicken foccacia sandwich with soup or salad is one of the favorites. The service here is fast and friendly.

El Porton Bar

3151 Broadway, between 124th and 125th Sts. (212) 665-7338. www.elportonbar.com.
Cuisine: Mexican. Lunch, Dinner, Brunch. $$. Daily 10am–2am. All major credit cards.
Bus—M4, M11, M60, M104, BX15. Subway—1 to 125th St.

El Porton is a neighborhood eatery that prepares south-of-the-border comfort food. Monday through Friday the Mexican restaurant features a luncheon special for $7.50 from 12pm to 4pm. The special includes a platter of traditional Mexican fare such as a burrito or quesadilla with a side, as well as a choice of a glass of sangria, wine, margarita, juice, or coffee. Also, on Monday and Tuesday night for $12.95 you can enjoy a beef, chicken, and veggie fajitas with sangria, margarita, or Mexican Tecate beer. At the prix-fixe brunch on Saturday and Sunday from 11am to 4pm you have a choice of various egg dishes with a salad, along with a glass of sangria, wine, margarita, soda, juice, or coffee.

Famous Fish Market

684 W. 145th St., at St. Nicholas Ave. (212) 491-8323. Cuisine: Seafood. Lunch, Dinner. $.
Mon–Wed 11am–10:30pm, Thu 11am–11pm, Fri 11am–12am, Sat 11:30am–12am, Sun
12pm–10pm. Cash only. Bus—M3, BX19. Subway—A, B, C, D to 145th St.

We don't know what came first, the name or—because the fried fish is so doggone good—the reputation. Some swear that this restaurant serves up the best fried fish in New York City. The take-out-only basement restaurant is literally a hole in the wall and can easily be missed if it weren't for the long line, especially for dinner, which snakes down St. Nicholas Ave. The portions of fried whiting fish and chips are more than generous.

FAMOUS FISH MARKET

Globle Trippin Coffeehouse-Bookstore-Kazbah

1689 Amsterdam Ave., between 143rd and 144th Sts. (917) 860-0237. www.
globetrippin.com. Cuisine: Coffee shop. Lunch, Dinner. $$. Tue–Sun 12pm–8pm.
Cash only. Bus—M4, M5, M100, M101, BX19. Subway—1 to 145th St.

The new kid on the block and very much welcomed, Globle Trippin Coffeehouse-Bookstore-Kazbah embraces all the charm and sense of community evoked in traditional coffeehouses throughout the world, and more. Not only does it offer up robust coffees, international fruit, and spiced and herbal teas, but it prepares different homemade savory dishes including salads, wraps, and sandwiches every day to balance a well-stocked pastry case of sweet treats that also change every day. What makes this establishment even more unique is its small bookstore that features works by authors with a foreign heritage or works about foreign countries, and the events such as book signings, artists salons, cooking classes, various kinds of workshops, and its game nights. There is a Sunday brunch from 12pm to 4pm and a Friday night wine club from 8pm to 11pm.

Heights Bar & Grill

2867 Broadway, 2nd Fl., between 111th and 112th Sts. (212) 866-7035. www. heightsnyc.com. Cuisine: American, Mexican. Lunch, Dinner, Brunch. $$$. Kitchen Daily 11am–11pm, Brunch Sat and Sun 11am–4pm, Rooftop Mon–Thu 5pm–11pm, Fri–Sun 11am–11pm, bar is open till 3am on Fri and Sat, Lunch 11:30am–4pm. All major credit cards. Bus—M4, M60, M104. Subway—1 to 110th St.

The Heights Bar & Grill is like an institution on Broadway. It's a classic Columbia University student hangout that offers cheap drinks and loud conversation. The hit here is the $4 frozen margarita in a rainbow of flavors during Happy Hour, 5pm to 7pm, which also includes stuffed-to-bursting burritos for $8.95 to $13.95. In 2009 *New York Magazine* listed the Heights as one of the "Best Rooftop Bars in New York City." The rooftop, while not high enough to give you a breathtaking view, is charming and intimate, with a semi-retractable roof and air-conditioning when it's humid. The mostly Mexican menu offers a wide array of inexpensive burritos, burgers, salads, and sandwiches for lunch, dinner, and brunch.

Jimbo's Hamburger Palace

1345 Amsterdam Ave., between 125th and 126th Sts. (212) 865-8777. Cuisine: Burgers, Sandwiches, American. Breakfast, Lunch, Dinner. $. Mon–Sat 5:30am–10pm, Sun 7am–9pm. Cash only. Bus—M4, M11, M60, M100, M01, M104, BX15. Subway—1 to 125th St.

This is where it all started, the original Jimbo's Hamburger Palace. Now this venerable hamburger joint has mushroomed into a local chain with numerous sites throughout Central, East, and West Harlem. This particular one is the smallest of them all—almost a hole in the wall. But boy, are the burgers great! There are hamburgers, cheeseburgers, turkey burgers, and veggie burgers with sautéed onions that can be ordered solo or deluxe (lettuce, tomatoes, fries), and you can watch as the short order cook prepares your order on an open grill. Other sandwiches that Jimbo's loyal customer base enjoys are the gyros and grilled tuna sandwiches. Breakfast here is cheap and good. Try the pancakes with a side of turkey bacon.

Kitchenette Uptown

1272 Amsterdam Ave., between 122nd and 123rd Sts. (212) 531-7600. www. kitchenetterestaurant.com. Cuisine: American, Baked Goods. Breakfast, Lunch, Dinner. $$$. Mon–Fri 8am–11pm, Sat and Sun 9am–11pm. All major credit cards. Bus—M4, M11, M60, M104. Subway—1 to 125th St.

The Kitchenette Uptown has cultivated a loyal following because it has consistently been serving up New England-style comfort food and bakery goods—and they are good at it. Its diverse menu is filled with homemade food is fresh, hearty, flavorful, and made with care. Their brunch has people lined up on Saturday and Sunday from 9am to 4:30pm. Reservations are not taken, so be prepared to wait. There are numerous egg dishes with sides of home-fries and garlic-roasted fries, various homemade griddle cakes, waffles, and French toast, creamy Southern cheese grits, fluffy buttermilk biscuits, homemade turkey sausage with apples and sage, just to name a few. While waiting just inside the door to be seated, there are abundantly filled pastry cases of made-from-scratch cakes, pies, cupcakes, and more to whet the appetite. The décor creates an ambience that instantly transports you to a small-town country kitchen with pressed-tin ceiling, polka-dot wainscoting, and salvaged doors for tables. Must-tries are the flaky cherry pie, turkey meatloaf, and Caesar salad with a hint of anchovies.

a Posada
3496 Broadway, at 143rd St. (212) 281-2164. Cuisine: Mexican. Breakfast, Lunch, Dinner. $$. Daily 9am–4am. V, MC. Bus—M4, M5, M100, M101, BX19. Subway—1 to 145th St.

La Posada prepares authentic and reasonably priced Mexican food in this unassuming site on bustling Broadway. Some dishes to consider include the pollo en chipotle, quesadillas, chicken tacos, and lip-smacking salsa. This restaurant delivers, but if you don't speak Spanish, you might get your order quicker if you choose take-out.

yla's Café
1270 Amsterdam Ave., between 122nd and 123rd Sts. (212) 280-0705. Cuisine: French, American. Breakfast, Lunch, Dinner. $$. Daily 8am–11pm. All major credit cards. Bus—M4, M11, M60, M104. Subway—1 to 125th St.

Lyla's Café serves breakfast all day and night. It stands out for the numerous crepes that are featured, including more than a dozen or so traditional French dessert crepes and buckwheat crepes that fold in cheeses, veggies, meat, chicken, ham, etc. Also, there is an impressive collection of omelets to choose from as well as pancakes and waffles. A debate has sprung up over the Internet regarding the "Best Burger" in New York, where Lyla's has been the chosen recipient of the title. The burger under discussion combines chopped beef and crisp onions with a firm brioche rather than a common burger bun. On Lyla's menu it is listed as a hamburger priced at $9.99 and served with salad, tomatoes, onions, and homemade fries.

assawa
1239 Amsterdam Ave., at 121st St. (212) 663-0505. www.massawanyc.com. Cuisine: Eritrean, Ethiopian. Lunch, Dinner. $$$. Daily 11:30am–11pm. V, MC, AmEx. Bus—M4, M11, M60, M104. Subway—1 to 116th St.

Massawa has for more than twenty years been preparing authentic Eritrean and Ethiopian cuisine in its location near Columbia University. Hearty chicken, seafood, beef, and lamb stewed with red spicy berbere and with a hot sauce called awaze are ladled on injera that serves as plate and utensil, and is home-baked flat bread made from the wheat grain teff. If a diner prefers rice and utensils, they are provided. There are several restaurants in New York that serve Ethiopian food, but few that feature food from Eritrea, which is a tiny nation that has an extensive coastline on the Red Sea, north of landlocked Ethiopia. Seafood dishes are usually not found on Ethiopian menus so it is a real treat to see salmon silsi (cubes of wine-glazed fish) and several spicy shrimp dishes on Massawa's menu. The combination platters allow you to sample multiple dishes.

ax Caffe
1262 Amsterdam Ave., between 122nd and 123rd Sts. (212) 531-1210. www.maxsoha.com. Cuisine: Salads, Sandwiches. Breakfast, Lunch, Dinner. $$. Daily 8am–12:30am. V, MC, AmEx. Bus—M4, M11, M60, M104. Subway—1 to 125th St.

This petite "little brother" of Max SoHa on the same block is a comfortable oasis where you can enjoy coffee or a good sandwich in lounge style, with comfortable velvet couches, loveseats, and coffee tables rather than dining tables. Compared to its heartier relative, Max Caffe's menu is lighter, with more sandwiches, wraps, salads, paninis, crostinis, and tapas prepared with an Italian touch. The restaurant features a "Wine of the Month," and on Wednesday and Friday from 5pm to 6pm wine and beer is half-priced. During the day you can find Columbia students hard at work on their laptops taking advantage of the free Wi-Fi service.

Max SoHa
1274 Amsterdam Ave., at 123rd St. (212) 531-2221. www.maxsoha.com. Cuisine: Italian. Lunch, Dinner. $$$. Daily 12pm–12am. Cash only. Bus—M4, M11, M60, M104. Subway—1 to 125th St.

Max SoHa offers Italian food with the comforts of home but the flair of a gourmet. In this unassuming brick-walled bistro, this Soho-styled eatery excels at preparing hearty soups, pasta, and Mediterranean specials. Because of its reasonable prices and the numerous daily specials, this restaurant is usually packed for dinner. The black ink seafood pasta stands out among the many uptown Italian restaurants. Rich lasagna, baked in individual pottery dishes, is mouthwatering. A special of lobster ravioli packs juicy morsels of seafood in a tomato-cream sauce, just to name one of the many fine specials. In addition, there is an extensive list of wines to choose from, and there are several varieties of beer. Max SoHa does not accept reservations, so come early.

Mi Floridita Restaurant
3219 Broadway, at 129th St. (212) 662-0090. Cuisine: Cuban, Latin American, Caribbean. Breakfast, Lunch, Dinner. $$. Daily 9am–2am. All major credit cards. Bus—M4, M100, M101, M104. Subway—1 to 125th St.

For over four decades Mi Floridita Restaurant has been upholding a family tradition—cooking good traditional Cuban food and selling it at reasonable prices. At one time, there were seven Floriditas that flourished in response to filling a niche for the large influx of Cubans to the area in the 1960s. Today, the eatery, which is more a diner, still prepares Cuban favorites but also accommodates other Caribbean cuisines like mangú, a Dominican breakfast dish composed of mashed plantains, olive oil, sautéed onions, and a hint of vinegar (can be eaten with sausage, beef, fruit, cheese, eggs). This is the restaurant to order the quintessential Cuban sandwich. A baguette is piled high with sliced ham and roast pork, relish, and Swiss cheese, and placed in a foil-wrapped sandwich press. During its toasting, the sandwich receives a flourish of butter. The end result is a gastronomic delight. Also, try the roast chicken-on-the-bone special, the sangria, and the garlic chicken plate.

Miss Mamie's Spoonbread Too
366 W. 110th St., between Columbus and Manhattan Aves. (212) 865-6744. www. spoonbreadinc.com/miss_mamies.htm. Cuisine: Southern, Soul Food. Lunch, Dinner. $$$. Mon–Thu 12pm–10pm, Fri and Sat 12pm–11pm, Sun 11am–9:30pm. All major credit cards. Bus—M3, M4, M7, M116. Subway—1 to 110th St.

Miss Mamie's (the owner's mother) is the sister restaurant to Miss Maude's (the owner's aunt), which is located in Central Harlem. It was opened by ex-Wilhelmina model, cookbook author Norma Jean Darden, who also runs a successful catering business. The restaurant serves comfort food based on family recipes from Ms. Darden's popular cookbook, *Spoonbread and Strawberry Wine*, which she co-authored with her sister Carole. It's Southern down-home cooking here. Students from nearby Columbia University, uptown church ladies, savvy New Yorkers, and VIPs like former President Bill Clinton all feel at home in this inexpensive soul-food restaurant. Try President Clinton's favorite: the "Miss Mamie Sampler" with shrimp, short ribs, and chicken. *The New York Post* says, "On its own or smothered in gravy, Spoonbread has the best fried chicken in NYC!"

Mi Tierra Cafeteria Restaurant

3569 Broadway, between 146th and 147th St. (212) 690-7505. Cuisine: Dominican, American. Breakfast, Lunch, Dinner. $$. Daily 7am–12am. All major credit cards. Bus—M4, M5, M100, M101, BX19. Subway—1 to 145th St.

Mi Tierra Cafeteria Restaurant is a popular hangout for the Dominican residents of this neighborhood that is west of the Hamilton Heights Historic District. The décor is nothing to write home about, but the traditional Dominican dishes are what keep people coming back. The flavorable mofongo, rotisserie chicken, stewed meats with sides of beans and yellow or white rice, and the fried plantain or yucca are served in huge portions. Sit at the bar and enjoy the friendly Latin vibe in this eatery.

Pasha Events at the Riverside Café

490 Riverside Drive or 91 Claremont Ave., at 120th St. Riverside Church, South Hall Lobby of the Martin Luther King Wing (212) 870-6820. www.theriversidechurchny.org/about/?cafe. Cuisine: International. Breakfast, Lunch, Brunch. $. Mon–Fri 8am–3pm; Sun Brunch 11:30am–3pm. All major credit cards. Bus—M4, M5, M60, M104. Subway—1 to 116th St.

Pasha Events is located in a place where old-world charm and elegance come together at the gothic-inspired Riverside Church. Their selection of hot and cold food is available at affordable prices. A full hot breakfast can be purchased for $4 and a hot lunch for $6. They also provide on- and off-premises full-service catering for diverse functions such as small gatherings, weddings, corporate events, meetings, and fundraisers for over 1,000 guests.

Pinnacle

2937 Broadway, at 115th St. (212) 662-1000. Cuisine: Pizza, Gourmet Deli, Juice Bar. Breakfast, Lunch, Dinner. $. 24 hours, except for summer 5:30am–12am. V, MC, AmEx. Bus—M4, M60, M104. Subway—1 to 116th St.

Pinnacle is a great place to grab a cheap slice of pizza quickly. What's even better is that this place is open twenty-four hours except in the summer months, when it closes at midnight. Orders also are delivered twenty-four hours. It's crowded in the morning for breakfast because menu items go no higher than $4.

Raw Soul

348 W. 145th St., between St. Nicholas and Edgecombe Aves. (212) 491-5859. www.rawsoul.com. Cuisine: Vegan and Juice Bar. Lunch, Dinner. $$. Tue–Sat 11am–9pm. All major credit cards. Bus—M3, M100, M101, BX19. Subway—A, B, C, D to 145th St.

Raw Soul prepares vegan and vegetarian meals and juices fresh daily with local organic fruits and vegetables from scratch. They use no dairy, refined sugars, tofu, preservatives, or processed foods. The menu changes daily and there is always a lunch special. Favorites include the veggie burger served on a flaxseed bun, the collard leaf wrap of pumpkin seed pate, and the raw pizza made of buckwheat crust, mushrooms, sun-dried tomatoes, black olives, and green and red peppers. Enjoy live entertainment during Sunday brunch.

Sezz Medi

1260 Amsterdam Ave., at 122nd St. (212) 932-2901. www.sezzmedi.com. Cuisine: Italian. Lunch, Dinner, Brunch. $$$. Sun–Wed 11:30am–10:30pm, Thu 11:30am–11:30pm, Fri–Sat 11:30am–12am. All Major Credit Cards. Bus—M4, M11, M60, M104. Subway—1 to 125th St.

This Italian eatery, which is located on a block of restaurants that has become a destination in West Harlem, features traditional brick-oven pizza with Italian-themed salads and antipasto. The pleasantly diverse menu has hidden treasures such as the prime rib for two, roasted salmon, and the seafood risotto. In addition to daily specials and a full bar, the restaurant offers a reasonably priced Sunday brunch that includes egg dishes with an Italian slant, pancakes and waffles, and fresh salads.

Sweet Chef Southern Style Bakery

122 Hamilton Pl., at 142nd St. (212) 862-5909. www.sweetchefbakeryny.com. Cuisine: Bakery. $. Mon–Sat 12pm–8pm. Cash only. Bus—M4, M5, M100, M101. Subway—1 to 145th St.

Sweet Chef Southern Style Bakery initially opened a wholesale operation and provided Southern baked goods to restaurants and gourmet supermarkets such as Amy Ruth's, Spoonbread, Fairway, and Westside Market. The wonderful aromas emanating from the shop prompted local residents to request that a retail bakery be opened. The tiny storefront is not much to look at but the scrumptious sweets inside have helped the shop owned by **Amadou "Jackie" Diakite** become a fixture in West Harlem. Diakite left his native Ivory Coast and his executive-chef position at the five-star Hotel Ivoire to move to New York. After holding down numerous jobs, in 1996 he decided to open a bakery where he could blend the baking skills learned from familial cooking in Africa and the Southern style his store espouses. He insists that many of the spices and ingredients are the same in both styles, just the tastes are different. The pumpkin, sweet potato, and pecan pies are divine, as are the buttery cookies and crumbly cobblers.

Terrace In The Sky

400 W. 119th St., between Amsterdam Ave. and Morningside Dr. (212) 666-9490. www.terraceinthesky.com. Cuisine: French, Mediterranean, American. Lunch, Dinner, Brunch. $$$$$. Tue–Thu and Sat 5:30pm–11pm, Fri 12pm–11pm, Sun 11am–3pm. All major credit cards. Bus—M4, M60, M104. Subway—1 to 116th St.

For decades Terrace In The Sky, which is located in the penthouse of Butler Hall on the Columbia University campus, has been consistently providing elegant dishes and impeccable service to discriminating diners. In addition to the exquisite French and Mediterranean cuisine, the breathtaking views of Manhattan from its glass-walled dining room and outdoor terrace draw the public here. The upscale prix-fixe Sunday brunch (two courses for $35 and three courses for $45) features items like crab cakes with white anchovies, warm duck confit with poached pears, roasted pork loin, and a rack of lamb with a black-olive puree. Add to this a voluminous wine list and various cocktails that are priced between $10 and $14. For dessert, try the bananas Foster, which is caramelized tableside. The dining experience is enhanced by a seductive ambience that includes the melodic strains of a harp.

Tom's Restaurant

2880 Broadway, at 112th St. (212) 864-6137. Cuisine: American. Breakfast, Lunch, Dinner. $. Sun–Wed 6am–1:30am, Thu–Sat 24 hours. Cash only. Bus—M4, M60, M104. Subway—1 to 110th St.

One of this restaurant's claims to fame is that its exterior appears in *Seinfeld*. However, the popular TV sitcom used a different location for the interior. Another claim to fame is that from Thursday through Saturday this restaurant remains open 24 hours and its Formica counter and old-fashioned booths fill up. Tom's serves American comfort food—burgers and fries, grilled cheese sandwiches, pancakes, eggs, old-fashioned milk shakes and ice cream sundaes, and the like—at extremely cheap prices.

Live Entertainment

El Morocco Theater & Nightclub

3534 Broadway, at 145th St. (212) 939-0909. www.elmorocconyc.com. Tues–Wed 6pm–2am, Thu–Sun 10pm–4am. All major credit cards. Bus—M4, M5, M100, M101, BX19. Subway—1 to 145th St.

The trademark of the original El Morocco club of the 1930s and 1940s was its zebra-stripe motif and palm trees. It was home to the rich and famous and also was the site where Tito Puente recorded his live *Cha Cha Cha* album in 1958. It was the first club to use a velvet rope. The new El Morocco with its over-the-top zebra motif, palm trees, and even a leopard motif lounge, is a 10,000-square-foot re-creation of the glamorous supper club of old, but this time with a contemporary Latino orientation. This hot spot is located in a building that housed **Club Caborrojeno**, a popular 1960s Latin club, and is outfitted with modern flourishes like plasma screens hung around the club. Like any good nightclub, this place stays open very late, which means things don't get to popping until well after 1am. Then guests can dance the merengue, bachata, salsa, and reggaeton into the wee hours of the morning. This club also provides live entertainment, including Latin jazz bands and comedy/variety shows. The place promises to expand its reach by hosting concerts and independent theater in the future.

Showman's

375 W. 125ᵗʰ St., between Morningside and St. Nicholas Aves. (212) 864-8941. Mon–Sat 1pm–4am. Wed and Thu: No cover charge, two-drink minimum, showtimes 8:30pm, 10pm and 11:30pm. Fri and Sat: $5 cover charge and two-drink minimum, showtimes 9:30pm, 11:30pm and 1:30am. All major credit cards. Bus—M2, M3, M10, M60, M100, M101, BX15. Subway—A, B, C, D to 125ᵗʰ St.

Founded in 1942, Showman's was a hangout spot for Apollo entertainers and performers and was located next door to the famed theater until 1985 when, due to a fire, it moved to Eighth Avenue between 124ᵗʰ and 125ᵗʰ Streets. The erection of the Harlem USA development, where the Magic Johnson theater complex is located, forced a move to its current location in 1999. The club is now much smaller than its previous incarnations, but the close-knit feel for which it was known remains. It has showcased legendary artists such as **Pearl Bailey**, Eartha Kitt, Sarah Vaughan, **Lionel Hampton**, Duke Ellington, and **Grady Tate**, just to name a few. It continues the tradition of booking quality blues and jazz performers, especially some of the best jazz organ musicians.

St. Nick's Jazz Pub

773 St. Nicholas Ave., at 149ᵗʰ St. (212) 283-9728. www.stnicksjazzpub.net. Daily 1pm–4am. Cash only. Bus—M3. Subway—A, B, C, D to 145ᵗʰ St. (front of train)

ST. NICHOLAS PUB

Since the 1940s St. Nick's has been putting it down like no other. It is the oldest continually operating jazz club in Harlem, and it's hardly changed since the 1940s, when it was **Luckey's Rendezvous** owned by Duke Ellington's piano player, **Luckey Roberts**. Not to be missed is the Monday night jam session, presided over by trumpeter **Melvin Vines** and his group, where some of the best players in the tri-state area show up to jam and participate in the "cutting contest." Tuesdays, Vines and his group return. Wednesdays has **Rahn Burton** on keys and **Vicky Kelly's** old-school vocals, and on Thursdays different bands rotate through. Friday night is the standing-room-only event of the week, as **Donald Smith**, brother of organist **Lonnie Liston Smith**, leads the best weekly session you're likely to see. Saturdays is West African music. And Sundays feature the TC III's singers' workshop. The crowd gets really thick here, so arrive early! On any night just remember to put the duckets in the bucket! Since there is no music charge, it is only fair that appreciation for the music be shown when the bucket is passed around.

Dining and Live Entertainment

Cotton Club

666 W. 125th St., at Riverside Dr. (212) 663-7980, (888) 640-7980 toll free. www.cottonclub-newyork.com. Cuisine: Soul Food. Dinner, Brunch. $$. Mon Swing Night 8pm–12am $20, Thu–Sat Blues and Jazz Buffet Dinner 8pm–12am $45, Sat and Sun Gospel Buffet Brunch 12pm and 2:30pm $34. All major credit cards. Bus—M4, M60, M104, BX15. Subway—1 to 125th St.

Do not be confused, this is not the Cotton Club of the Harlem Renaissance that was owned by Mafia mogul **Owney Madden.** The famous site at 142nd Street and Lenox Avenue was razed in the 1960s. This 125th Street supper club opened in the late 1970s and does a brisk business catering to tourists and to Harlemites who book it for special events. It is a legend itself, boasting the best mouthwatering soul food buffet and American fare in town. Today, the Cotton Club has recreated the nostalgia of a swing dancing party on Monday featuring an á la carte menu and the thirteen-piece Cotton Club Allstars band, blues concerts, and supper club entertainment, and an all-you-can-eat Sunday gospel buffet brunch.

Covo Trattoria Pizzeria and Lounge

701 W. 135th St., at Twelfth Ave. (212) 234-9573. www.covony.com. Cuisine: Italian, Pizza. Lunch, Dinner, Brunch. $$$. Daily 10am–12am. All major credit cards. Bus—M4, M60, M100, M101, BX15. Subway—1 to 125th or 137th St.

Located in a giant warehouse space that has been softened and made cozy with candlelight and antique bric-a-brac, Covo Trattoria Pizzeria and Lounge anchors a new commercial complex that was once a meatpacking district. The menu features delicious puffy-crusted brick-oven pizzas, pasta dishes including black ink fettuccine with crab and spaghetti carbonara, and hearty main courses like prime short ribs braised in Barolo wine and grilled, marinated New Zealand rack of lamb. There is a popular prix-fixe brunch held every Saturday and Sunday from 10am to 2pm that for $14.95 includes a choice of orange juice, bellini, or mimosa and coffee, plus a main course selection from a menu of various egg dishes, grilled items, and griddle breads. After enjoying a meal downstairs, diners can retire upstairs to Covo Lounge, which sports an eclectic collection of sofas and chairs, to enjoy a classic cocktail or a simple glass of wine from an extensive list. The lounge features live jazz and half-price drinks and pizza every Thursday from 8:30pm to 11:30pm. The lounge operates a Happy Hour on Wednesday from 5pm to 8pm, when signature cocktails and wine by the glass are priced at $5, domestic and imported beer for $3, and half-price pizza.

Dinosaur Bar-B-Que

777 W. 125th St., at Twelfth Ave. (212) 694-1777. www.dinosaurbarbque.com/nycIndex.php. Cuisine: Barbecue. Lunch, Dinner. $$$. Mon–Thu 11:30am–11pm, Fri and Sat 11:30am–12am, Sun 12pm–10pm. All major credit cards. Bus—M4, M60, BX15. Subway—1 to 125th St.

Dinosaur Bar-B-Que, which was founded as a hangout for Syracuse's biker population, put down stakes in West Harlem in 2004, making it the third outpost for this legendary "honky-tonk" rib joint that is situated along the Twelfth Avenue wasteland, which was once home to a thriving meatpacking industry. In addition to serving up succulent ribs and fixings, Dinosaur Bar-B-Que is a place to hear live blues on Saturday starting at 10:30pm while enjoying an array of signature drinks and an impressive selection of imported and domestic beers. The rustic décor includes outdoor picnic tables for seating, stacks of firewood placed strategically throughout the place, exposed beams with ornamental motorcycles hanging, and "Beef" and "Pork" painted in faded lettering on the brick wall to serve as an appropriate reminder that this space was once a meatpacking factory. As for the food, the pork ribs stand out, along with the pulled pork sandwich. During the day, this is the place to take the kids because the wait staff is infinitely patient.

Havana Central at the West End

2911 Broadway, between 113th and 114th Sts. (212) 662-8830. www.havanacentral. com. Cuisine: Cuban. Lunch, Dinner, Brunch. $$$. Sun and Mon 11am–10pm, Tue– Thu 11am–11pm, Fri and Sat 11am–12am. V, MC, AmEx. Bus—M4, M60, M104. Subway—1 to 116th St.

The legendary West End bar and restaurant was a former beatnik hangout and perennial dive bar that hosted writers **Allen Ginsberg** and **Jack Kerouac** as well as legions of Columbia students. Now it has reopened as a vibrant Cuban restaurant and bar. Havana Central is part of a chain of Manhattan restaurants that serve up Cuban cuisine drawn from family recipes that have been preserved over generations. The best dishes are those that stay close to traditional Cuban cooking—ropa vieja, the classic stew of shredded beef spiced with plenty of pepper and onions, and pernil, tender pieces of roasted pork laden with garlic. Live Latin music abounds on Friday and Saturday from 9pm to 12am, and during Sunday brunch from 1pm to 4pm. This lively eatery features several weekly specials that are easy on the wallet, including the $12.95 prix-fixe lunch from Monday through Saturday that offers a choice of appetizer, entrée, and dessert. During Happy Hour, Monday through Friday from 4pm to 8pm, mojitos are $5, sangria $4, and beer $3. Churros (fried glazed donuts) are $1 on Tuesday, empanadas are $1 on Wednesday, and mojitos are $6 on Thursday.

La Pregunta Arts Cafe

1528 Amsterdam Ave., between 135th and 136th Sts. (347) 591-6387. www.lapregunta. net. Cuisine: Latin American. Lunch, Dinner. $$. Mon–Fri 11am–10pm, Sat 10am–12am, Sun 10am–6pm. All major credit cards. Bus—M100, M101. Subway—1 to 137th St.

The Latin American theme would be hard to miss with sandwiches named for revolutionaries—including the "Castro," "Duarte," and "Che"—and beers from Uruguay, Mexico, Brazil, and Costa Rica at the vibrant La Pregunta Arts Cafe. Located across the street from City College, La Pregunta was opened to provide a venue for creative and intellectual expressions for and by uptown and other working-class and immigrant communities. Truly a neighborhood café, La Pregunta, which means "the question" in Spanish, explores contemporary issues through poetry, music, film, and the visual and performing arts in a relaxed atmosphere with food and drink. Events and performances run Thursday through Saturday nights, and though there's not always a cover charge, admission may cost you up to $10; call ahead for details. Artisan coffees and teas, delicious pastries, fresh sandwiches on specialty bread, and a variety of fresh salads are served. The full bar features their signature guava martini and sugarcane mojito and an á la carte menu of mouthwatering appetizers during the evenings. Beers and drinks are only $5, and all tapas run under $10.

Pisticci

125 La Salle St., between Broadway and Claremont Ave. (212) 932-3500. www.
pisticcinyc.com. Cuisine: Italian. Lunch, Dinner, Brunch. $$$. All major credit cards.
Daily 11am–11pm. Bus—M4, M11, M60, M104, BX15. Subway—1 to 125th St.

At Pisticci, which is easy to miss because it is off the beaten path, you will enjoy good Italian cucina that will leave you well satisfied. Regular diners want to keep this place a secret, but the word is out because there is always a wait for a table on most weekend evenings. The wait is worth it for just the Caprese salad filled with fresh mozzarella di bufala, flown in along with cerignola olives every Wednesday from Naples. Then there is the homemade fettuccine with wild mushrooms and truffle oil that is one of the memorable dishes. The pastas, mozzarellas, and desserts are prepared daily from scratch, which has helped establish a following for the food here. Rotating art installations, the live jazz performances on Sunday from 6:30pm to 9:30pm, frequent wine tastings, and opera nights are features at this restaurant that also provides outdoor seating in the summer. Combine the good cooking with warm service and you have a winner.

Apparel

B. Jay's
540 W. 145th St., between Broadway and Amsterdam Ave. (212) 283-9208. Mon–Sat 10am–9pm, Sun 10am–7:30pm. V, MC. Bus—M4, M5, M100, M101, BX19. Subway—1 to 145th St.

Large selection of sneakers, including Nike, Fila, Puma, Adidas, Converse, Diesel, Vasque, and many more for men, women, and children.

Blue Jeans
3528 Broadway, between 144th and 145th Sts. (212) 690-1880. Mon–Sat 10am–9pm, Sun 10:30am–7:30pm. V, MC. Bus—M4, M5, M100, M101, BX19. Subway—1 to 145th St.

Large selection of jeans, including Buffalo, 7 Jeans, Citizen, Mek Denim, Diesel, True Religion, as well as T-shirts.

Blue Magic
3542 Broadway, at 145th St. (212) 694-4441. Mon–Sat 10am–9pm, Sun 11am–8pm. V, MC, AmEx. Bus—M4, M5, M100, M101, BX19. Subway—1 to 145th St.

Trendy name-brand clothes, sneakers, sportswear, and accessories for men and women.

Harlem 145
3534 Broadway, between 144th and 145th Sts. (212) 491-7446. Mon–Thu 10am–9pm, Fri and Sat 10am–9:30pm, Sun10:30–7:30pm. V, MC. Bus—M4, M5, M100, M101, BX19. Subway—1 to 145th St.

Brand-name clothes and sneakers for men and women.

Jay's Sportswear
3542 Broadway, at 145th St. (212) 281-1807. Mon–Sat 10am–9pm, Sun 11am–7:30pm. All major credit cards. Bus—M4, M5, M100, M101, BX19. Subway—1 to 145th St.

Brand-name clothes, sneakers, sportswear, and accessories for men and women.

Liberty House III
2878A Broadway, at 112th St. (212) 932-1950. www.libertyhousenyc.com. Daily 10am–6:45pm. All major credit cards. Bus—M4, M60, M104. Subway—1 to 110th St.

Boutique with eclectic clothing, jewelry, accessories, and gifts. A nice selection of well-made one-of-a-kind children's clothing.

V.I.M.
508 W. 145th St., between Broadway and Amsterdam Ave. (212) 491-1143. www.vim.com. Mon–Sat 9:30am–7pm, Sun 11am–6pm. V, MC, Dis. Bus—M4, M5, M100, M101, BX19. Subway—1 to 145th St.

Large selection of brand-name sneakers and jeans for men, women, and children.

Books

Bank St. Bookstore

610 W. 112th St., at Broadway. (212) 678-1654. www.bankstreetbooks.com. Mon–Thu 11am–7pm, Fri and Sat 10am–6pm, Sun 12pm–6pm. V, MC, AmEx. Bus—M4, M60, M104. Subway—1 to 110th St.

Owned and operated by Bank Street College of Education, Bank Street Bookstore offers an extensive array of books for children, parents, and teachers. Referrals are available by grade level at the helpful Web site, or visit in person to query the knowledgeable staff. Events include storytelling and music for children ages five to ten, and the store has a large selection of games, books, and toys.

Discount Stores

El Mundo

3300 Broadway, between 133rd and 134th Sts. (212) 234-6387. Mon–Sat 9:30am–7:30pm, Sun 10am–6pm. All major credit cards. Bus—M4, M5, M11, M100, M101. Subway—1 to 137th St.

Hamilton Palace/El Mundo

3560 Broadway, between 145th and 146th Sts. (212) 862-6032. Mon–Sat 10am–7:30pm, Sun 10am–6:30pm. All major credit cards. Bus—M4, M5, M100, M101, BX19. Subway—1 to 145th St.

El Mundo has band-name clothes for men, women, and children, housewares, and much more at deeply discounted prices. If you have patience, you can find some really good deals here!

Food

Fairway

2328 Twelfth Ave., at 130th St. (212) 234-3883. www.fairwaymarket.com. Daily 8am–11pm. All major credit cards. Bus—M4, M100, M101, BX15. Subway 1 to 125th St.

A specialty gourmet market that stocks just about everything, from produce delivered fresh from the farm every day to items from the full-service butchers to gourmet organic coffees, and much more.

Westside Market

2840 Broadway, at 110th St. (212) 222-3367. www.wmarketnyc.com. 24 Hours. All major credit cards. Bus—M4, M60, M104. Subway—1 to 110th St.

A gourmet market that features affordable fresh produce, and a wide assortment of prepared foods, cheeses, breads, meat, poultry, and seafood.

Sneakers/Shoes

Aerosoles

2913A Broadway, between 113th and 114th Sts. (212) 665-5353. www.aerosoles.com. Mon–Sat 9:30am–8pm, Sun 11am–6pm. All major credit cards. Bus—M4, M60, M104. Subway—1 to 116th St.

(See Central Harlem description.)

Foot Locker
3549 Broadway, at 145ᵗʰ St. (212) 491-0927. www.footlocker.com. Mon–Sat 10am–8pm, Sun 11am–
7:30pm. All major credit cards. Bus—M4, M5, M100, M101, BX19. Subway—1 to 145ᵗʰ St.

Brand-name men's, women's, and children's athletic footwear, men's athletic apparel, and accessories.

Payless
3554 Broadway, between 145ᵗʰ and 146ᵗʰ Sts. (212) 368-8717. www.payless.com. Mon–Fri 9:30am–8pm,
Sat 9am–8pm, Sun 10am–7pm. All major credit cards. Bus—M4, M5, M100, M101, BX19. Subway—1 to
145ᵗʰ St.

(See Central Harlem description.)

Toys

Madame Alexander Doll Company
615 W. 131ˢᵗ St., between Riverside Dr. and Broadway. (212) 283-5900. www.madamealexander.com.
Daily 9am–5pm. All major credit cards. Bus—M4, M5. Subway—1 to 137ᵗʰ St.

Designer and manufacturer of Alexander Dolls and fine quality collectible dolls, baby dolls, and
play dolls.

Wine/Liquor

Brand's Wines and Liquors
550 W. 145ᵗʰ St., between Broadway and Amsterdam Ave. (212) 234-1460. Mon–Sat 10am–12am, Sun
12pm–9pm. All major credit cards. Bus—M4, M5, M100, M101, BX19. Subway—1 to 145ᵗʰ St.

Nice selection of wines and liquors at affordable prices.

International Wines & Spirits
2903 Broadway, between 113ᵗʰ and 114ᵗʰ Sts. (212) 280-1850. www.internationalwinesandspirits.com.
Mon–Sat 10am–10pm, Sun 12pm–7pm. All major credit cards. Bus—M4, M60, M104. Subway—1 to
116ᵗʰ St.

Nice selection of wines, beer, and liquors.

Wine and Liquor Authority
574 W. 125ᵗʰ St., between Broadway and Amsterdam Ave. (212) 663-9015. Mon–Thu 9am–11pm, Fri
and Sat 9am–12am, Sun 12pm–9pm. All major credit cards. Bus—M4, M60, M100, M101, M104, BX19.
Subway—1 to 125ᵗʰ St.

Newly opened discount wine and liquor shop. Lots of space and a good selection of wines and spirits.

SIGNIFICANT FAITH-BASED INSTITUTIONS
AND BURIAL GROUNDS

The Church of The Intercession

550 W. 155th St., at Broadway. (212) 283-6200. www.intercessionnyc.dioceseny.org.
Bus—M4, M5, M100, M101, BX9. Subway—1 to 157th St.

The Church of the Intercession was established in 1847, four years after **Old Trinity Church** in lower Manhattan purchased a 24-acre tract for use as a cemetery in **Carmansville** (the name of a village that lined the Hudson River from 140th St. to 158th St., which is now West Harlem). The current building, which was the third one built, was supported by Trinity Church, which agreed to make Intercession its cemetery chapel after the IRT subway brought an influx of residents that the previous building could not accommodate. Designed by **Bertram Goodhue**, of **Cram, Goodhue & Ferguson**, the structure was designed as a large English Gothic complex consisting of the cathedral-like church and tower, a full cloister, vicarage, vestry, and parish house. It was built between 1911–1914 and named the Chapel of the Intercession. The nave, which features an altarpiece that is embedded with hundreds of stones from holy places throughout the world that were collected by the church's first rector, **Dr. Milo Hudson Gates**, is a work of unsurpassed beauty and not to be missed. In 1976, the chapel became the Church of the Intercession after once again receiving its independence from Trinity Church. In 1966 the church was designated a landmark.

Trinity Church Cemetery and Mausoleum

770 Riverside Drive, at 155th St. (212) 368-1600. www.trinitywallstreet.org/
congregation/cemetery. Bus—M4, M5, M100, M101, BX9. Subway—1 to 157th St.

The Trinity Church Cemetery and Mausoleum, overlooking the Hudson River from upper Riverside Drive, is the only remaining active cemetery in Manhattan and is where the affluent residents of Manhattan's past are buried. Such names as Astor, Schermerhorn, **Eliza Jumel** (who owned the oldest standing mansion in Manhattan), naturalist **John James Audubon**, and writer **Clement Clarke Moore** are inscribed on the headstones and mausoleum entrances. The cemetery has a west and east division, and in 1871 a bridge was built to connect them after Broadway was cut through it. The architects were **Vaux, Withers and Co.** and the engineer was **George C. Radford**. The bridge was torn down in 1913 during the construction of the Church of the Intercession. In 1969 the cemetery was designated a historic landmark.

Church of the Annunciation

88 Convent Av., at 131st St. (212) 234-1919. Bus—M11, M100, M101. Subway—A, B, C, D to 125th St.

The Church of the Annunciation was the first Catholic church that was built in Manhattan's West Side above Second Street. The church was founded in 1854 by the **Christian Brothers** to primarily minister to the Irish Catholic laborers on the Hudson River Railroad. The first building was erected next to Manhattan College (formerly the Academy of Convent of the Sacred Heart) at 131st Street and the Bloomingdale Road (Old Broadway). The brothers subsequently sold the adjoining church and rectory sites to **John Hughes**, the first Catholic Archbishop of New York. The present stone building, built in 1906–07 by the architectural firm of **Lynch & Orchard**, is the church's second structure, to which the congregation moved from two blocks east in 1907.

Convent Avenue Baptist Church
420 W. 145th St., at Convent Ave. (212) 234-6767. www.conventchurch.org. Bus—M3, M100, M101, BX19. Subway—A, B, C, D, to 145th St.

CONVENT AVENUE BAPTIST CHURCH

In 1942 the "Kingdom Builders" proudly walked into the former **Washington Heights Baptist Church**, a neo-Gothic building faced in blocks of Georgia marble that was designed by **Lamb & Rich** 1897–99, and named it Convent Avenue Baptist Church. Under the leadership of **Dr. John W. Saunders** the church continued to flourish and purchased three additional townhouses around the church. **Rev. Mannie L. Wilson** led the congregation after Dr. Saunders' passing and continued to be a leading force within the Harlem community, as well as established missions in Liberia, Nigeria, and Guyana, where a chapel is named in his honor. Rev. Wilson was also the first African American Protestant to preach in St. Patrick's Cathedral and the White House. Under Rev. Wilson the church continued to purchase buildings, including 425 W. 144th Street, a large six-story structure that now serves as the John W. Saunders Education Building and is connected to the church by a walkway. Both the Hamilton Grange Senior Citizens Center and the Boys and Girls Club of Harlem are housed in the building. The church is developing a center for the club as well as affordable housing in a nearby vacant school on 145th Street that it purchased in 1980 under the leadership of the late **Rev. Clarence P. Grant**. Convent is home to the world-renowned Harlem Opera Theater and provides administrative space to the Baptist Ministers Conference of Greater New York and Vicinity that meets there weekly. Each year in January, they hold their prestigious Martin Luther King, Jr., services.

Old Broadway Synagogue
15 Old Broadway, between 125th and 126th Sts. (212) 662-9767. Bus—M4, M11, M60, M100, M101, M104, BX15. Subway—1 to 125th St.

The Old Broadway Synagogue is the only synagogue operating in Harlem. Tucked away on Old Broadway, this Orthodox Jewish synagogue was incorporated in 1911 under the name of **Chevra Talmud Torah Anshei Ma'aravi** (Torah Study Society, People of the West Side of Harlem) by a Polish immigrant named **Morris Schiff**. The synagogue was built in 1923 by the architectural firm of **Meisner & Uffner** and is listed on the National Register of Historic Places. It was mostly used by the Ashkenazic Jewish population of Russian and Polish immigrants who began living in Harlem during the 1880s. Prior to the purchase of the building, the congregation would meet in storefronts and the back room of a nearby bar until it purchased a house on Old Broadway, which eventually was demolished to make room for the current structure. The congregation had an active Talmud Torah (Hebrew school) probably from its founding until the 1960s or 1970s. The most well-known rabbi, **Jacob Kret** (1909–2007), was

OLD BROADWAY SYNAGOGUE

a Holocaust survivor and became the spiritual leader of the synagogue in 1950. With most of the founding families gone, he recruited other Holocaust survivors who had immigrated to New York. Over time Rabbi Kret became the *mashgiach* (kosher food supervisor) in the nearby Barnard College dining hall as well as a *Talmud* tutor at the Jewish Theological Seminary. He had a deep influence on many Columbia University, Barnard College, and Jewish Theological Seminary students until he retired from the synagogue in 1997. Since 2000, the synagogue has attracted young people who live in Harlem and Washington Heights, as well as those from Morningside Heights and the Upper West Side. Old Broadway offers a weekly class on *Pirkei Avot* (Ethics of the Fathers), a section of the Talmud containing ethical maxims.

Riverside Church

490 Riverside Drive, at 120th St. (212) 870-6700. Gift Shop (212) 870-6972. www.theriversidechurchny.org. Daily 7am–10pm. Bus—M4, M5, M60, M104. Subway—1 to 116th St.

Riverside began as a small Baptist church on the Lower East Side and moved several times before building at its current location. Built largely with funds from **John D. Rockefeller, Jr.**, it is modeled after the thirteenth-century Gothic cathedral in Chartres, France. Construction on the Riverside Church began in 1927 with some of the finest stone, stained glass, carving, and woodwork of its time. The first service was held in 1930. Today, the church has 2,400 members and affiliates representing forty different denominational, national, ethnic, and cultural backgrounds. Riverside, designated a landmark in 2000, is the tallest church in the United States, standing 392 feet high. One of only three churches in New York that have carillons, which were donated by Rockefeller, it contains the largest collection (seventy-four) ranging from ten pounds to twenty tons.

Tours—After Sunday morning Service of Worship, there is a free tour of the church. Beginning at 12:15pm, the tour lasts about one hour. No advance reservations are necessary for individuals or groups.

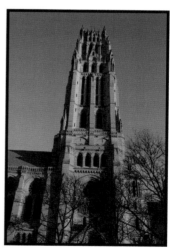

RIVERSIDE CHURCH

St. Mary's Episcopal Church

521 W. 126th St., at Old Broadway. (212) 864-4013. www.stmarysharlem.org. Bus—M4, M11, M60, M100, M101, M104, BX15. Subway—1 to 125th St.

St. Mary's Episcopal Church, located in Manhattanville, is the oldest congregation in continuous service on its original site in Harlem. Originally founded in 1823, its present stone building was erected in 1909 by **T. E. Blake** in association with the architectural firm of **Carrere & Hastings**. This modest neo-Gothic structure features herringbone brickwork trimmed with concrete. The gabled-roof porch contains a bell that was presented to St. Mary's by Jacob Schiefflein, Manhattanville founder and the church's land donor. Historically known as a champion for the poor, in 1831, St. Mary's was the first church in the Episcopal Diocese to abolish pew rentals. Clearly visible to passersby is the marble seal, inlaid into the church's porch, and burial vault in which Schieffelin and his wife, Hannah, are interred. In 1998, the church, its adjacent frame parish house (circa 1851), garden, and brick school building (1890) were officially designated a New York City landmark. The church continues its social activism, is a leader in the environmental justice movement in Harlem, and operates several outreach programs that assist working-class and low-income residents.

The Cathedral Church of Saint John the Divine

1047 Amsterdam Ave., at 112th St. (212) 316-7490. Tours: (212) 932-7347. Cathedral Hours: Mon–Sat 7am–6pm, Sun 7am–7pm, July and August the Cathedral closes at 6pm on Sunday. Grounds and Gardens: Open during daylight hours. www.stjohndivine.org. Bus—M4, M11, M60, M104. Subway—1 to 110th St.

THE CATHEDRAL CHURCH OF SAINT JOHN THE DIVINE AND PEACE FOUNTAIN

The Cathedral Church of St. John the Divine is the mother church of the Episcopal Diocese of New York and is the largest Gothic church in the world. The cathedral is almost two football fields in length, 601 feet, and has 121,000 square feet of area space. The construction of the cathedral began in 1887, but due to the financial panic, wars, and money problems it was not completed—it is still a work in progress. Now in its fourth phase of construction, which began in 1998, over a century after its cornerstone was first laid in 1892, the original Romanesque-Byzantine design by **Heins & La Farge** was replaced by a Gothic design of architect **Ralph Adams Cram**, who was hired to complete the building after Heins' passing. The founders of the cathedral insisted it be built as a "house of worship for all nations" and that ideology comes to life in the church's slogan, "A House of Prayer for All People," as well as in its diverse congregation and traditions. Stop off in the garden to see the Peace Fountain, a sculpture and fountain which depicts the struggle of good and evil, as well as a battle between Archangel Michael and Satan.

Public Tours

Individuals and groups of fewer than ten people can tour from Tuesday through Saturday between 11am and 11pm and Sunday at 2pm. Call the tour number above to find out about public tours that are offered.

CHURCHES WITH GOSPEL SERVICES

Antioch Baptist Church
515 W. 125th St., between Broadway and Amsterdam Ave. Sunday, 11am. Bus—M11, M60, M100, M101, M104, BX15. Subway—1 to 125th St.

Child's Memorial Temple Church of God in Christ
1763 Amsterdam Ave., between 147th and 148th Sts. Sunday, 11am. Bus—M4, M5, M100, M101, BX19. Subway—1 to 145th St.

Convent Avenue Baptist Church
420 W. 145th St., at Convent Ave. Every first Sunday of the month, 11am. Bus—M3, M100, M101, BX19. Subway—A, B, C, D to 145th St.

St. John's Baptist Church
448 W. 152nd St., between Amsterdam and Convent Aves. Winter, Spring, and Fall: Sunday 11am. Summer: Sunday 10:30am. Bus—M3, M100, M101. Subway—1 to 157th St.

Morningside Park

Bus—M3, M4, M7, M11, M116. Subway—B, C to 110th St.

Morningside Park is located between 110th and 123rd Streets and Morningside Drive and Manhattan Avenue, and is 30 acres in size. The park takes its name from its eastern side—where the sun rises in the morning. The city commissioned **Frederick Law Olmsted** and **Calvert Vaux** (co-designers of Central and Prospect Parks) to produce a design for the park in 1870, but construction did not begin until 1883 after their original design was revised. The Morningside Ave. side of the park is tucked underneath a massive buttressed masonry retaining wall with a parapet. A series of esplanades, with 30-foot-wide walkways linked by steps, lead down to the Manhattan Ave. side of the park. The park is home to the following statues: *Lafayette and Washington* by **Frederic-Auguste Bartholdi** (1900), the *Carl Schurz Memorial* by **Karl Bitter** and **Henry Bacon** (1913), and the *Seligman (Bear and Faun) Fountain* by **Edgar Walter** (1914). The park also contains an arboretum and an ornamental pond and waterfall. On July 15, 2008, the park was designated a New York Scenic Landmark, the city's first since 1983. On Saturdays, from the end of May to mid-December, a Farmers Market is open at the plaza entrance to the park at 110th Street and Manhattan Ave. from 9am to 5pm, rain or shine.

Facilities: Baseball diamond, dog run, playgrounds, basketball courts, handball courts, volleyball court, and a small recreation center.

Riverside Park

W. 72nd Street to St. Clair Place (125th St.) and 135th to 158th Streets and Riverside Drive to Hudson River. Bus—M4, M5, M11, M60. Subway—1 to 110th, 116th, 145th Sts.

In the early 1870s, the original Riverside Park could be found between W. 72nd Street and 125th Street, and was designed by Frederick Law Olmsted. Then, it stretched more than two miles; today, it stretches four miles, ending at 158th Street. While it retains much of what Olmstead designed, the park also made use of several other landscape architects' designs, including Calvert Vaux and Samuel Parsons. Riverside Park is Manhattan's most spectacular waterfront park and was designated a scenic landmark in 1980. The park has a long and storied history, and continues today as one of New York City's best unknown parks to tourists. Today, the park consists of 267 acres and has sweeping views of New Jersey and the George Washington Bridge. In the park you can find countless outdoor cultural and musical events. A visit to the park when the sun is setting is truly an experience that one will not forget.

In the portion of the park in Harlem on Riverside Drive, you will find four monuments. The larger-than-life bronze statue of statesman **Samuel Tilden** (1814–1886), who was elected New York State Governor in 1874, and whose bequest of an extensive collection of books and $6 million led to the formation of the New York Public Library, is located at 112th Street. The statue was created by **William Ordway Partridge** and dedicated October 4, 1926. Grant's Tomb is the largest mausoleum in the world and contains the remains of Ulysses S. Grant (1822–1885), the 18th U.S. President and Civil War General. The granite and marble structure, which was designed by architect **John Duncan**, was completed in 1897 and is located at 122nd Street. The **Amiable Child Monument** is a grave marker for a five-year-old child who died in 1797 and consists of a small, simple urn on a pedestal surrounded by an iron fence. It is located at 123rd Street. The **Ralph Ellison Memorial**, or **Invisible Man**, by celebrated African American artist **Elizabeth Catlett**, is located at 150th Street. The 15-foot-high and 7.5-foot-wide bronze cutout silhouette of a man that was unveiled on May 1, 2003, was inspired by the landmark 1952 novel *Invisible Man* by African American author and scholar Ralph Ellison (1914–1994).

Facilities: Baseball fields, soccer fields, volleyball courts, playgrounds, dog runs, basketball courts, kayak, canoe and sailboat launch sites, 110-slip marina, handball courts, tennis courts, running tracks, skate parks, fishing, a large portion of the Manhattan Waterfront Greenway (for bicycles), and seasonal cafes.

Riverbank State Park
Bus—M4, M5, M11, BX19. Subway—1 to 145th Street

Riverbank State Park, located from 137th Street to 145th Street, is 28 acres in size, and is the only park of its kind in the Western Hemisphere. Its design was inspired by urban rooftop designs in Japan. The park, which is built on the top of the **North River Wastewater Treatment Plant**, is 69 feet above the Hudson River and is the only state park in Manhattan. Riverbank was designed by **Dattner Architects** and **Abel Bainnson Butz Landscape Architects**, and opened in 1993.

Riverbank boasts acres of green roofs and is the largest "green" roof in NYC today. The location of the park offers breathtaking views of New York's skyline, the Hudson River, New Jersey, the Palisade Mountains, and the George Washington Bridge.

Facilities: Totally Kid Carousel, a covered skating rink for roller skating in the summer and ice skating in the winter, cultural theater, athletic complex with fitness room, restaurant (River Park Café), amphitheater, docking facilities for excursion and fishing boats, Olympic-sized pool, wading pool, tennis courts, basketball courts, softball field, hand/paddleball courts, running track with a football/soccer field, playgrounds, and picnic areas.

St. Nicholas Park

Bus—M3, M10. Subway—B, C, to 135th St.

St. Nicholas Park is located between 128th and 141st Streets and St. Nicholas Avenue and St. Nicholas Terrace, and is 23 acres in size. Some of the land for the park was acquired in 1835. Additional property was assembled between 1900 and 1909 that included the area at 128th Street known as **"The Point of Rocks,"** where General George Washington had positioned himself during the Battle of Harlem Heights in 1776. The name of the park is taken from adjacent streets St. Nicholas Terrace to the west and St. Nicholas Avenue to the east. These streets honor New Amsterdam patron saint **St. Nicholas of Myra**, whose likeness adorned the masthead of the *New Netherland* ship that brought the first

Dutch settlers to New Amsterdam, and who is the inspiration for Father Christmas or Santa Claus. Landscape architect and Parks Commissioner Samuel Parsons designed the park himself. The park was built on a rugged mass of Manhattan schist following the steep and irregular topography of northern Manhattan. The imposing and Gothic-inspired City College of New York campus overlooks the park. Hamilton Grange, the summer home of our first Secretary of the Treasury and one of the nation's Founding Fathers, Alexander Hamilton, was moved from nearby Convent Avenue into the park in 2008.

Facilities: Basketball courts, dog runs, playgrounds, barbecue area, and handball courts.

West Harlem Piers Park

Bus—BX15. Subway—1 to 125th St.

West Harlem Piers Park, a two–acre waterfront oasis that connects West Harlem to the Hudson River, officially opened May 30, 2009. Located from St. Clair Place to 132nd Street between Marginal Way and the Hudson River, this new park supports various activities, including fishing, water tours, boating, and ecological exploration. The piers can also accommodate a variety of vessels, allowing excursion boats and water taxis to dock in West Harlem. The bicycle and pedestrian paths provide a critical link in the waterfront greenway, creating a continuous path from the Battery to Dyckman Street.

Public art displayed in the park by local artist **Nari Ward** include a series of sculptures titled *Voice,* which were inspired by the local residents who frequently fish at this site. The sculptures are accompanied by **Signage Barriers**, a series of street-sign-inspired text.

Facilities: Bicycle path, fishing, public art.

GARAGES

126th Street Parking Corp.
418 W. 126th St., between Amsterdam and Morningside Aves. 24 Hrs/Outdoor/Valet/Credit and Cash.

Central Parking System
250–256 Bradhurst Ave., between 154th and 155th Sts. 24 Hrs/Indoor/Valet/Cash-Only.

GMC
532–538 W. 122nd St., between Broadway and Amsterdam Ave. 24 Hrs/Indoor/Valet/Credit and Cash.

GMC West 129th Street Garage
605–611 W. 129th St., between Broadway and 125th St. 24 Hrs/Outdoor/Valet/Credit and Cash.

Laz L Park 2
457 W. 150th St., at Convent Ave. 24 Hrs/Indoor/Valet/Credit and Cash.

Manhattan Parking
543 W. 110th St., between Broadway and Amsterdam Ave. 24 Hrs/Indoor/Self/Credit and Cash.

Morningside Heights Housing Corp.
102 La Salle St., between Broadway and Amsterdam Ave. 24 Hrs/Indoor/Valet/Cash-Only.

MPG Uptown 2, LLC
3333 Broadway, at 134th St. 24 Hrs/Indoor/Self-Park/Credit and Cash.

MTP 129th St. Parking
627 W. 129th St., between Riverside Drive and Broadway. 24 Hrs/Outdoor/Valet/Cash-Only.

Propark
502 W. 114th St., between Broadway and Amsterdam Ave. 24 Hrs/Indoor/Valet/Cash-Only.

Rapid Park
621 W. 120th St., between Riverside Dr. and Claremont Ave. 7am–12am/Indoor/Valet/Credit and Cash.

Stable Car Parking
614 W. 153rd St., between Riverside Drive and Broadway. 24 Hrs/Indoor/Valet/Cash-Only.

The Lionsgate
512 W. 112th St., between Broadway and Amsterdam Ave. 6am–1am, Sun 7am–1am/Indoor/Valet/Credit and Cash.

Uni. Facility Corp.
631–635 W. 131st St., between Riverside Dr. and Broadway. 6am–12am/Outdoor/Valet/Cash-Only.

Uptown Parking
475 W. 145th St., between Amsterdam and Convent Aves. 8am–6pm/Indoor/Valet/Cash-Only.

Y & H Garages
526 W. 134th St., between Broadway and Amsterdam Ave. 24 Hrs/Indoor/Valet/Cash-Only.

SERVICE STATIONS

Mobil Service Stations
800 St. Nicholas Ave., between 151st and 152nd Sts.

3260 Broadway, at 131th St.

LIBRARIES/INTERNET/WI-FI

Libraries with Free Internet

George Bruce Branch
518 W. 125th St., at Amsterdam Ave. (212) 662-9727. Mon and Wed 11am–7pm, Tue 10am–6pm, Thu 10am–7pm, Fri 12pm–5pm, Sat 10am–5pm.

Hamilton Grange Branch
503 W. 145th St., between Broadway and Amsterdam Ave. (212) 926-2147. Mon and Wed 11am–7pm, Tue and Thu 10am–6pm, Fri 12pm–5pm, Sat 10am–5pm.

Morningside Heights Branch
2900 Broadway, at 113th St. (212) 864-2530. Mon–Thu 10am–7pm, Fri and Sat 10am–5pm.

Wi-Fi

Starbucks
(Free Wi-Fi available for existing T-Mobile subscribers, AT&T DSL subscribers and AT&T mobile devices that are Wi-Fi enabled. You also can purchase two consecutive hours of Wi-Fi access for $3.99.)

2929 Broadway, at 114th St. Daily 6am–12am.

2853 Broadway, at 111th St. Mon–Thu 6am–11pm, Fri and Sat 6am–11pm, Sun 7am–10pm.

Internet Café

Dollar Internet Café
1687 Amsterdam Ave., at 143rd St. (718) 213-4677. Bus—M4, M5, M100, M101. Subway—A, B, C, D, 1 to 145th St.

POSTAL SERVICES

FedEx Authorized Ship Centers
Tiemann Mail Center. 52 Tiemann Pl. between Broadway and Claremont Ave. (212) 222-3573. Mon–Fri 7am–7pm, Sun 9am–4pm.

600 W. 116th St. between Broadway and Claremont Ave. (212) 749-3515. Mon–Fri 8:30am–9pm.

Copy Experts. 3062 Broadway, between 121st and 122nd Sts. (212) 864-6501. Mon–Fri 8am–9pm, Sat 10am–3pm.

U.S. Postal Service/Columbia University Post Office
534 W. 112th St., between Broadway and Amsterdam Ave. (212) 864-7813. Mon–Fri 9am–5pm, Sat 9am–4pm.

U.S. Postal Service/Hamilton Heights Station
521 W. 146th St., between Broadway and Amsterdam Ave. (212) 281-1338. Mon–Fri 8am–5pm, Sat 8am–4pm.

UPS Store #1786
603 W. 115th St., at Broadway. (212) 865-9601. Mon–Fri 8am–8pm, Sat 9am–5pm.

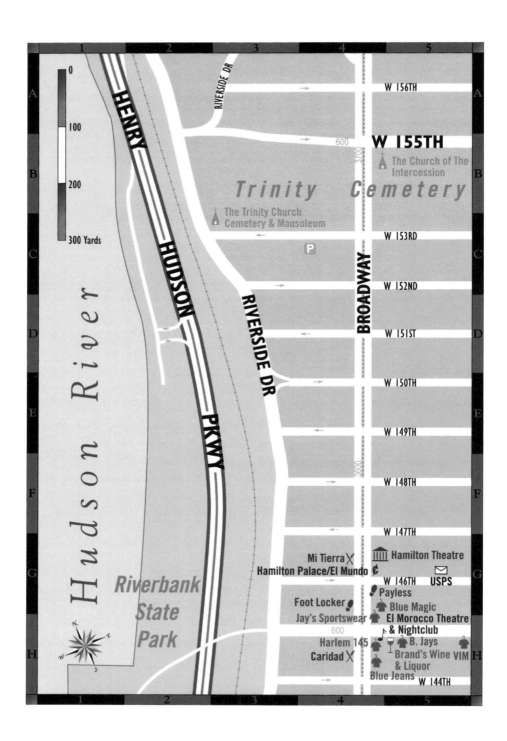

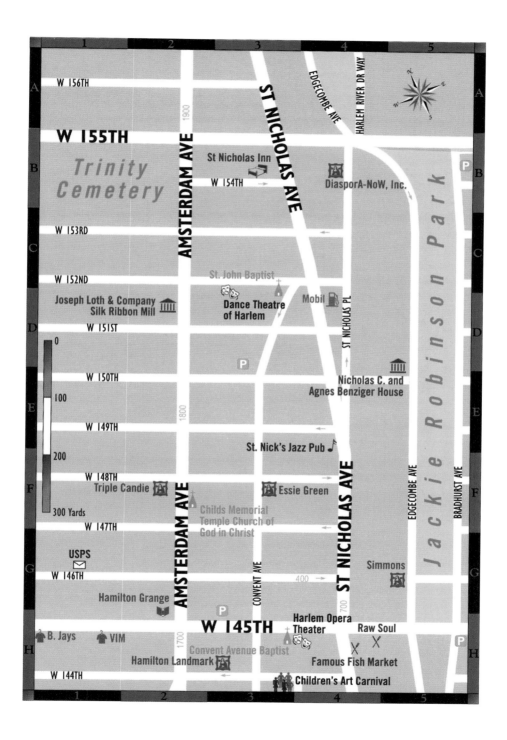

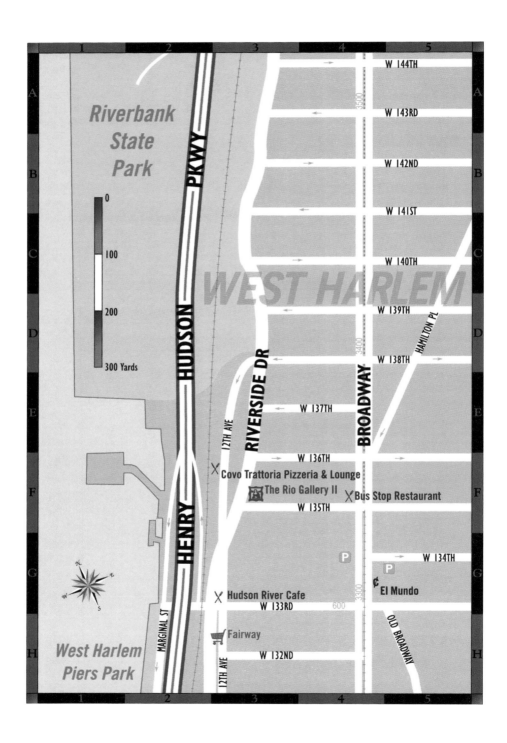

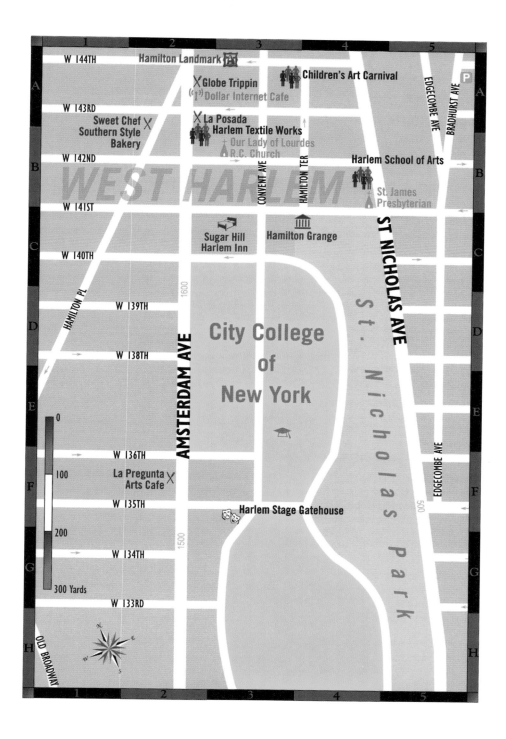

West Harlem Map A1

B. Jays, H5
Blue Jeans, H4
Blue Magic, G4
Brand's Wine & Liquor, H5
Caridad, H4
El Morocco Theatre & Nightclub, H4
Foot Locker, G4
Hamilton Palace/El Mundo, G4
Hamilton Theatre, G4
Harlem 145, H4
Jay's Sportswear, H4
Mi Tierra, G4
Payless, G4
Riverbank State Park, G2
The Church of The Intercession, B4
The Trinity Church Cemetery & Mausoleum, C3
Trinity Cemetery, B3
USPS, G5
VIM, H5

West Harlem Map A2

B. Jays, H1
Children's Art Carnival, H3
Childs Memorial Temple Church of God in Christ, F2
Convent Avenue Baptist, H3
Dance Theatre of Harlem, D3
DiasporA-NoW, B4
Essie Green, F3
Famous Fish Market, H4
Hamilton Grange Branch NYPL, G2
Hamilton Landmark, H3
Harlem Opera Theater, H4
Jackie Robinson Park, F5
Joseph Loth & Company Silk Ribbon Mill, D2
Mobil, D4

Nicholas C. and Agnes Benziger House, D5
Raw Soul, H4
Simmons, G5
St. John Baptist, C3
St Nicholas Inn, B3
St. Nick's Jazz Pub, E4
Trinity Cemetery, B1
Triple Candie, F2
USPS, G1
VIM, H1

West Harlem Map A3

Bus Stop Restaurant, F4
Covo Trattoria Pizzeria & Lounge, F3
El Mundo, G4
Fairway, H3
Riverbank State Park, B2
The Rio Gallery II, F3
West Harlem Piers Park, H1

West Harlem Map A4

Children's Art Carnival, A3
City College of New York, E3
Dollar Internet Cafe, A2
Globe Trippin, A2
Hamilton Grange, C4
Hamilton Landmark, A3
Harlem School of Arts, B4
Harlem Stage Gatehouse, F3
Harlem Textile Works, B2
La Posada, A2
La Pregunta Arts Cafe, F2
Our Lady of Lourdes R.C. Church, B3
St. James Presbyterian, B4
St. Nicholas Park, F4
Sugar Hill Harlem Inn, C3
Sweet Chef Southern Style Bakery, A2

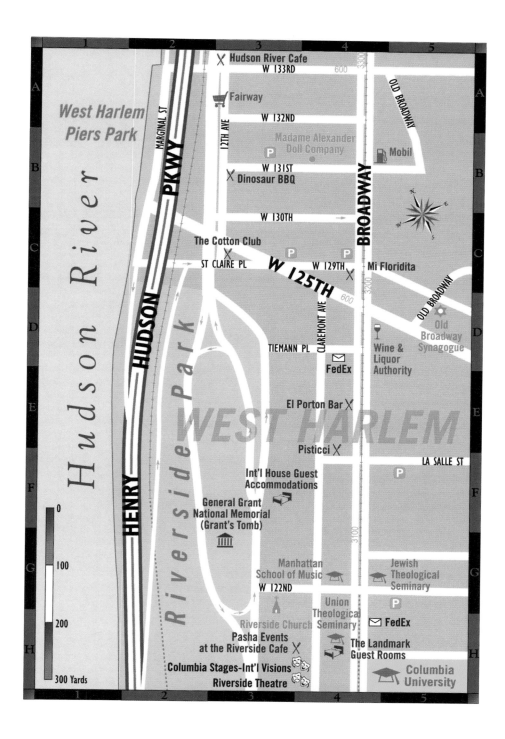

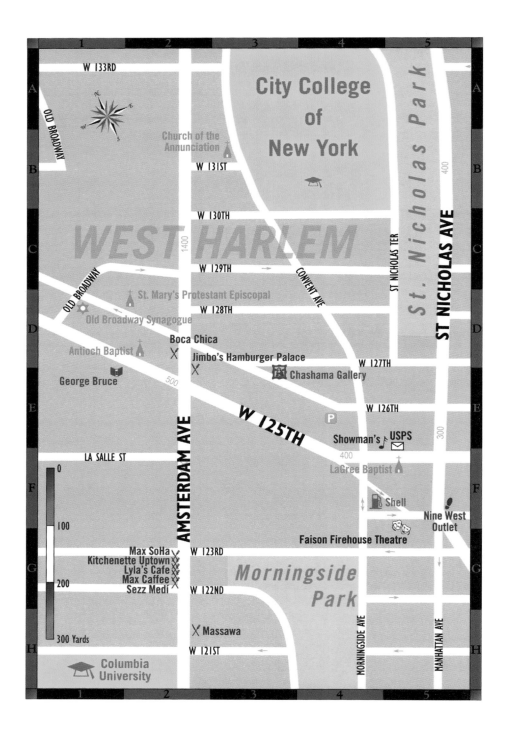

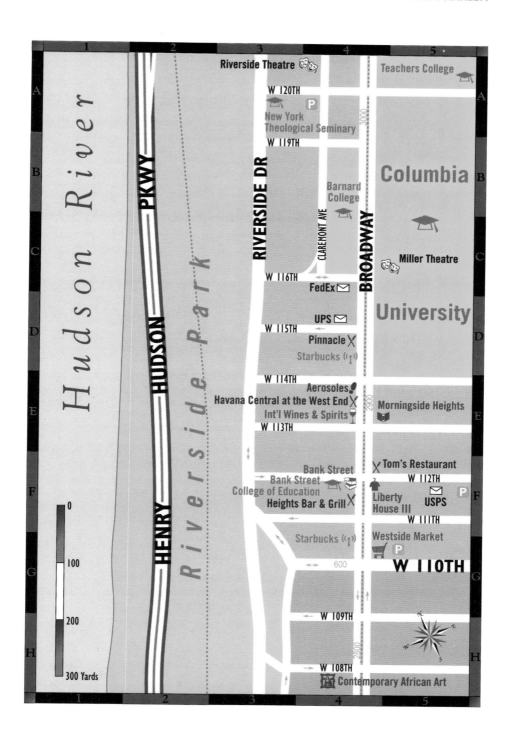

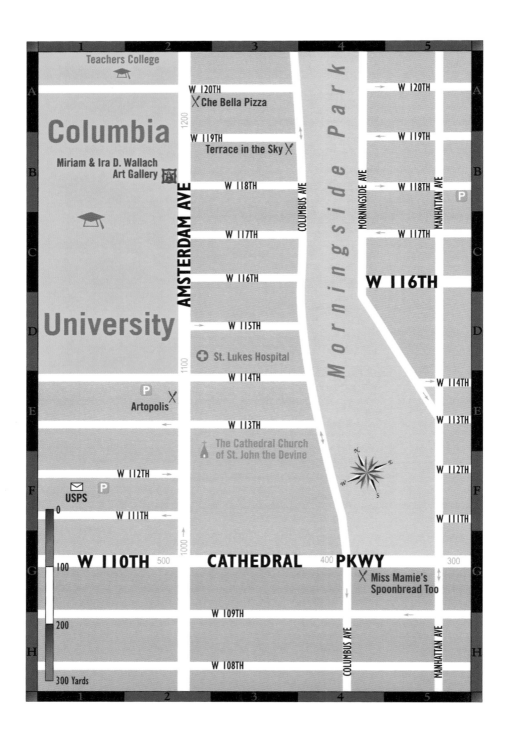

West Harlem Map B1

Columbia Stages-Int'l Visions, H4
Columbia University, B3
El Porton Bar, E4
Fairway, D4
FedEx, H4
General Grant National Memorial
 (Grant's Tomb), F3
Int'l House Guest Accommodations, F3
Jewish Theological Seminary, G4
Madame Alexander Doll Company, B4
Manhattan School of Music, G4
Mi Floridita, C4
Mobil, B4
Old Broadway Synagogue, D5
Pasha Events at the Riverside Cafe, H4
Pisticci, E4
Riverside Church, H3
Riverside Park, G2
Riverside Theatre, H4
The Cotton Club, C3
The Landmark Guest Rooms, H4
Union Theological Seminary, H4
West Harlem Piers Park, A1
Wine & Liquor Authority, D4

West Harlem Map B2

Antioch Baptist, D2
Boca Chica, D2
Chashama Gallery, E3
Church of the Annunciation, B3
City College of New York, B4
Columbia University,   H1
Faison Firehouse Theatre, F5
George Bruce Branch NYPL, E1
Jimbo's Hamburger Palace, D2
Kitchenette Uptown, G2
LaGree Baptist, F5
Lyla's Cafe, G2
Massawa, H2
Max Caffee, G2
Max SoHa, G2
Morningside Park, G4
Nine West Outlet, F5
Old Broadway Synagogue, D1
Sezz Medi, G2

Shell, F5
Showman's, E4
St. Mary's Protestant Episcopal, D2
St. Nicholas Park, C5
USPS, E5

West Harlem Map B3

Aerosoles, E4
Bank Street Bookstore, F4
Bank Street College of Education, F4
Barnard College, B4
Columbia University, B5
Contemporary African Art, H4
FedEx, C4
Havana Central at the West End, E4
Heights Bar & Grill, F4
Int'l Wines & Spirits, E4
Liberty House III, F4
Miller Theatre, C5
Morningside Heights Branch NYPL, E4
New York Theological Seminary, A3
Pinnacle, D4
Riverside Park, F2
Riverside Theatre, A3
Starbucks, D4
Starbucks, G4
Teachers College, A5
Tom's Restaurant, F4
UPS, D4
USPS, F5
Westside Market, G4

West Harlem Map B4

Artopolis, E2
Che Bella Pizza, A2
Columbia University, C1
Miriam & Ira D. Wallach Art Gallery, B2
Miss Mamie's Spoonbread Too, G4
Morningside Park, C4
St. Lukes Hospital, D2
Teachers College, A1
Terrace in the Sky, B3
The Cathedral Church of St. John the
 Devine, F2
USPS, F1

GRAFFITI HALL OF FAME

INTRODUCTION

EAST HARLEM RIVER

The East Harlem community stretches for 2.2 square miles from FDR Drive to Fifth Avenue between East 96th to East 142nd Streets. Also included in East Harlem are **Randall's** and **Ward's Islands** in the East River, opposite the stretch from 103rd to 125th Streets that is accessible by the Triborough Bridge and a foot bridge at 103rd Street. Known as **El Barrio** ("the neighborhood") or **Spanish Harlem**, this historically working-class area is home to one of the largest predominantly Latino communities in New York City. It includes the area formerly known as **Italian Harlem** and still harbors a small Italian American population along Pleasant Avenue. However, since the 1950s it has been dominated by residents of Puerto Rican descent, sometimes called Nuyoricans. Puerto Rican immigration after the First World War established an enclave at the western portion of Italian Harlem (around 110th Street and Lexington Avenue). The area slowly grew to encompass all of Italian Harlem as they moved out and Hispanics moved in during another wave of immigration after the Second World War. Many more

154

African Americans also moved to **East Harlem** after World War II, and have remained. Other area residents are made up of a diverse tapestry of ethnic groups including Latinos from Mexico, the Dominican Republic, Central and South America, Blacks and Africans from the Caribbean and West Africa, Turks from Eastern Europe, and Chinese.

EAST HARLEM BUILDING

The mix of population and economic dis-investment, called "red-lining," had a devastating effect on the housing stock, making the area a prime target for federal slum clearance. As early as 1938 and then after World War II, the New York City Housing Authority (NYCHA) razed buildings in neighborhoods, block by block, to make way for twenty-four high-rise public housing projects. The neighborhood contains the highest geographical concentration of low-income public housing projects in the United States. The total land area is 1.5 square miles. Many residents felt that whatever the inadequacy of their housing, they could not stand by and watch the wholesale demolition of homes and neighborhoods. They were joined by others who, ineligible for public housing, were faced with the threat of homelessness. Together, they organized protests and blocked additional destruction of property. The last large-scale housing project in East Harlem was completed in 1965. Such activism gave rise to political groups like the **Young Lords**, which came to prominence in 1969 when they used confrontational tactics to bring services and attention to the residents of East Harlem. Some of the Young Lords alumni include journalists **Juan Gonzalez**, **Felipe Luciano**, **Geraldo Rivera**, and **Pablo Guzmán**.

Historically, 116th Street (**Luis Muñoz Marín Blvd.,** named for the first elected governor of Puerto Rico, who lived in East Harlem before returning to Puerto Rico in 1940 and ushered in Commonwealth status to the island) has been the primary business hub of Spanish Harlem. From Lexington to First Avenues the street is lined with businesses selling food, clothing, and other specialty and ethnically specific goods. East 116th Street terminates at FDR Drive, the site of the East River Plaza, a retail mall that opened in 2009 with large commercial tenants—Costco, Target, Best Buy, and Marshalls. Along Park Avenue between East 111th and 116th Streets is the famous **La Marqueta,** an enclosed market that once housed 500 mostly Puerto Rican merchants who presided over stalls in five buildings under the elevated Metro-North tracks selling fresh tropical produce, meats, fish, and dairy products. Once the spiritual heart of East Harlem, La Marqueta was a vibrant regional center for Spanish food and groceries during the 1950s and 1960s. But a long decline began in the 1970s, and today, despite repeated efforts at revitalization, the old atmosphere has all but disappeared. East Harlem's commercial and business district has expanded to encompass Third Avenue between 112th and 124th Streets.

LA MARQUETA

The cultural crossroads of East Harlem is located from 104th to 108th Streets between Fifth and Madison Avenues. In addition to **El Museo del Barrio** and the **Museum of the City of New York**, other organizations that strengthen East Harlem's cultural identity include the artist collective **Taller Boricua,** the Afro-Dominican folklore group Palo Monte, Los Pleneros de la 21 (a performing ensemble which preserves the Afro-Puerto Rican traditions of the Bomba and Plena), and the **Puerto Rican Traveling Theater** (which presents and produces bilingual professional theater and offers artistic development through its Raúl Juliá Training Unit to emerging and established artists).

EAST HARLEM STREETSCAPE

155

The **Harbor Conservatory for the Performing Arts**, home to the **Raices Latin Music Museum**, a Smithsonian Affiliate, serves as a focus for theatre, dance, and musical performance in the neighborhood; it also hosts the annual competition to award the Charlie Palmieri Memorial Piano Scholarship, which was established in Palmieri's memory by Tito Puente for the benefit of intermediate and advanced young (aged twelve to twenty-five) pianists' study of Latin-style piano.

Of the three Harlem areas, Spanish Harlem is recognized most in popular songs, including **Ben E. King's** R&B song "Spanish Harlem," **The Mamas & the Papas'** song "Spanish Harlem," **Louie Ramirez's** Latin soul song "Lucy's Spanish Harlem," and **Bob Dylan's** song "Spanish Harlem Incident." It was also mentioned in **Elton John's** song "Mona Lisas and Mad Hatters" and **Carlos Santana's** song "Maria Maria." Spanish Harlem has given birth to everything from sixties-era boogaloo to mind-bending salsa and many grooves in between. It inspired the formation of Oscar Hernandez's Grammy Award–winning **Spanish Harlem Orchestra**. The feature film *Vote For Me!* takes place in current-day Spanish Harlem, and was written and directed by former New York State Assemblyman **Nelson Antonio Denis**. The area is also the setting for the **J. D. Robb** book *Salvation in Death*, the twenty-seventh book in the popular "in Death" crime series.

East Harlem is also home to one of the few major television studios north of midtown, **Metropolis** (106th St. and Park Ave.), where shows like BET's *106 & Park* and *Chappelle's Show* have been produced. Many famous artists have lived and worked in Spanish Harlem, including the renowned timbalero Tito Puente (110th Street was renamed **"Tito Puente Way"**), musicians **Charlie** and **Eddie Palmieri**, **Ray Barretto**, **Mario Bauza**, **Johnny Colon**, **Machito**, and Father of Boogaloo **Joe Cuba**, among others. Actors who at one time called East Harlem home include **Al Pacino**, **Rita Moreno**, **Burt Lancaster**, and Esther Rolle. **Miguel Algarin**, co-founder of the Lower East Side Nuyorican Poets Café, also was raised in East Harlem. Probably the most famous author from East Harlem was **Henry Roth**, whose family moved uptown from the Lower East Side. **Piri Thomas** wrote a best-selling autobiography titled *Down These Mean Streets* in 1967. Also, the contemporary artist **Soraida Martinez**, the painter and creator of "Verdadism," was born in Spanish Harlem. Baseball Hall of Famer **Lou Gerhig** was raised in East Harlem.

HISTORIC SITES NOT TO MISS

7 East 128th St.
Between Fifth and Madison Aves. Bus—M1. Subway—4, 5, 6 to 125th St.

Designated a landmark in 1982, this charming wood-frame house is one of a handful of buildings still standing that relate to Harlem's early history as a rural village. Erected around 1864, this French Second Empire building is remarkably well preserved. It retains its original stoop, decorated porch, double doors, shutters, and multicolored slate roof. Harlem Renaissance High School is located across the street at 22 E. 128th St. When it was P.S. 24, author **James Baldwin** (1924–1987) attended school here.

17 EAST 128TH STREET

Harlem Court House
170 E. 121st St., at Sylvan Place. between Lexington and Third Aves. Bus—M101, M103. Subway—4, 5, 6 to 125th St.

The Harlem Court House, a vibrant Romanesque Revival brick structure that was completed in 1893, is one of the most impressive buildings in East Harlem. This structure was designed by the architectural firm of **Thom & Wilson** and once housed the 9th District Civil Court, the Fifth District Prison (a jail with temporary holding cells), a magistrate's court, and a small claims court, but now is home to the Harlem Community Justice Center, which opened in 2001. Designated a landmark in 1967, the courthouse has elements of the Victorian Gothic, most notably in its pinnacles and multiple steeped gables. Romanesque Revival characteristics include the blocky massing and typical round arched door and window openings. The four-story masonry structure has a granite base with a red-brick facade trimmed with bluestone and terra-cotta. The corner tower is topped by eight small gables with two clocks below. Inside, a marble and iron spiral staircase leads from the lobby to the top of the tower. Other interior features include marble mosaic floors and oak door and window trim. The double-height third-floor

HARLEM COURT HOUSE

courtroom has a vaulted ceiling, oak paneling and trim, and federal Works Progress Administration (WPA) murals by **David Karfunkle**. Not far from rejuvenated courtrooms and staircases are age-encrusted steps, dimly lit corridors, and a heavy metal door. Few people ever venture there. Just beyond that door beckon the empty cells of perhaps New York City's oldest complex of still-standing jail tiers.

Langston Hughes House

20 E. 127ᵗʰ St. between Fifth and Madison Aves. Bus—M1, M60, M100, M101, BX15. Subway—2, 3, 4, 5, 6 to 125ᵗʰ Sts.

This ivy-clad residence was the only home that celebrated Harlem Renaissance poet and writer Langston Hughes ever purchased. The 1869 brownstone was designated a landmark in 1980. Hughes purchased the property in 1947 with funds he earned as lyricist of *Street Scene*, a Broadway opera that was based on **Elmer Rice's** play about the pungent life of people living in a Manhattan tenement, which won him a Pulitzer Prize in 1929. Rice collaborated with German-born composer **Kurt Weill** and they surprisingly invited Hughes to work on this project as the lyricist. Designed by architect **Alexander Wilson** and constructed as part of the post–Civil War building boom in the district by two real estate developers **James Meagher** and **Thomas Hanson**, the row house eventually passed into the hands of **Eino and Alina Lehto**, who were among the last survivors of what had once been a thriving Finnish community. Hughes, who lived here on the top floor until his death in 1967, shared this house with his longtime family friends, **Ethel (Toy) and Emerson Harper**, whom he lived with since the 1920s when he was in Harlem for any length of time. In the mid-2000s the house was renovated. For a short while it was used as a cultural site for spoken word and musical performances, but has since been purchased for private use. Hughes was the first African American author to support himself through his writing. He earned critical attention for his portrayal of realistic Black characters and he became one of the dominant voices speaking out on issues concerning Black culture.

Marcus Garvey Park Fire Watchtower

Entryway at 124ᵗʰ St. and Fifth Ave. Bus—M1, M7, M60, M100, M101, M102, BX15. Subway—2, 3 to 125ᵗʰ St.

The fire watchtower was built in 1856 by engineer **Julius Kroehl**. Fire watchtowers like this one once dotted the city, but became obsolete because buildings grew taller and fire alarm call boxes were installed on the streets. However, when they were used, lookouts would sit in the semi-enclosed tower to scout for fire. When a fire was spotted, the lookout would send a message by Morse Code, and ring the bell to alert the volunteer firefighters. In the late 1880s, the towers were torn down, except this one, which was protected on park land. The tower was designated a landmark in 1967 and placed on the National Register of Historic Places. The post-and-lintel cast-iron constructed frame provided the prototype for the modern-day skyscraper. After fire watchtowers became obsolete, the residents of Mount Morris Park continued to ring the bell twice a day, and this practice continued for the African American residents who rang the bell well into the 1960s when Easter Sunrise services were organized by the area churches. The structure is now braced to keep it from falling until it can be revitalized, a priority project of the Marcus Garvey Park Alliance, which

MARCUS GARVEY PARK FIRE WATCHTOWER

is working closely with the City Parks Foundation and the New York City Department of Parks and Recreation to make this happen.

Saint Nicholas Russian Orthodox Cathedral
15 E. 97th St., between Fifth and Madison Aves. (212) 996-6638. www.russianchurchusa.org.
Bus—M96, M101, M102, M103. Subway—6 to 96th St.

Saint Nicholas Russian Orthodox Cathedral, the diocesan seat of the Russian Orthodox Church in North America, was built in 1902 with funds collected throughout the Russian empire. Designed by **John Bergesen**, an architect of Russian descent, the building was designed according to the characteristic Russian model, with seven domes above a dark redbrick facade trimmed with limestone and glazed tile in green, blue, and yellow. The curving ribs of the domes are of gilt bronze, contrasting with the green painted galvanized iron surface. The building's features derive from seventeenth-century Baroque churches in Moscow. The "Moscow Baroque" style was revived in Russia in the late nineteenth century. The church's cross came from a sunken Russian navy ship, the *Retvizan*, which went down during the Russo-Japanese war.

SAINT NICHOLAS RUSSIAN ORTHODOX CATHEDRAL

Sylvan Court Mews
121st St., between Lexington and Third Aves. North of The Harlem Court House.
Bus—M101, M103. Subway—4, 5, 6 to 125th St.

There is always a charming surprise hidden in Harlem, and the Sylvan Court Mews is one of those jewels. Ten late nineteenth-century two-story townhouses are tucked away on an unpaved, unmapped blind alleyway right off 121st Street between Lexington and Third Avenues. The half-block area, which is reminiscent of some parts of Greenwich Village, once had an iron arched sign noting "Sylvan Court" as old photographs show. It is necessary to be on foot so as not to miss this forgotten piece of Old Harlem. Sylvan Court is an extension of the equally obscure Sylvan Place, which is a small art park that runs from 120th to 121st Streets. The charming little redbrick houses in Sylvan Court, of which three are vacant and boarded up, were probably used as stables in the late 1800s, when Harlem was more of a sleepy village than the expansive urban neighborhood it has become. Mews are typically former nineteenth-century stable yards that end abruptly in an alley-like layout. The carriage houses are only two levels or so and have historically been converted to cottage-like living quarters. The alleys of the West Village and Brooklyn Heights feature similar carriage houses that have been lovingly restored and landmark-protected. Unlike them, Sylvan Mews does not have landmark protection.

MUSEUMS

El Museo del Barrio

1230 Fifth Ave., at 104th St. (212) 831-7272. www.elmuseo.org. Suggested Admission: Adults $9, Students $5, Members and Children Under 12 Free, Seniors Free all day Wed, Free Admission every third Sat of each month. Wed–Sun 11am–6pm; Café Wed–Sun 11am–5pm. Tours: (212) 660-7113 or visit Web site, and a gift shop. Wheelchair accessible. Bus—M1, M2, M3, M4, M106. Subway—6 to 103rd St.

Founded in 1969 as a place of cultural pride for the Puerto Rican community, today the museum has expanded its mission to represent the diversity of art and culture in all of the Caribbean and Latin America. The northern most Museum Mile institution boasts an extremely wide-ranging 8,000-object collection which includes Pre-Columbian art, traditional artwork, works on paper, paintings, sculptures and installations, photography, and film. Deeply rooted in the community, El Museo provides quality educational programs through its guided tours, hands-on workshops, school partnerships, family programs, cultural festivals, and adult public programs. Carefully designed to be accessible to all audiences, the museum offers something for everyone among the many community events, festivals, and book readings on the museum's calendar.

International Salsa Museum

2127 Third Ave., at 116th St. (212) 289-1368. Tue–Sun 12pm–8pm. Bus—M101, M102, M103, M116. Subway—6 to 116th St.

Imagine holding the congas which Joe Cuba once played. You can do this and more at the International Salsa Museum. Founded in 1999, the museum documents the evolution of salsa music and dance and pays homage to artists (living and dead) who are part of its chronological development. The collection includes vintage LPs, concert posters, musical instruments, T-shirts, photographs, and books. Especially noteworthy are the life-sized bronze sculpture of **Celia Cruz** and smaller busts of **Yomo Toro** and **Ruth Hernandez**. Cuba, who also serves as the assistant director of the museum, has generously donated his first set of congas (which are suspended in midair), and other mementos of his career. Much of the collection has been donated by everyday people who want to pass on their joy and pride in the Afro-Latin music legacy. It is suggested that you call first before visiting the museum, which is located in the back of the Made in Puerto Rico store. Once you get there, there is no telling who you might run into, as the museum is a popular meeting place for the living musical legends who are still performing and creating.

Museum of the City of New York

1220 Fifth Ave., at 103rd St. (212) 534-1672. www.mcny.org. Suggested Admission: Adults $10, Seniors and Students $6, Families $20 (max. two adults), Members and Children under 12 Free, and free admission on Sundays between 10am and 12pm. "I'm a Neighbor"—If you live or work in East Harlem above 103rd St., simply walk in the entrance, say "I'm a neighbor," and the suggested admission charge will be waived. Tue–Sun 10am–5pm. Open on Monday holidays including Martin Luther King, Jr. Day, Presidents' Day, Memorial Day, Labor Day, and Columbus Day. Tours: (212) 534-1672, ext. 3406. Wheelchair accessible. Bus—M1, M2, M3, M4, M106. Subway—6 to 103rd St.

All you ever wanted to know about New York and then some. The Museum of the City of New York says it all and has it all. The museum's mandate is to explore the past, present, and future of New

York City and celebrate its heritage of diversity, opportunity, and perpetual transformation. While a mouthful for most, the museum accomplishes this feat with grace and style through its rich collection, exhibitions, and programs for children and adults. The permanent collections include Decorative Arts; Photography, Prints and Drawings; Theater and Broadway; Toy; Fashion, Costumes and Textiles; and Paintings and Sculptures.

Raices Latin Music Museum

1 E. 104th St., at Fifth Ave. (212) 427-2244 ext. 578. www.harborconservatory.org/m_raices.html. Bus—M1, M2, M3, M4, M106. Subway—6 to 103rd St.

The Raíces (Roots) Latin Music Museum is a comprehensive, multimedia collection that documents the history and the growth of Latin music in New York City, underscoring its roots in Afro-Caribbean rhythms and trends. Founded in 1979 by musician/educators **Ramon Rodriguez, Louis Bauzo**, and **Joe Conzo**, Raices has been declared an American Treasure by the White House and the National Trust for Historic Preservation. The collection concentrates on the contributions of Cuba, Puerto Rico, and the Dominican Republic. The collection acknowledges African roots and European influences in Latin music and holds over 15,000 artifacts, including original manuscripts by major artists, rare photos, video and audio recordings, periodicals, oral histories, artifacts, instruments, and a photo exhibition on the folkloric roots and history of salsa music. Currently used by students and scholars, Raíces served as a major research source for the feature film *Mambo Kings*, based on Oscar Hijuelos' Pulitzer Prize–winning novel, *The Mambo Kings Play Songs of Love*. The museum is temporarily being housed at the Harbor Conservatory for the Performing Arts until a permanent home is found.

The National Jazz Museum in Harlem

104 E. 126th St., Suite 2D. (212) 348-8300. www.jazzmuseuminharlem.org. Mon–Fri 10am–4pm. Visitor Center. Bus—M35, M60, M100, M101, M103, BX15. Subway—4, 5, 6, Metro North to 125th St.

This is the place where the history of jazz is learned and appreciated by visitors and students alike. The best instruments to bring to the National Jazz Museum in Harlem are your ears—to hear the strains of America's classical music or to hear some veteran jazz musician expound upon its history. Programs include Harlem Speaks, Jazz for the Curious Readers, Jazz for the Curious Listener, Saturday Panels, Harmony in Harlem, Harlem in the Himalayas, and Jazz in the Parks. The museum visitor's center is chock-full of books, CDs, and DVDs for your perusal. There is also a first-class exhibit of photos on the walls. Now housed in temporary quarters, the museum is the lead cultural component in the redevelopment of Mart 125, which is across the street from the Apollo Theater. Upon completion of the project, the museum will have about 10,000 square feet of exhibit space on the street level. There'll also be a restaurant and a small performance venue.

GALLERIES

MediaNoche
1355 Park Ave., 1st Fl., at 102nd St. (212) 828-0401. www.medianoche.us. Wed–Sat 3pm–7pm, and by appointment. Bus—M1, M2, M3, M4, M106. Subway—6 to 103rd St.

MediaNoche, a project of PRdream (see Theatre and Cultural Institutions), is a new media project and digital gallery that offers residencies and exhibition space for artists working in new media. The Digital Film Studio at MediaNoche is a space for independent filmmakers to converge. Works-in-progress screenings, screenplay readings, and a variety of workshops are offered. Production equipment and offline digital post are also available. Past exhibitions include The Making of Golden Warriors, a video installation by Francisca Benitez, Desktop Metaphor, and an exhibition by Mateo Zlatar.

Somniac Art Gallery
332 E. 116th St., between First and Second Aves. (212) 876-7303. www.somniacgallery. com. Tue–Fri 12pm–6pm. Private showing call (646) 320-5210. Bus—M15, M101, M102, M103, M116. Subway—6 to 116th St.

Somnicc Art Gallery, founded by art enthusiasts and artists **Richard Lasdon** and **Marina Thomas**, exhibits contemporary works from emerging and established artists. The gallery is sometimes host to small performances, readings, and other events.

The Taller Boricua Galleries at the Julia de Burgos Cultural Center
1680 Lexington Ave., between 105th and 106th Sts. (212) 831-4333. www.tallerboricua. org. Tue, Wed, Fri, Sat 12pm–6pm, Thu 1pm–7pm. Bus—M101, M102, M103, M106. Subway—6 to 106th St.

Taller Boricua is a multicultural institution providing artists with the opportunity to share ideas with their peers and it collaborates with other not-for-profit organizations and the community. The gallery exhibits works from artists that represent the diversity and richness of East Harlem.

THEATERS AND CULTURAL INSTITUTIONS

Julia de Burgos Cultural Arts Center

1674 Lexington Ave., between 105ᵗʰ and 106ᵗʰ Sts. (212) 831-4333. Bus—M101, M102, M103, M106. Subway—6 to 103ʳᵈ St.

The Julia de Burgos Cultural Arts Center was originally built as Public School 72 and is one of the oldest intact school structures in Manhattan. The neo-Grec style building, which was designed by **David I. Stagg**, was completed in 1882 while the annex, designed by **C. B. J. Snyder**, was completed in 1913. Designated a landmark in 1996, architectural features include a series of interlocking patterned brickwork capped by handsome towers. The building extends along the entire Lexington Avenue block front. It was built to serve a rapidly growing immigrant community. Now serving a new immigrant community, this building was brought back to life in 1995 with a $5.5-million infusion of money provided through a public/private partnership to serve the cultural needs of its Spanish-speaking residents. Architects **Lee Borrero's** and **Raymond Plummey's** design work created an attractive restoration of the venerable school house to establish a cultural arts center that is named for **Julia de Burgos**, a vibrant Puerto Rican poet and journalist who intermittently lived in East Harlem from the 1930s to the 1950s. She is commemorated in a mosaic wall mural by **Manny Vega** near the corner of 106ᵗʰ Street and Lexington Avenue. The cultural center, founded in 1994, provides space for the Taller Boricua (Puerto Rican Workshop) gallery, first launched as an artists' collective in the late 1960s. The center also sponsors plays, Latin jazz performances, dances, poetry jam sessions, and classes of all kinds.

Art for Change

1699 Lexington Ave., between 106ᵗʰ and 107ᵗʰ Sts. Basement North. (212) 348-7044. www.artforchange.org. Bus—M101, M102, M103, M106. Subway—6 to 103ʳᵈ St.

Art for Change (AfC) is an organization that uses artistic expression as a catalyst for social change. AfC provides space for other organizations, artists, and activists to congregate, rehearse, network, and interact with the East Harlem community. There are four major programs that help East Harlem youth and adults preserve and appreciate their culture. *CALLE (Creating Artistic Links to Liberation and Expression)* is a bilingual (Spanish/English) street theater project for high-school-aged youth who develop and perform plays about their visions and opinions. *Art Belongs to Everyone* is a year-round program that mounts art exhibits, interventions, workshops, and discussions in nontraditional spaces in East Harlem. *ExplorArte* is a two-year cultural exchange program between New York youth and youth from other countries, which culminates with a cultural performance or exhibition in various East Harlem sites and in performance spaces located in participating countries around the world. *Hacia Afuera* is a public art festival held annually in East Harlem in August. Public spaces like gardens, sidewalks, or walls are used for dance and music performances, art workshops for kids and adults, site-specific art installations, and interactive media pieces.

Harbor Conservatory for the Performing Arts

I E. 104th St., at Fifth Ave. (212) 427-2244 ext. 573. www.harborconservatory.org. Bus—M1, M3, M4, M106. Subway—6 to 103rd St.

The Harbor Conservatory for the Performing Arts is a nonprofit performing arts center that offers a complete education in music, dance, and theater to children and teens. It is especially noted for its Latin music curriculum, which provides instruction in almost every instrument in the Latin playing style. The Harbor was founded in 1970 and currently has an annual enrollment of over 1,000 students; operates four pre-professional ensembles (two in dance, two in theater), nearly 100 group classes, and numerous workshops; and provides over 300 private music lessons. The music department offers instruction in classical, jazz, Latin, and popular style music in private, group, and workshop sessions. The dance department focuses on classical ballet, modern, jazz, and tap for youth between the ages of four and eighteen. The Theatre Arts Program provides training in original, classical, contemporary, and musical theatre. The Harbor also awards the Charlie Palmieri Memorial Piano Scholarship for intermediate and advanced pianists ages twelve to twenty-five for the study of Latin-style piano. The scholarship was established in memory of Charlie Palmieri by Tito Puente.

La Casa de la Herencia Cultural Puertorriqueña

1230 Fifth Ave., Ste. 458, between 104th and 105th Sts. (212) 722-2600. www.lacasapr.org. Bus—M1, M3, M4, M106. Subway—6 to 103rd St.

La Casa de la Herencia Cultural Puertorriqueña, Inc. is a nonprofit community-based cultural institution that for more than twenty years has promoted Puerto Rican art, culture, and history. La Casa hosts and sponsors seminars, lectures, contests, literary and artistic workshops, and concerts. The organization also offers weekly classes that instill an appreciation for traditional music and instruments, dance, and arts and crafts to keep these art forms alive through generations. Its Puerto Rican Heritage Library is an important scholarly resource that documents Puerto Rican history in New York and Puerto Rico. The collection consists of approximately 14,000 books, periodicals, newspapers, microfilms, photographs, sound and visual recordings, government documents, and doctoral dissertations in Spanish and English. The library is open to members, students, and professionals by appointment.

National Black Theater

2031–33 National Black Theatre Way, Fifth Ave., between 125th and 126th St. (212) 722-3800. www.nationalblacktheatre.org. Wheelchair accessible. Bus—M1, M7, M60, M100, M101, M102, BX15. Subway—2, 3, Metro North to 125th St.

The National Black Theatre (NBT) complex is a 64,000-square-foot cultural hub centrally located at the intersection of Fifth Avenue and 125th Street. Founded by producer/actress/cultural activist **Dr. Barbara Ann Teer** (1937–2008), NBT was the first theater company in the nation to perform ritual theatre based on West African traditions. NBT offers theatrical and cultural programs throughout the year and also hosts workshops, symposia, and special events. The building houses the largest collection of contemporary Yoruba sacred art in the Western Hemisphere—with much of it created in Harlem. Dr. Teer arranged for Nigerian craftsmen to design the theater's interior as well as create many of the sculptures and paintings outside and inside the building. The wooden sculptures on the landings actually began life as trees in Connecticut.

Puerto Rico and the American Dream (PRdream.com)

161 E. 106ᵗʰ St., between Lexington and Third Aves. (212) 828-0401. www.prdream.com. Bus—M1, M2, M3, M4, M106. Subway—6 to 106ᵗʰ St.

Puerto Rico and the American Dream or PRdream.com is an award-winning digital organization that provides content via a Web site on the history, culture, and politics of Puerto Rico and the Puerto Rican Diaspora in both Spanish and English. Original content includes film screenings, an art gallery, discussion boards, historical timelines, and oral histories, along with announcements and current events postings. In cooperation with the Center for Puerto Rican Studies at Hunter College/City University of New York, which hosts CentroTalks that brings scholars to New York to discuss significant issues, PRdream.com presents a digest of these talks. The organization also holds the annual Summer Film Fest that screens world cinema in the 103ʳᵈ Street Community Garden at sunset. The original curator of Nuyorican Cinema, PRdream.com provides a permanent online exhibition of these independent films along with critical essays about them. PRdream also launched MediaNoche, a new media project and digital gallery (see Galleries/East Harlem).

Teatro Heckscher

1230 Fifth Ave., at 104ᵗʰ St. (212) 831-7272. www.elmuseo.org/theater. Wheelchair accessible. Bus—M1, M2, M3, M4, M106. Subway—6 to 103ʳᵈ St.

The historic and beautifully restored Teatro Heckscher, formerly the Heckscher Theatre, is the only theatre of its kind on the Upper East Side of Manhattan. Consisting of a proscenium arch stage and seating 599, the theater was intended primarily for children's theatre when built in 1921. The interior contains *Scenes from Children's Literature*, a series of monumental murals designed by the gifted illustrator and painter **Willy Pogany** (1882–1955). Rendered in oil on canvas, these invaluable murals range in size to approximately 16 feet by 25 feet, and depict legendary children's tales, including "Jack and the Beanstalk," "Hansel and Gretel," "Little Red Riding Hood," and "Cinderella." Other splendid treasures in the theatre include eight luminous circular stained-glass fixtures on the ceiling painted with children's motifs and two charming chandeliers in the shape of castles. The theatre has been home to many Broadway tryouts during the 1930s, was the original site for the Joseph Papp New York Shakespeare Festival, was the site for a special tribute to Tito Puente during the 39ᵗʰ Annual Grammy awards, and is now part of the New York City's Historic Music Trail.

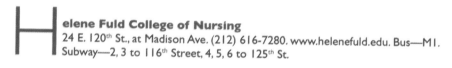

EDUCATIONAL INSTITUTIONS

Helene Fuld College of Nursing
24 E. 120th St., at Madison Ave. (212) 616-7280. www.helenefuld.edu. Bus—M1.
Subway—2, 3 to 116th Street, 4, 5, 6 to 125th St.

The Helene Fuld College of Nursing specializes in educating licensed practical nurses to advance to the associate degree registered nurse level. It was established in 1945 as a "training school" for practical nurses as part of the Hospital for Joint Diseases. In 1964, the school started the first program in the country for licensed practical nurses to become diploma registered nurses. In 1975, the school received its permanent charter from New York State with the authority to confer the AAS degree in nursing. As of November, 2007, more than 4,300 AAS degrees in nursing have been awarded. The college now functions as an independent not-for-profit college under the authority of the New York State Board of Regents.

Mount Sinai School of Medicine
One Gustave L. Levy Place, 100th St., and Fifth Ave. (212) 241-6500. www.
mountsinai.org. Bus—M1, M2, M3, M4. Subway—6 to 96th St.

The Mount Sinai Hospital was founded in 1852 as the Jews' Hospital, but it was another century before a school of medicine was created. After establishing a School of Medicine in 1963, the school now enjoys the distinction of being ranked among the leading medical schools in the nation. When it was organized, the school was the first medical school to be formed by a hospital without a university affiliation. However, by 1967 it entered into an affiliation agreement with the City University of New York, and graduated its first class in 1968. Today, the school encompasses the post-graduate and house staff training programs of the hospital, as well as maintains a graduate school for biological sciences, a Medical Scientist Training Program (M.D.–Ph.D.), and many master- and doctoral-level degree programs. The school is currently affiliated with many different institutions around the metropolitan area to provide a variety of practice settings for its educational programs, undergraduate and graduate. The school and hospital occupy a four-block area on Fifth Avenue adjacent to Central Park, with architecture designed by **I. M. Pei**.

Touro College
Taino Towers (Harlem) Campus. 240 E. 123rd St., between Second and Third Aves. (212)
722-1575. www.touro.edu/nyscas/. Bus—M60, M100, M101, M103, BX15. Subway—4,
5, 6 to 125th St.

The Taino Towers campus of Touro College was opened in 1979 under the umbrella of the New York School of Career and Applied Studies, which is a division of the college. At Taino Towers students can pursue a wide range of career-oriented college programs covering business management and administration, human services, education concentration from K through sixth grade, and computer science. Students can obtain Associate of Arts degrees and Bachelor of Science degrees. Since the new medical school opened on 125th Street, the school is gearing up to offer a four-year undergraduate degree program that will prepare students for admission to the Osteopathic Medical School. Touro College is an independent school of higher learning established to "strengthen Jewish life and perpetuate the Judaic tradition on the college campus," as well as to contribute to building a better society.

ACCOMMODATIONS

 ew York Apartments to Let
239 E. 120th St., between Second and Third Aves. (646) 468-3463. www.newyork-apt2let.com. Bus—M15. Subway—4, 5, 6 to 125th St.

New York Apartments to Let offers newly refurbished air-conditioned two-bedroom apartments (non-smoking), each with living room, dining room, kitchen, and bathroom on a quiet side street in the heart of El Barrio, or Spanish Harlem. The two ground-floor units also share a back garden, where smoking is permitted. Proprietors provide the basics of chilled water the first night, milk, coffee, and tea, as well as shampoo, hair conditioner, towels, television, and local phone access. The location is convenient to brand-name stores on 116th Street and 125th Street, unique Harlem markets, and the Apollo Theater, and is close to transportation that can take you virtually anywhere

else in New York City. Also for rent is a board room that accommodates four to thirty people for meetings. The space includes a conference table, video TV, flip charts, and complimentary beverages of coffee, tea, and water. The owners, John and Rose Maloney, live in the building and are more than happy to recommend good shopping, bars, and restaurants in the area. The posted rate is $300 per night (two-night minimum stay).

pper Yorkville Suites
1876 Third Ave. between 103rd and 104th Sts. (646) 330.5472. www.upperyorkvillesuites.com. Bus—M101, M102, M103. Subway—6 to 103rd St.

The owners of this upscale establishment strive to provide superior accommodations and comforts at affordable prices. It's like a home away from home. Every suite in Upper Yorkville has a minimum of 500 square feet of space and features exposed brick walls, high ceilings, ceiling fans, private kitchens and bathrooms, air-conditioning, and flat panel TVs with cable. To ensure a pleasant stay, each of the five suites is fully furnished with a full range of large and small appliances, cooking utensils, bath and bed linens, cutlery, crockery, and other necessities like free Wi-Fi. Most of the suites can comfortably accommodate a family as large as five. If you have a party larger than five, please call for details. Upper Yorkville Suites is only one block away from major public transportation or private car service. Located minutes from all points of interest in New York City, it's an easy walk to Central Park, Museum Mile, and great restaurants and clubs. Rates range from $135 to $275 depending on the season (two-night minimum stay).

Virginia's Guest House

128 E. 112ᵗʰ St., between Park and Lexington Aves. (212) 369-4572. www.tripadvisor.com/Hotel_Review-g60763-d628066. Bus—M101, M102, M103. Subway—6 to 110ᵗʰ St.

Virginia's offers an affordable, safe, clean, and comfortable home away from home in New York City. Accommodations include single and double rooms with shared bathrooms and showers. Each room has a TV and there is also free Internet and breakfast available. Room rates range from $50 to $60 a night.

DINING AND LIVE ENTERTAINMENT

Creole Restaurant and Music Supper Club

2167 Third Ave., at 118th St. (212) 876-8838. www.creolenyc.com. Cuisine: Creole. Lunch, Dinner, Brunch. $$$$. Tue–Thu 12pm–12am, Fri and Sat 12pm–4am, Sun 1pm–9pm. V, MC. Bus—M101, M102, M103, M116. Subway—6 to 116th St.

It's like being in the French Quarter of New Orleans when you step into Creole Restaurant and Music Supper Club. Owner **Kevin Walters** serves up Creole dishes that are reminiscent of the specialties found in the French Quarter. This eatery offers an exquisite and unique dining and entertainment experience where Creole cuisine, an American-created style of cooking out of Louisiana that blends French, Spanish, African, and Native American influences, is merged with jazz entertainment and a revolving art gallery of works by local artists. Dishes, such as spicy blackened catfish, Creole stew chicken, blackened shrimp Napoleon, New Orleans–style crab cakes, several gumbo variations including a vegetarian one, and sweet potato beignets (fried doughnuts), are signature dishes here. Don't miss out on one of East Harlem's great bargains—either a $7 or $8 luncheon special served Mon–Fri from 12pm–4pm.

Since opening, Creole has invigorated the uptown jazz scene and most recently the booking focus has been on Latin Jazz, which is very appropriate since the restaurant and club is located in the heart of Spanish Harlem, or as the locals say, El Barrio. This place is always jumping with top-notch entertainment, so check the Web site calendar for the schedule.

Dining

A Taste of Seafood

59 E. 125th St., between Madison and Park Aves. (212) 831-5584. www.atasteofseafood.com. Cuisine: Seafood. Lunch, Dinner. $$$. Mon–Thu 7am–9pm, Fri and Sat 7am–4am, Sun 1pm–11pm. All major credit cards. Bus—M1, M60, M100, M101, BX15. Subway—2, 3, Metro North to 125th St.

For more than fifteen years, A Taste of Seafood has been frying up some of the best fish in Harlem. Originally located across the street from its new location on 125th St. in a small space with a few seats at its luncheonette counter, the crowds would stretch down the block for what would be at least a twenty-minute wait to order fried-to-perfection fish or shrimp. Recently the fish joint morphed into a full-fledged seafood restaurant when it moved into its glamorous new digs—a deluxe two-story space with purple light fixtures and a nautical décor. The move did not affect the quality of the food—the fried whiting, which is its signature offering, is as good as ever. In addition to the fact that customers can now dine in, a greater variety of fried fish is offered: catfish, porgies, and red snapper. The menu also lists some even higher-end items, including steamed king crabs, snow crabs, ocean scallops, and lobster tails. Just remember, this is a restaurant that made its reputation on its fried fish.

Charlie's Place

1960 Madison Ave., between 125th and 126th Sts. (212) 410-0277. Cuisine: Japanese, Sushi. Lunch, Dinner. $. Mon–Sat 11:30am–8pm. Cash only. Bus—M7, M60, M100, M101, M102, BX15. Subway—2, 3, Metro North to 125th St.

There are not a lot of options for sushi in East and Central Harlem, so when Charlie's Place opened the residents were beside themselves—they didn't have to travel "downtown" for sushi. This restaurant is a take-out spot for not only sushi, but teriyaki and wings. The sushi rolls are priced at $10 each. The favorite is the spicy salmon roll. Also, there are good combo deals for around $6 and $7 that come with salad, lo mein or rice, a meat dish of either teriyaki chicken, shrimp or beef, and a can of soda. The only complaint about this place is that it closes too early.

East Harlem Café

1651 Lexington Ave., at 104th St. (212) 996-2080. www.eastharlem-cafe.com. Cuisine: Sandwiches, pastries, and beverages. $. Mon–Fri 7:30am–7pm, Sat 10am–7pm, Sun 11am–5pm. Cash only. Bus—M101, M102, M103, M106. Subway—6 to 103rd St.

Opened in the fall of 2008, the East Harlem Café has become a destination for a taste of Latino culture. In addition to organic coffees and teas, pastries, and sandwiches, this café hosts book signings and readings, film screenings, and the East Harlem Comedy Hour. Every Saturday tea tastings are hosted but require advance booking. The $15 per person charge includes a pot of coffee or tea, tea sandwiches, and cakes and scones. An added plus here are the comfy couches, convenient outlets along the wall to plug in laptops, and free Wi-Fi access.

El Barrio Juice Bar

308 E. 116th St., between First and Second Aves. (212) 828-0403. Cuisine: Juices, Smoothies. Breakfast, Lunch. $. Daily 8am–8pm. Cash only. Bus—M15, M101, M102, M103, M116. Subway—6 to 116th St.

El Barrio Juice Bar is a take-out haven that serves healthy juices, sandwich wraps, and fresh vegetable and fruit salads for lunch. This busy spot specializes in customized coolers, both the traditional and the health-shake variety, in 16 oz. servings. There are a dozen flavors of the thin shakes called licuados which blend milk and sugar with fruits and berries for $3.50. The good thing is that soy and rice milk can now be substituted for milk in both the licuados and the $4 smoothies. Fresh fruits and vegetables are juiced and blended for $3.50 and $4, and energy and protein juices for $4 each. In the front of the store, fruits and vegetables and health food staples are sold, along with the customary bottles of Latin sodas—Jarritos and Mirinda—and their Western counterparts, plus a freezer case of popsicles flavored with guava, lime, and almond.

El Paso Taqueria

64 E. 97th St., between Fifth and Madison Aves. (212) 996-1739. www.elpasotaqueria.com. Cuisine: Mexican. Breakfast, Lunch, Dinner. $$$. Daily 9am–11pm. V, MC. Bus—M1, M2, M3, M4, M96, M106. Subway—6 to 96th St.

237 E. 116th St., between Second and Third Aves. (212) 860-9753. Bus—M101, M102, M103, M116. Subway—6 to 116th St.

El Paso Taquería and Cevichería

1643 Lexington Ave., between 104th and 105th Sts. (212) 831-9831. Bus—M101, M102, M103, M106. Subway—6 to 103rd St.

If you are looking for authentic Mexican cuisine prepared by authentic Mexican cooks, El Paso Taquería is the place. El Paso, which has the best guacamole in town, is located in three sites in East Harlem, and most recently moved its tiny and cramped Lexington Ave. site across the street to a much larger and finely appointed space that contains nearly ninety more seats, including an enclosed patio garden that is divine. This expanded site has a more ambitious menu and slightly higher prices. Besides a wide range of traditional Mexican dishes like quesadillas, stuffed chilis, and tacos, four types of ceviches (citrus-marinated seafood), fresh oysters, and the famous Oaxaca mole have been added to the menu. Even with the move, the food in all three locations continues to stand out. Authenticity also extends to the beverages such as aguas frescas (fresh-squeezed and blended juices), homemade sangria, a wide variety of Mexican beers, and of course the quintessential margarita. Possessing a loyal fan base of locals, a Zagat rating and a good review from the *New York Times* have helped attract a broader following for these taquerias. Not bad for a business that started out peddling its food from a wooden pushcart in 1993!

Fishers of Men

32 E. 130th St., between Fifth and Madison Aves. (212) 828-4447, Cuisine: Seafood. Breakfast, Lunch, Dinner. $. Mon–Wed 10am–8pm, Thu and Fri 10am–9pm, Sat 9am–9pm. Cash only. Bus—M1, M7, M102. Subway—2, 3 to 135th St.

(See Central Harlem for description.)

Giovanna's Restaurant and Pizzeria

1567 Lexington Ave., at 100th St. (212) 360-6300. Cuisine: Italian, Pizza, Pasta. Lunch, Dinner, Brunch. $$$$. Daily 11am–11pm. All major credit cards. Bus—M101, M102, M103. Subway—6 to 103rd St.

Fast becoming a neighborhood favorite, this charming restaurant makes some divine brick-oven pizza with toppings that serve anyone's taste. Chef and owner **Divino Seno**, who previously was the head chef at Nick's on the Upper East Side, prepares great pastas, veal and chicken dishes, and a fish of the day entrée. Please try the homemade tiramisu, which many swear is the best. Giovanna's offers a $6.99 lunch special of salad, and a choice of pizza, pasta, or chicken. There's a special brunch menu which includes paninis, egg dishes, and pancakes. Whatever you choose to eat, don't forget the coffee, which is served with warm milk. The wine bar has a good selection of Italian wines, and beer is also served.

Green Apple BBQ

362 E. 112ᵗʰ St., between First and Second Aves. (212) 410-6915. www.
greenapplebbq.com. Cuisine: Barbecued Ribs, Chicken. Lunch, Dinner. $$. Tue–Sun
12pm–9pm. Bus—M15, M101, M102, M103, M116. Subway—6 to 116ᵗʰ St.

Green Apple BBQ ribs are smoked over chunks of apple and hickory wood, giving them an authentic Texas barbecue flavor. The Mexican chef, who hails from down the coast in Veracruz, prepares some succulent ribs, slathered with a sweet peppery sauce, that pull free from the bone with only gentle resistance. The menu includes American and Mexican dishes that make the place all the better. Primarily a take-out spot, the tiny restaurant does have five tables for eating in. Luncheon specials are reasonably priced—for example, the Texas-style barbecued beef ribs come with one side for $9.

Itzocan Bistro

1575 Lexington Ave., between 100ᵗʰ and 101ˢᵗ Sts. (212) 423-0255, www.itzocanbistro.com.
Cuisine: French-Mexican Fusion. Lunch, Dinner, Brunch. $$$. Daily 11am–11pm. All major
credit cards. Bus—M101, M102, M103. Subway—6 to 103ʳᵈ St.

When Itzocan Café moved from the East Village and set down stakes in East Harlem as the Itzocan Bistro, chef and co-owner **Anselmo Bello** also brought with him his Franco-Mexican fusion cooking that won him a loyal following. No chips and salsa here, but bistro fare creatively infused with south-of-the-border ingredients is served at modest prices and with gracious service. A few inventive creations include: mussels steamed in tequila-and-serrano-pepper broth, grilled filet mignon with potatoes au gratin and Rioja anche chile sauce, pistachio-crusted salmon with string beans, jalapeno ragout, and duck confit, and mushrooms quesadilla with brie and baby greens. There is always something to sample because the menu changes with the seasons. A nice weekend brunch is served from 12pm–3pm and a prix-fixe dinner can be enjoyed Mon–Thu 5pm–7pm.

La Fonda Boricua

169 E. 106ᵗʰ St., between Lexington and Third Aves. (212) 410-7292. www.fondaboricua.
com. Cuisine: Puerto Rican. Lunch, Dinner. $$. Daily 11am–9pm. All major credit cards.
Bus—M101, M102, M103, M106. Subway—6 to 103ʳᵈ St.

La Fonda Boricua, which literally means "Puerto Rican diner," serves classic Puerto Rican food in a spacious homelike atmosphere and décor where seventy-five can be seated comfortably. The **Ayala brothers**, who in 1996 purchased George and Gina's small luncheonette and expanded in 2001, worked with the kitchen crew to preserve many of the restaurant's traditional and favorite dishes like pernil (roasted pork), arroz con pollo (rice with chicken), citrus-marinated steak smothered in onions, succulent chicarrones (fried chicken chunks), and octopus and codfish salads. Until recently it was home to some of the greatest live, improvisational Latin music being performed in New York City. This feature was moved across the street when the brothers opened the FB Lounge (see Dining & Entertainment). In 2008 La Fonda beat the starch out of chef Bobby Flay's rice when he brought his Food Network show *Throwdown with Bobby Flay* uptown to challenge La Fonda to an arroz con pollo battle.

a Tropizienne Bakery

2131 First Ave., at 110th St. (212) 860-5324. Cuisine: Gourmet Baked Goods. $. Daily 6am–8pm. Cash only. Bus—M15, M101, M102, M103. Subway—6 to 110th St.

La Tropezienne chose its name for a luscious custard-filled pastry that is available in two sizes at this authentic French bakery owned and operated by a real Frenchman. At this low-profile spot that has been in operation since 1991, you will find a myriad of breads, sandwiches, and cookies, spanning French classics like boule, pain bagnat, langues de chat, and hometown favorites like poppy rolls, roast beef sandwiches, and rugelach. Also, a fine croque monsieur is made here. But the tarts and cakes are the heart of the bakery's oeuvre—the tart au citron and the shop's namesake cake, la Tropezienne, are especially worth sampling. What's marvelous about this place is you won't pay anything like the sticker prices you'll find in the few high-end bakeries in the city.

echonera Sandy

2261 Second Ave., at 116th St. (212) 348-8654. Cuisine: Cuban, Dominican, Puerto Rican. Breakfast, Lunch, Dinner. $. Daily 6am–3am. Cash only. Bus—M15, M101, M102, M103, M116. Subway—6 to 116th St.

Want fast delivery? Call Lechonera Sandy, which can get a succulent whole rotisserie chicken and some traditional sides like beans and rice and plantain to you in a zip if you are in East Harlem or nearby. Located on one of East Harlem's busiest corners, Sandy's draws a crowd of regulars not simply for a lengthy menu of Latin favorites but especially as a lechonera—a destination for platefuls of crisp-skinned roast suckling pig, or lechon asado. The mofongo, served with chicarrones, is cheaper than most. If you come here for take-out and you don't speak Spanish, read the menu which translates into English the dishes found on the steam table. Better still, point to what you want.

loyd's Carrot Cake

2051 Second Ave., at 105th St. (212) 831-9156. www.lloydscarrotcake.com. Cuisine: Bakery, Salads, and Paninis. $. Mon, Wed, and Thu 9:30am–8pm, Tue, Fri, and Sat 9:30am–7pm, Sun 10am–3pm. All major credit cards. Bus—M15, M101, M102, M103, M106. Subway—6 to 103rd St.

Lloyd's Carrot Cake opened in Riverdale in 1987, and the carrot cake is so good that most folks do not mind making a trip to this exclusive Bronx neighborhood once in a while to buy a cake—especially for a special occasion. At one point the bakery operated a take-out-only site in Central Harlem. Now there is a bakery/café in East Harlem. Lloyd's offers three choices of its moist carrot cake, made from scratch and void of preservatives—with nuts, without nuts, and sugar-free. All carrot cakes are certified Kd (Kosher dairy), too. You can also purchase cakes by the slice. Other items sold here are coconut and red velvet cakes, sweet potato, pecan and apple pies, paninis, smoothies, and salads.

anna's Soul Food and Salad Bar

54 E. 125th St., between Madison and Park Aves. (212) 360-4975, www. mannasrestaurants.com, Cuisine: Soul Food. Lunch, Dinner. $. Mon–Sat 11am–9pm, Sun 11am–8pm. Cash only. Bus—M1, M60, M100, M101, BX15. Subway—2, 3, Metro North to 125th St.

(See Central Harlem for description.)

Moustache Pitza

1621 Lexington Ave., at 102nd St. (212) 828-0030. www.moustachepitza.com. Cuisine: Middle Eastern. Lunch, Dinner. $$. Daily 12pm–12am. All major credit cards. Bus— M101, M102, M103. Subway—6 to 103rd St.

With two other locations in the East and West Village, Moustache Pitza has now come to East Harlem. The big attraction at this restaurant is the fantastic jazzed-up versions of pizza—Middle Eastern-style. The oven-baked pizzas are prepared on pita bread and come with appropriate Middle Eastern toppings— ground lamb, onion, tomato, parsley, and spices, or one with walnuts, dried yogurt, onions, and olive oil. There are kebabs, sandwiches, salads, and some of the best baba ghanoush outside the Middle East. The décor is light and airy with burnished copper table tops, and when it's warm, there is outdoor seating.

Ottomanelli Bros.

1325 Fifth Ave., between 111th and 112th Sts. (212) 828-8900. www.nycotto.com. Cuisine: Italian, Barbecue. Lunch, Dinner, Brunch. $$$. Daily 11am–10pm. V, MC, AmEx. Bus—M1, M2, M3, M4. Subway—2, 3 to 110th St.

The name Ottomanelli in New York is synonymous with fine meats, and the butcher shop opened by the family more than ninety years ago in Yorkville is still open. Today the family operates several meat markets, cafes, and bakeries in Manhattan and sells packaged goods online. The East Harlem location, close to Duke Ellington Circle where Central Park ends, is one of two grills that the family operates. Here you can enjoy their famous steaks and steak burgers, barbecued ribs, hearty pastas from family recipes, and grilled chicken. There is a great prix-fixe brunch served on Saturday and Sunday from 11am–4pm. For $9.95 you get a choice of a mimosa, Bloody Mary, or Prosecco sparkling wine; coffee or tea; and a choice of challah French toast, buttermilk pancakes, frittata, omelet, or a steak burger. All these items are served with house potatoes and bacon or sausage.

Patsy's Pizzeria

2287 First Ave., at 118th St. (212) 534-9783. www.patsyspizzeriany.com. Cuisine: Italian, Pizza. Lunch, Dinner. $$$. Mon–Thu 11am–11pm, Fri and Sat 11am–12am, Sun 12pm– 10pm. Cash only. Bus—M15, M101, M102, M103, M116. Subway—6 to 116th St.

Many argue that it's the type of oven used that determines the authentic taste of pizza. In the case of Patsy's Pizzeria, it's the coal oven it uses to impart an unmistakable smoky flavor to the crust that is characteristic of the classic New York pizza. Patsy's is one of the holdouts from the old Italian Harlem days, established in 1933. In business for more than seventy-five years, Patsy's still proudly serves its superb old-world pizza, with a smooth, thin, light crust, blackened and blistered by the heat, crisp all the way through, and topped with creamy mozzarella, plump red tomatoes, and fragrant fresh basil. There are few misses with the numerous pasta dishes that are available at Patsy's because they are lovingly prepared with the freshest vegetables, herbs and spices, meats, poultry, and seafood. The place stays crowded, which is a testament to its popularity with fans, who come from near and far to enjoy great Italian cuisine in an old-world environment replete with the original wood wainscoting, pressed tin ceiling, and scores of photographs hanging on the wall of 1930s and 1940s celebrities who frequented the establishment.

Pee Dee Steak House

2006 Third Ave., between 110th and 111th Sts. (212) 996-3300. Cuisine: Steak house. Lunch, Dinner. $$$. Mon–Thu 11am–11pm, Sat and Sun 11am–12am. All major credit cards. Bus—M101, M102, M103. Subway—6 to 110th St.

(See Central Harlem for description.)

Piatto d'Oro II Ristorante Italiano

1 E. 118th St., at Fifth Ave. (212) 722-7220. www.restaurantpiattodoro.com. Cuisine: Italian. Lunch, Dinner. $$$. Sun–Wed 11am–10pm, Thu–Sat 11am–11pm. All major credit cards. Bus—M1, M7, M102, M116. Subway—2, 3 to 116th St.

349 E. 109th St., between First and Second Aves. (212) 828-2929. Bus—M15, M101, M102, M103. Subway—6 to 110th St.

Gran Piatto d'Oro

1429 Fifth Ave., between 116th and 117th Sts. (212) 722-2244. Bus—M7, M102, M116. Subway—2, 3 to 116th St.

Piatto d'Oro translates to "golden dish" and the dishes do shine at these establishments, which have brought Italian soul food to Harlem. When the owners closed their Il Bocconcino Restaurant in SoHo and opened their first Uptown location on 109th St., residents met them with open arms and said, "Thank you for bringing Downtown to Uptown." All three locations produce old-world "cucina con amore" dishes. The fifty different dishes include homemade pastas topped with a variety of sauces, pizzas, and multiple chicken, veal, and seafood platters. But the risottos are the true standouts. The Risotto ai Funghi Porcini is heavy, creamy, and overflowing with mushrooms, while an artichoke white sauce makes the Risotto ai Carciofi a lighter choice. There is outdoor seating at all three restaurants. The largest of the three and the newest addition, Gran Piatto D'oro, is a spacious and elegant affair that comfortably seats over a hundred diners and has space in the basement to accommodate private parties.

Rao's Restaurant

455 E. 114th St., between Pleasant and First Aves. (212) 722-6709. www.raos.com. Cuisine: Italian. Dinner. $$$$. Mon–Fri 5pm–11pm. Cash only. Bus—M15, M101, M102, M103, M116. Subway—6 to 116th St.

Unless you have connections, you will not land a reservation at Rao's, a family restaurant opened in 1896 when East Harlem or El Barrio was Italian Harlem. Rao's is the most in-demand restaurant in the city, with a Who's Who list of celebrities who have dined here. It was known as an eatery where mobsters went—when the actor **Michael Nouri** played Mob boss **Lucky Luciano** in a 1980s TV series, owner **Frank Pellegrino** showed him Luciano's table. Rao's is also renowned for its great homestyle Neapolitan cuisine—luscious pastas, chicken in vinegar and lemon, and meatballs—and its unmatched hospitality, including serenades by Pellegrino, who once earned his living singing and was a regular FBI agent on HBO's *The Sopranos*. For decades Rao's existed as a neighborhood restaurant where its local customers would regularly fill the tables until they were given standing reservations—much like owning a condominium—that persevere to this day. The demand for reservations exploded after an extremely favorable review in the *New York Times* in 1977. Since Rao's has only ten tables and one seating per night, you have to know someone who "owns" one of the tables to get a reservation. However, to experience the ambience this slice of old New York engenders, you can enjoy a drink at the bar which has a charm of its own. Bartender **Nick "The Vest" Zaloumis,** so called because of the 136 vests he owns, will serve you one of his classic drinks and entertain you with stories about serving celebrities. Tip: Come dressed to impress.

Ricardo's Steakhouse

2145 Second Ave., between 110th and 111th Sts. (212) 289-5895. www. ricardosteakhouse.com. Cuisine: Steakhouse, American. Dinner. $$$$. Tue and Wed 4pm–11pm, Thu–Sun 4pm–12am. All major credit cards. Bus—M15, M101, M102, M103. Subway—6 to 110th St.

An East Harlem gem, Ricardo's Steakhouse has become one of the in-demand restaurant-lounges in East Harlem. This new-world Latino open kitchen steak house serves juicy steaks, lamb and pork chops, and seafood in an upscale spacious interior that features colorful Cuban and local artists' works on the exposed brick walls and a charming covered open-air terrace in the back that is heated when it gets cool. There isn't a bad cut of steak here, but the oysters and the mixed grill are also worth a try. You can also order some of the best lip-smacking mojitos and margaritas here. Another plus is that the service is fast and gracious. Reservations are recommended to avoid having to wait too long to be seated.

Savoy Bakery

170 E. 110th St., between Lexington and Third Aves. (212) 828-8896. www.savoybakery. com. Cuisine: Bakery. $. Mon–Fri 7am–7pm, Sat and Sun 8am–6pm. All major credit cards. Bus—M101, M102, M103. Subway—6 to 110th St.

Known for its fresh-baked breads and a gorgeous selection of pastries and cakes that taste as good as they look, the Savoy Bakery crossed the bridge from Tenafly, New Jersey, to open its first New York City location in East Harlem. It has been a good marriage for both the bakery and the East Harlem community. All the baked goods, which are prepared on-site to guarantee freshness, contain no trans fats, and the prices are very reasonable! Also, local residents are employed here. For all this Savoy has earned the loyal patronage of the neighborhood residents, who crowd the place especially in the morning for coffee and pastries. Soup is also available for lunch.

Sister's Caribbean Cuisine

1931 Madison Ave., at 124th St. (212) 410-3000. Cuisine: Caribbean. Breakfast, Lunch, Dinner. $$. Mon–Fri 11am–9pm, Sat and Sun 11am–8pm. Cash only. Bus—M101, M103, M104, M60, BX15. Subway—2, 3, 4, 5, 6, Metro North to 125th St.

Sister's Caribbean Cuisine has been serving up a variety of eats from various Caribbean islands since the late 1990s when the strip on Madison Ave. from 120th St. to 124th St. was revitalized, thanks to the development of North General Hospital and the Maple Court and Maple Gardens co-ops. Such delicacies include the Guyanese version of chicken, goat or vegetable roti wrapped in an in-house griddle curry-flavored flatbread after split chickpeas and potatoes have been added, jerk chicken with a mild bite, and dark brown masala curry chicken flavored with Caribbean and East Indian spices. Entrées are served with peas and rice infused with coconut milk and a choice of vegetables, including calaloo made with leafy dasheen greens stewed in coconut milk, and okra. North General Hospital staff crowd this place at lunchtime, so stake out your seat early at this tiny, attractively decorated, and sunny eatery.

SpaHa Café

1872 Lexington Ave., between 116th and 117th Sts. (212) 427-1767. Cuisine: Café. Breakfast, Lunch, Dinner. $. Mon–Fri 8:30am–7pm, Sat and Sun 8:30am–8pm. V, MC. Bus—M101, M102, M103, M116. Subway—6 to 116th St.

A bit of Paris landed in East Harlem when SpaHa (short for Spanish Harlem) Café opened its door. At this comfortable and friendly space, you can find great breads, pastries, coffees, and savory food (sandwiches, quiches, etc.) that have been sourced from some of the best gourmet suppliers like authentically French La Tropezienne Bakery, and the famous Balthazar Bakery, both of which bake from scratch every day. For lunch, dinner, and brunch, crisp salad bowls and gourmet soups complement paninis and sandwiches. An incredible farmers market filled with truffle oils, gourmet vinegars, mustards, sauces, homemade marmalades, soy products, organic, gluten-free, and sugar-free products, cage-free eggs, and tofu makes this café stand out in the neighborhood.

Uptown Veg

14 E. 125th St., between Fifth Ave. and Madison Aves. (212) 987-2660. Cuisine: Vegetarian, Smoothies, Juice Bar. Breakfast, Lunch, Dinner. $$. Daily 8am–10pm. All major credit cards. Bus—M1, M7, M60, M100, M101, M102, BX15. Subway—2, 3, Metro North to 125th St.

Formerly known as Uptown Juice Bar, Uptown Veg is probably Harlem's most popular vegetarian restaurant, judging from the long lines for buffet and made-to-order food or for the juice bar during lunch and dinner. The best deal is an option of three choices from the hot food bar for $6—it's a massive plate of food. The hot food bar has choices ranging from steamed broccoli to curries, rice and beans, plantain, and a lot of faux-chicken, such as barbecued "chicken" wings and faux-beef options. The juice bar offers a wide variety of juices named after ailments they apparently cure.

Yo In Yo Out

1569 Lexington Ave., between 100th and 101st Sts. (212) 987-5350. www.yoinyoout. com. Cuisine: Bistro. Breakfast, Lunch, Dinner, Prix Fixe. $$. Mon–Fri 8:30am–10pm, Sat 8:30am–11pm, Sun 9am–9pm. All major credit cards. Bus—M101, M102, M103. Subway—6 to 103rd St.

YO IN YO OUT

A traditional French bistro in terms of menu but with an ambience that is much more informal and laid back, Yo In Yo Out opened its small and cozy environment with crepes, salads, and sandwiches on the menu. The owner and chef **Yoanne** (which explains the Yo) **Magris**, who hails from France, shops daily at the market so the prix-fixe special is always a surprise and the desserts are simply scrumptious. The crepes, of which there is an impressive variety, rule here. Everything on the menu is reasonably priced with nothing exceeding $14, and the $1.20 house coffee is unheard of in New York. Also, if more than one dessert strikes your fancy, try the Assiette mini-dessert, which allows you to sample several tinier versions.

Dining and Live Entertainment

Amor Cubano Restaurant

2018 Third Ave., at 111th St. (212) 996-1220. www.amorcubanorestaurant.com. Cuisine: Cuban. Lunch, Dinner, Brunch. $$$. Daily 12pm–12am, Wed–Sun 7pm–11pm live entertainment. All major credit cards. Bus—M101, M102, M103. Subway—6 to 110th St.

Amor Cubano is the best place to go for an authentic night of Cuban entertainment and cuisine. Live music and dancing fill the front of the restaurant. In back, where the décor evokes a Cuban backyard patio complete with outdoor furniture and faux laundry hanging on clotheslines, you can hold quiet conversations while dining on typical Cuban dishes. Favorites include garlicky lechon asado—roast pork with bitter orange mojo sauce; vaca frita—shredded bits of steak fried with onions and garlic; the hearty garbanzos fritos—chickpeas crisped with smoked ham and bacon; or the more contemporary Cubano frito—Cuba's take on the hamburger, presented as two sliders made from ground beef, pork, and Spanish sausages. However, it is the music, not the food, that make the locals flock here. Live Latin music abounds from Wed–Sun, 7pm–11pm. On weekends, the talented house band, **Ray y Su Son Sonete**, belts out great son (Afro Cuban music), salsa, and rumba. On Thursdays the club's signature drink, mojitos in five different flavors, flows all night at the bar for $5. Every Tuesday trovadores (Cuban folksingers) are invited to perform starting at 7:30pm. Sunday brunch provides unlimited sangria in pineapple or red wine versions and bottomless mimosas.

Aurum Mediterranean Bar & Grill

2252 First Ave., between 115th and 116th Sts. (646) 719-1157. www.aurumnyc.com. Cuisine: Mediterranean, American. Dinner. $$$$. Mon–Thu 5pm–12pm, Fri–Sun 5pm–1am. All major credit cards. Bus—M101, M102, M103, M116. Subway—6 to 116th St.

A hidden gem in East Harlem, Aurum Mediterranean Bar & Grill offers fine dining with European ambience. This eatery prepares great Mediterranean dishes. Favorites include appetizers such as bruschetta with carmelized mushrooms and prosciutto, or the grilled merguez (lamb sausage) with sliced cucumber, tsatsiki (tangy yogurt), and fresh feta cheese drizzled with a balsamic reduction, and grilled entrees like rack of lamb, skirt steak and chicken, beef, and pork kabobs. The pastas and the sides of either garlic or yucca fries are a must-order. An added plus here is the romantic enclosed outdoor patio which offers exclusive privacy that outdoor sidewalk cafés lack. On Friday there is a jazz band and on Saturday there is a belly dancer entertaining.

Camaradas el Barrio Bar & Restaurant

2241 First Ave., at 115th St. (212) 348-2703. www.camaradaselbarrio.com. Cuisine: Latin American, Caribbean, sandwiches. Dinner, Sunday Brunch. $. Mon–Wed 4pm–1am, Thu–Sat 4pm–3:30am, Sun 12pm–10pm. Cash only. Bus—M15, M101, M102, M103, M116. Subway—6 to 116th St.

When it comes to rock en Español and Spanish-language pop, a scene has gradually been developing with the emergence of Camaradas El Barrio. It's a workers' public house where camaraderie is built atop a fine selection of wine, great beers from around the world, excellent music and a menu featuring "Puerto Rican pub food." The club books groups like **Yerbabuena**, an Afro-Rican band which plays Boricua roots music every Thursday night, and on Fridays various bands are booked including **Navegante**, an en Español–playing, turbocharged power trio fronted by singer and instrumentalist Jean Shepherd, who is of Puerto Rican and Peruvian descent. Among the band's fans is Carlos Santana, who recorded one of Shepherd's songs on his album *All That I Am*. In an environment that has a downtown chic look of exposed brick, a vintage sewing machine, and rough-hewn wooden benches, mouthwatering delights such as alcapurrias (meat fritters), mofongo (plantain mashed with pork rind and garlic), an array of salads, skewed satay chicken and shrimp, spicy calamari, Barrio burgers, and chocolate empanadas are served.

Chimney Barbecue and Sushi Bar & MILK Lounge

2056 Second Ave., between 105ᵗʰ and 106ᵗʰ Sts. (212) 360-1988. www.chimneybbq. com. Cuisine: Barbecue, French Asian Fusion, Sushi. Dinner. $$$$. Daily 5:30pm–11:30pm. Bar open 5pm–6pm and 2-for-1 drinks 6pm–7pm. V, MC, AmEx. Bus—M15, M101, M102, M103, M106. Subway—6 to 106ᵗʰ St.

Chimney Barbecue and Sushi Bar & MILK Lounge is located on the site of the legendary Christopher's, a Latin music dance club that featured artists such as Tito Puente, Eddie Palmieri, Ray Barretto, and Joe Cuba during its heyday in the seventies and eighties. Today, the new establishment pays homage to those roots while adding a twenty-first-century spin. A double-level room complete with a full-service bar, and an exotic menu of French/Asian fusion food served on the main level, while the MILK lounge above boasts an all-white lounging and dance area, together makes the Chimney a swinging 3,400 square feet of sensory sound, spirits, and gastronomic experience. Melding French cuisine with an Asian flair and just a twist of his African roots is Senegalese chef **Malik Fall**, who was executive chef at the East Village Boucarou Lounge. The eclectic menu includes appetizers like the Tango Mango ceviche, crab and corn cake, sugarcane grilled shrimp, with complementing entrees such as asado (Argentinean barbecued short ribs) Korean short ribs, spicy pork ribs, smoked barbecued ribs, pan-seared lamb chops, and every conceivable combination of sushi and salads. Lounge events include an after-work salsa dance party with live bands every Wednesday, and jazz, spoken word, house, and karaoke nights scheduled during the week.

Don Pedro's

1865 Second Ave., at 96ᵗʰ St. (212) 996-3274. www.donpedros.net. Cuisine: Euro Caribbean. Lunch, Dinner, Brunch. $$$$. Mon–Thu 11am–11pm, Sat and Sun 11am–1am. All major credit cards. Bus—M96, M101, M102, M103. Subway—6 to 96ᵗʰ St.

Don Pedro's, a Caribbean bistro that fuses Dominican, Cuban, and Puerto Rican cuisine, has become a neighborhood favorite since it opened in 2003. Diners can enjoy new takes on classic dishes such as mofongo and pernil or opt for one of chef **Rene Hernandez's** original signature dishes, such as Montadito Don Pedro (an appetizer of cured pork tenderloin, mancheo cheese, and piquillo pepper) and the flaming T-bone steak. The attractive two-level restaurant has a full-service bar that serves an array of cocktails including the popular mojito, which is made with champagne, and several varieties of sangria. Brunch is served from 11am to 3pm on Sunday. Most nights there is dancing á la DJ music.

FB Lounge

172 E. 106th St., between Lexington and Third Aves. (212) 348-3929. www.fondaboricua. com. Cuisine: Puerto Rican. Dinner. $$$. Tue–Sat 5pm–2am. All major credit cards. Bus—M101, M102, M103. Subway—6 to 103rd St.

In response to the overwhelming popularity of Latin Jazz Thursdays, the owners of La Fonda Boricua opened the FB Lounge right across the street. The lounge has become home to some of the most authentic live improvisational Afro-Caribbean and Latin music being played today. This is where New York City's best come to jam in the tradition of Machito and the Afro-Cubans of the 1940s, and on Thursday through Sunday night, you never know who is going to drop by to sit in. The lounge offers an exciting menu of both the new and the traditional, and continues in the La Fonda Boricua tradition of combining great food, music, and art in El Barrio. Oh yes, those who come to experience the unique sounds and flavors of the lounge are encouraged to let go and dance.

Kiosk

70 E. 116th St., between Madison and Park Aves. (212) 348-9010. www.mnkiosk.com. Cuisine: Moroccan, Mediterranean. Dinner. $$$. Sun–Thu 4:30pm–10pm, Fri and Sat 4:30pm–11pm. All major credit cards. Bus—M1, M102, M116. Subway—6 to 116th St.

North Africa has come to Harlem! Kiosk is the first Moroccan restaurant to come to East Harlem, adding to the recent multicultural dining and entertainment establishments to open in El Barrio. Host/owner **Mounir Najd**, a native of Casablanca, has blended Moroccan/Moorish design elements in the eatery's décor with classic Moroccan and Mediterranean cuisine and cultural offerings of hookah (water filtration smoking of herbal fruits) to create a unique and memorable dining experience. Some of the menu favorites are the savory tagines (which are slow-cooked casseroles of chicken, lamb, or fish), kabobs, couscous, and hummus dishes typical to the region. Every Saturday belly dancing is featured at 8pm and 10pm. Call to find out when Brazilian jazz is scheduled.

Mojito's Bar & Grill

227 E. 116th St., between Second and Third Aves. (212) 828-8635. Cuisine: Mexican. Lunch, Dinner. $$. Sun–Wed: 1pm–12am, Thu–Sat 1pm–3am. All major credit cards. Bus—M15, M101, M102, M103, M116. Subway—6 to 116th St.

Mojito's Bar & Grill lives up to its name by mixing up some amazing mojitos. And the Mexican establishment also mixes up a variety of delicious specialty drinks that can be chosen from a large cocktail menu. This bar and grill features a variety of moderately priced appetizers and entrees, cocktails, and live entertainment. The appetizers—especially the ceviches and the guacamole—are the winners here. Every Thursday, Friday, and Saturday you can dance to live Latin salsa, Cuban son, or R&B music provided by local bands. During the summer months there is an outdoor garden that patrons are welcome to enjoy.

Orbit East Harlem

2257 First Ave., at 116th St. (212) 348-818. www.orbiteastharlem.com. Cuisine: American. Dinner, Brunch. $$$. Sun–Tue 11am–11pm, Wed–Thu 11am–11:30pm, Fri–Sat 11am–12am. All major credit cards. Bus—M15, M116. Subway—6 to 116th St.

Part of what makes Orbit special is that it offers local residents and visitors alike weekly live music, drink specials, and a unique menu at reasonable prices in a relaxed atmosphere. Designated one of the Best Brunch Spots in New York by the *New York Post* in 2008, every brunch dish at this eatery comes in at $10 or less. Popular choices include the cornflakes French toast crunch, breakfast pasta, and a 10-ounce burger. All cocktails during brunch are priced at $5 and feature eleven different flavors of the popular mimosa. While the prices are wallet-friendly and the portions are generous, the best thing is the speed at which orders are delivered. There are also weekly specials prepared for dinner each night. Handmade pastas fill out a large chunk of the dinner menu, with daily raviolis like cod in sage and butter sauce representing the most unusual. Live salsa bands entertain every Friday night.

SHOPPING

Apparel

109-St. Inc.
1974 Third Ave., between 108th and 109th Sts. (212) 369-8360. Mon–Sat 10am–7pm, Sun 11am–6pm. All major credit cards. Bus—M101, M102, M103. Subway—6 to 110th St.

Large selection of Pelle/Pelle and other name-brand jeans, T-shirts, jackets, and more for men.

Ashley Stewart
1905 Third Ave., at 105th St. (212) 987-2630. www.ashleystewart.com. Mon–Sat 10am–7pm, Sun 11am–6pm. All major credit cards. Bus—M101, M102, M103, M106. Subway—6 to 103rd St.

(See Central Harlem description.)

Bolton's
175 E. 96th St. between Lexington and Third Aves. (646) 672-9253. www.boltonsstores.com. Mon–Fri 10am–8pm, Sat and Sun 10am–7pm. All major credit cards. Bus—M96, M101, M102, M103. Subway—6 to 96th St.

Brand-name women's clothes and accessories at discounted prices.

Cityline Footware
2154 Third Ave., at 116th St. (212) 369-7493. Mon–Thu 10:30–7pm, Fri and Sat 10:30–7:30pm, Sun 11am–5:30pm. All major credit cards. Bus—M101, M102, M103, M116. Subway—6 to 116th St.

Brand-name sneakers, boots, and sportswear for men.

HARLEM UNDERGROUND

Harlem Underground
20 E. 125th St., between Fifth and Madison Ave. (212) 987-9385. www.harlemunderground.com. Mon–Thu 10am–7pm, Fri and Sat 10am–8pm, Sun 12pm–6:30pm. V, MC, AmEx. Bus—M1, M7, M60, M100, M101, M102, BX15. Subway—2, 3, Metro North to 125th St.

Stylish designer and custom-made T-shirts.

Harlem Universal
2311 Second Ave., between 118th and 119th Sts. (212) 722-2200. Daily 9am–9pm. V, MC. Bus—M101, M102, M103, M116. Subway—6 to 116th St.

Custom T-shirts, clothes, sneakers, caps with embroidery/airbrush, and more.

Jans
2234 Third Ave., between 121st and 122nd Sts. (212) 427-4456. Mon–Sat 10am–7pm, Sun 11am–5pm. V, MC. Bus—M101, M102, M103. Subway—4, 5, 6 to 125th St.

Large selection of brand-name sneakers, jeans, polo shirts, and sportswear for men.

Motherhood Maternity

163 E. 125th St., between Lexington and Third Ave. (212) 987-8808. www.motherhood.com. Mon–Sat 10am–8pm, Sun 11am–6am. All major credit cards. Bus—M60, M100, M101, M103, BX15. Subway—4, 5, 6 Metro North to 125th St.

Maternity fashions at affordable prices.

Sociallite Accessories

1699 Lexington Ave., between 106th and 107th Sts. (212) 348-1384. Mon–Sat 11:30am–8pm. All major credit cards. Bus—M101, M102, M103. Subway—6 to 103rd St.

Nice boutique tucked away on Lexington Avenue which offers affordable costume jewelry, shoes, handbags, and so much more. The deals on the handbags make visiting this shop worthwhile.

THE BROWNSTONE

The Brownstone

24 E. 125th St., between Fifth and Madison Aves. (212) 996-7980. www.thebrownstonewoman.com. Mon–Sat 11am–7:30pm, Sun 11am–7pm. All major credit cards. Bus—M1, M7, M60, M100, M101, M102, BX15. Subway—2, 3, Metro North to 125th St.

Fashionable women's clothes and accessories; if you are looking for that special something, start here! Carries one-of-a-kind African American designer clothing and jewelry. Ask about the Harlem charm bracelet, a fine sterling silver bracelet with the 125th St. sign, chicken and waffles, brownstone charms, and a new line of charms that have recently been developed.

The Children's Place

153 E. 125th St., between Lexington and Third Aves. (212) 348-3607. www.childrensplace.com. Mon–Sat 9am–8pm, Sun 10am–6pm. All major credit cards. Bus—M60, M100, M101, M103, BX15. Subway—4, 5, 6 Metro North to 125th St.

(See Central Harlem description.)

V. I. M.

2239 Third Ave., at 122nd St. (212) 369-5033. www.vim.com. Mon–Sat 9:30am–7pm, Sun 11am–6pm. V, MC, Dis. Bus—M60, M100, M101, M103, BX15. Subway—4, 5, 6 to 125th St.

(See West Harlem description.)

Cosmetics/Salons/Spas/Skin Care

Exotic Fragrances

1645 Lexington Ave., at 104th St. (212) 787-3645. www.exoticfragrances.com. Mon–Sat 9:30am–6pm. V, MC. Bus—M101, M102, M103, M106. Subway—6 to 103rd St.

Fragrance oils, essential oils, lotions, bath oils, soaps, incense, accessories, and more, wholesale and retail.

Nicholas Variety
5 E. 125th St., between Fifth and Madison Aves. (212) 289-3628. www.nicholasreggae.com. Mon–Sat 9am–8pm, Sun 12pm–6pm. All major credit cards. Bus—M1, M7, M60, M100, M101, M102, BX15. Subway—2, 3, Metro North to 125th St.

2035 Fifth Ave., between 125th and 126th Sts. (212) 289-3628. www.nicholasreggae.com. Mon–Sat 9am–8pm, Sun 12pm–6pm. All major credit cards. Bus—M1, M7, M60, M100, M101, M102, BX15. Subway—2, 3, Metro North to 125th St.

Bath and body oils, incense and scented candles, oils, T–shirts, books, cultural posters and statues, and all things Bob Marley, wholesale and retail.

The Body Shop
One E. 125th St., at Fifth Ave. (212) 348-4900. www.thebodyshop-usa.com. Mon–Sat 10am–8pm, Sun 11am–7pm. All major credit cards. Bus—M1, M7, M60, M100, M101, M102, BX15. Subway—2, 3, Metro North to 125th St.

Natural products for your body, bath, skin care, makeup, hair, fragrances, and more.

Discount Stores

V & M American Outlet Center
1950 Third Ave., at 107th St. (212) 423-1066. Mon–Sat 9:30am–7:30pm, Sun 10am–6:30pm. All major credit cards. Bus—M101, M102, M103. Subway—6 to 110th St.

2228 Third Ave., at 120th St. (212) 987-6749. All major credit cards. Bus—M101, M103, M106. Subway—6 to 116th St.

Factory outlet and discount department store featuring home furnishings, furniture, electronics, clothing, and more.

Food

Pathmark Supermarket
160 E. 125th St., at Lexington Ave. (212) 427-3741. www.pathmark.com. 24 hours. All major credit cards. Bus—M60, M101, M103, BX15. Subway—4, 5, 6, Metro North to 125th St.

Supermarket with rooftop parking that is free for two hours when grocery receipt is shown.

Home Furnishings

H & M Art & Home Furnishing Center
17 E. 125th St., between Fifth and Madison Aves. (212) 831-9176. Mon–Sat 10am–8pm, Sun 12pm–6pm. All major credit cards. Bus—M1, M7, M60, M100, M101, M102, BX15. Subway—2, 3, Metro North to 125th St.

Home decorations and furniture, unframed and framed art, posters, and more. They also offer custom framing services.

Latino Specialties

Hand Made in Puerto Rico

2127 Third Ave., at 116th St., (212) 289-1368. Tue–Sun 12pm–7pm. Cash only. Bus—M101, M102, M106, M116. Subway—6 to 116th St.

The small shop serves as the community welcome and information center. It's somewhat of a museum for historical and cultural artifacts from Puerto Rico—you'll need to ask exactly what's for sale or what's just on display. Spanish and English are spoken.

Raices Dominicanas Cigars

2250 First Ave., between 115th and 116th Sts. (212) 410-6824. Daily 10am–11:30pm. Cash only. Bus—M101, M102, M103, M116. Subway—6 to 116th St.

Cigar shop offering hand-rolled cigars.

Music

Casa Latina Music Shop

151 E. 116th St., between Lexington and Third Aves. (212) 427-6062. www.casalatinamusic.com. Mon–Thu 10am–6:30pm, Fri and Sat 10am–7pm. V, MC, AmEx. Bus—M101, M102, M103, M116. Subway—6 to 116th St.

A family-owned business for more than thirty years, this dying breed of retail music stores still thrives in East Harlem. The shop sells Latin music CDs, musical instruments, books, DVDs, videos, and even carries a line of jackets and jewelry.

Rincon Musical

1936 Third Ave., at 107th St. (212) 828-8604. www.rinconmusical.com. Mon–Thu 10am–7pm, Fri and Sat 10am–8pm, Sun 11am–6pm. All major credit cards. Bus—M101, M102, M103, M106. Subway—6 to 103rd St.

Music CDs, musical instruments, books, sheet music, DVDs, videos, and more.

Sneakers/Shoes

Danny K. Fashions

1992 Third Ave., between 109th and 110th Sts. (212) 464-8377. Mon–Fri 10am–7pm, Sat 10am–7pm, Sun 10am–6pm. All major credit cards. Bus—M101, M102, M103. Subway—6 to 110th St.

2026 Third Ave., between 111th and 112th Sts. (212) 464-8377. Bus—M101, M102, M103. Subway—6 to 110th St.

Large selection of brand-name sneakers for men, women, and children. They also have leather jackets, T-shirts, and more.

Foot Locker

1911 Third Ave., between 105th and 106th Sts. (212) 828-3871. www.footlocker.com. Mon–Sat 10am–8pm, Sun 11am–7pm. All major credit cards. Bus—M101, M102, M103, M106. Subway—6 to 103rd St.

(See West Harlem description.)

Footaction
165 E. 125th St., between Lexington and Third Aves. (646) 672-0205. www.footaction.com. Mon–Sat 10am–8pm, Sun 11am–7pm. All major credit cards. Bus—M60, M100, M101, M103, BX15. Subway—4, 5, 6, Metro North to 125th St.

Brand-name sneakers, jeans, clothes, and accessories for men, women, and children.

New Shoe World
2115 Third Ave., between 115th and 116th Sts. (212) 876-8088. Mon–Sat 10am–7:30pm, Sun 11am–5pm. V, MC. Bus—M101, M102, M103, M116. Subway—6 to 116th St.

Brand-name sneakers, including Nike, Timberland, Reebok, Adidas, New Balance, and many more.

Payless
163 E. 125th St., between Lexington and Third Aves. (646) 672-9894. www.payless.com._Mon–Sat 9am–8pm, Sun 10am–6pm. All major credit cards. Bus—M60, M100, M101, M103, BX15. Subway—4, 5, 6 to 125th St.

1897 Third Ave., at 105th St. (212) 876-2826. Mon–Fri 9:30am–8pm, Sat 9am–8pm, Sun 10am–7pm. Bus—M101, M102, M103, M106. Subway—6 to 103rd St.

2143 Third Ave., at 117th St. (212) 289-2251. Mon–Fri 9:30am–8pm, Sat 9am–8pm, Sun 10am–7pm. Bus—M101, M102, M103, M116. Subway—6 to 116th St.

(See Central Harlem description.)

Pro Trend II
155 E. 116th St., between Lexington and Third Aves. (212) 369-3292. Mon–Sat 9:30am–7:30pm, Sun 10:30am–6:30pm. All major credit cards. Bus—M101, M102, M103, M116. Subway—6 to 116th St.

Large selection of brand-name sneakers, boots, and clothes for men.

Thrift Stores

Goodwill Third Avenue
2231 Third Ave., between 121st and 122nd Sts. (212) 410-0973. Mon–Sat 9:30am–8pm, Sun 10am–7pm. All major credit cards. Bus—M101, M103. Subway—6 to 125th St.

One of the most well-known thrift stores in the country, this Goodwill store features gently used and often brand-new home goods, furniture, accessories, and clothing for men, women, and children.

Wine/Liquor

K&D Wines & Spirits
1366 Madison Ave., between 95th and 96th Sts. (212) 289-1818. www.kdwine.com_. Mon–Sat 9am–9pm, Sat 9am–9pm. All major credit cards. Bus—M1, M2, M3, M4, M96. Subway—6 to 96th St.

Great wine selection, a knowledgeable and friendly staff, and free delivery in Manhattan. Also holds regular wine tastings.

Lexington Wine & Liquor
2010 Lexington Ave., at 122nd St. (212) 348-1313. Mon–Thu 9am–10pm, Fri and Sat 9am–12am, Sun 12pm–5pm. All major credit cards. Bus—M101, M103. Subway—4, 5, 6 to 125th St.

Nice selection of wines and spirits.

Madison Avenue Wines

1793 Madison Ave., at 116th St. (212) 987-0099. Mon–Thu 11am–9pm, Fri and Sat 11am–10pm, Sun 1pm–7pm. All major credit cards. Bus—M1, M102, M116. Subway—2, 3 to 116th St.

Large selection of affordable wines and spirits, with free delivery and free wine tasting on Sat 4pm–7pm.

Rivera Liquor

2025 First Ave., at 104th St. (212) 876-6007. Mon–Sat 8am–12am, Sun 12pm–9pm. V, MC, Dis. Bus—M15, M106. Subway—6 to 106th St.

Nice selection of wines and spirits.

SIGNIFICANT FAITH-BASED INSTITUTIONS AND BURIAL GROUNDS

St. Cecilia's Church

112–120 E. 106th St., between Park and Lexington Aves. (212) 534-1350. www.saint-cecilia-parish.org. Bus—M101, M102, M103, M106. Subway—6 to 103rd St.

St. Cecilia's Church was built in 1883 and was originally the church of the German and Irish community that resided in the area. It was the second Roman Catholic Church built in East Harlem, and has always served a diverse parish. First Germans, then the Irish worshipped here until the nineteenth century, followed by a Spanish-speaking congregation in the twentieth century. Using the plans of **Napoleon Le Brun**, the same architect who designed the Metropolitan Life Building, **Father Michael J. Phelan** acted as general contractor to construct the current building. He commissioned the services of carpenters, plasterers, tinsmiths, bricklayers, etc., who were mostly members of the parish, and thereby saved parishioners almost $50,000 in contracting fees. The Romanesque Revival structure, which was completed in 1887, reflects the masterful use of brick and terra-cotta especially evident in the arched panel depicting Saint Cecilia, patron saint of music, playing an organ. The Regina Anglo-reum was designed by architects Neville & Bagge and completed in 1907. The building was designated a landmark in 1976. Today the congregation consists of Italians, Jamaicans, Philippinos, Puerto Ricans, Dominicans, Africans, Germans, and Irish, to name a few. The parish's reverence and love for music, both sacred and secular, is exemplified by chorister Gilbert Price, who continues to sing at St. Cecilia's, in addition to his stage and television commitments, whenever he is in New York. There are four Folk Masses at St. Cecilia's every Sunday, and three different Folk Masses for young people. The "cuatro," an instrument of Puerto Rican heritage, is used together with the organ at the 11:15am Sunday Mass or on special occasions, such as the exceptionally beautiful Mass of Thanksgiving, or Christmas Midnight Mass, when the Nativity scene is reenacted.

Church of All Saints

47 E. 129th St., at Madison Ave. (212) 534-3535. Bus—M1, M7, M102. Subway—2, 3, 4, 5, 6 to 125th St.

CHURCH OF ALL SAINTS

Dedicated in 1893, the Church of All Saints is an imposing and quite grand church that is often called the **"St. Patrick's of Harlem."** The ornate Venetian Gothic building was designed by James Renwick, Jr., who was also the architect for St. Patrick's Cathedral, Grace Episcopal Church, and the Smithsonian Institution in Washington, DC. Designated a landmark in 2007, All Saints is noted for its patterned brickwork, terra-cotta details, wheel windows at the clerestory level, and tall bell tower. The vaulted interior is also rich in details, including comfortable hand-carved pews, murals, and stained glass. All Saints was built as a parish for the neighborhood's Irish immigrants. Today, the congregation is predominantly African American and Nigerian. Its Gospel Mass including gospel singing is an outstanding experience not to be missed.

Elmendorf Reformed Church

171 E. 121ˢᵗ St., at Third Ave. (212) 534-5856. www.elmendorfrca.org. Bus—M101, M103. Subway—4, 5, 6 to 125ᵗʰ St.

The Reformed Low Dutch Church of Haarlem or **"First Church of Harlem"** was organized under a Royal Charter granted in 1660 and was also known as the **First Collegiate Church**. It is now the Elmendorf Reformed Church, the oldest functioning church in Harlem. The first church, originally located at 127ᵗʰ Street and First Avenue, was built between 1655–67 and connected to the **"Negro Burying Ground"**. The second church built of stone was erected between 1685–87 and was destroyed during the Revolutionary War. The only remaining trace of the second church is a bell that was cast in Amsterdam, Holland, in 1734, and it is on display in the rear of the current sanctuary. After the country gained its independence in 1776, the denomination broke away from the old-world structure and became the Reformed Church in America. In 1824 the fourth church was completed by celebrated architect **Martin E. Thompson** at Third Avenue and E. 121ˢᵗ Street. It was altered in 1852 and later in 1884 was turned to face the side street enabling the congregation to sell their valuable corner lot. A modern parish house was erected in 1890 with the thought that the two buildings would serve as a mission and settlement house. In 1886 **Dr. Joachim Elmendorf** came to the economically disadvantaged church. Under his leadership a parish house and Sunday school building was designed in a neo-Classical style by John Ireland and built between 1893–94. Unfortunately, Elmendorf died in 1908, the collegiate system was abandoned, and the church designed by Thompson was razed. The parish was redesigned as the Elmendorf Reformed Chapel, named after Dr. Elmendorf. As the community began to racially change, the more affluent members left for the Upper East Side. **Rev. Donald DeYoung**, who led the church from 1957–1975, dug in his heels and the church became known as a "Protestant parish for all people" that served everyone. In 1978 the first African American pastor was installed. The first woman pastor, who is also African American, **Rev. Patricia A. Singletary**, was installed in 2002.

Harlem's African Burying Ground

127ᵗʰ St., at First Ave. Bus—M15, M116. Subway—6 to 116ᵗʰ St.

Under the direction of Governor **Peter Stuyvesant, Haarlem** was the second village organized in Manhattan. In 1658, slaves were used to construct a ten-mile road from **Greenwich Village** to the village of Haarlem. The village consisted of the Reformed Low Dutch Church, an inn, a mill, homes, farms, a ferry landing, and an Indian trail. Recently, when construction began to replace the Willis Avenue Bridge and to rehabilitate the 126ᵗʰ Street Bus Depot, the "Negro Burying Ground" was discovered between 126ᵗʰ and 127ᵗʰ Streets and First Avenue from old maps used to survey the land. The community is hoping that a park, promenade, or plaza will be built to properly honor the history of the cemetery and the history of early Haarlem. There will be no way to know for certain until the soil is dug up if there are remains and artifacts, but the prospect of such a discovery is being greeted both anxiously and eagerly. This would make it one of the exceptionally few remaining African American historical sites from the Colonial period.

Holy Rosary Church

444 E. 119ᵗʰ St., between First and Pleasant Aves. (212) 534-0740. www.nyholyrosary.org. Bus—M15, M116. Subway—6 to 116ᵗʰ St.

In 1884 His Eminence **John Cardinal McCloskey** established a new parish in East Harlem. At that time there was no Catholic church in East Harlem east of Third Avenue. It was inevitable that the rapidly

developing area would see the founding of two ethnic churches: **Our Lady of Mount Carmel** on 115th St. for the Italians and **Our Lady of the Holy Rosary** on E. 119th St. for the Germans and the Irish. It was called Holy Rosary in honor of **Mary, Queen of the Most Holy Rosary**. Under the first pastor, the **Rev. Joseph A. Byron**, four lots were purchased on 119th Street. Fortunately, St. Cecilia's Parish had finished the basement of their new church and no longer needed the old wooden church. In the summer of 1884 the old church was dismantled, floated up the East River to 119th Street, and reassembled at the site where the present church now stands. The work on the rectory was completed in the summer of 1887. The current church building, constructed in the Byzantine-Romanesque style of architecture, was completed in 1900. To accommodate the diversity of the parish, Holy Rosary now conducts services in Italian, Spanish, and English.

HOLY ROSARY CHURCH

Our Lady of Mount Carmel
449 E. 115th St., at First Ave. (212) 534-0681. Bus—M15, M116. Subway—6 to 116th St.

Even though East Harlem was the site of the third *Little Italy* in New York City, the Church of Our Lady of Mount Carmel is the first Italian parish established in the city. Also known in the early days as *the parish of the Italians in New York*, the history of the Our Lady of Mount Carmel is closely associated with the immigration of Italians to America. Typical of all of the *Little Italys* was the celebration of the popular feasts that were enjoyed in their native Italian towns and villages. The feast of Our Lady Of Mount Carmel was first held in East Harlem in 1881. This celebration led to the establishment of a church dedicated to the Blessed Mother in 1887. With the completion of the church came the arrival of the **Statue of the Blessed Mother**. The statute came from Italy and was adorned with precious garments, including the Madonna's dress made in India and valued at $8,000, and the gold crowns for the Madonna and child that are adorned with precious stones. In 1905 the papacy held an official coronation for the statue, making it one of only three images that enjoy the honor bestowed by pontifical authority. The other coronations include Our Lady of Perpetual Help in New Orleans, Louisiana, and the Lady of Guadalupe in Mexico. The Feast of Our Lady of Mount Carmel is held annually in July and includes a festival and procession from the Church through the streets of East Harlem. Although the procession has dwindled down to a few hundred people, at one time more than 500,000 people attended. Catholics from around the world visit the statue due to several documented miracles it is believed have been performed by the Blessed Mother.

St. Paul's Church
121 E. 117th St., between Park and Lexington Aves. (212) 534-4422. www.stpaulchurchive. org. Bus—M101, M102, M103, M116. Subway—6 to 116th St.

St. Paul's Church is one of the pioneer Catholic churches in New York City. It ranks among the first six Catholic churches erected in the city. Founded in 1834 when Harlem was little more than wilderness, for many years before its founding, St. Patrick's Old Cathedral was the only church in Manhattan north of Canal Street. It was necessary for some of the priests attached to St. Patrick's to attend to all the Catholics scattered throughout the forest-like parts of Manhattan's northern sections. They said mass in private homes and in barns. St. Paul's current imposing late Romanesque Revival structure, designed

by Neville & Bagge, is built of brick, with a facade of Indiana limestone. It was completed in 1905 and spans 160 feet in length and 5,060 feet in breadth, with nine exits. There is seating for 1,300, with individual seats and individual kneelers. Underneath the brick and stone is a steel frame, the cross beams of which are encased in solid oak that are artistically carved. This grand old parish has undergone tremendous population changes. Of the founding Irish who were in the vast majority during the first century of its life, only a sparse few hundred of their line remain at the church. Catering to the Spanish-speaking residents who now reside in the area, Sunday Mass is conducted in Spanish, and Spanish-speaking priests are available for confession. Though the area is now predominantly Puerto Rican, and more and more Mexicans have settled in the area, every nation under the sun is represented in this Catholic parish.

ST. PAUL'S CHURCH

CHURCHES WITH GOSPEL SERVICES

Bethel Gospel Assembly
2–26 E. 120th St., between Fifth and Madison Aves. Bus—M1, M7, M116, M102. Subway—2, 3, 6 to 116th St. Sun 8am and 11:30am.

East Ward Missionary Baptist Church
2011 First Ave., between 103rd and 104th Sts. Bus—M15, M106. Subway—6 to 103rd St. Sun 11am.

Second Spanish Baptist Church
163 E. 102nd St., between Lexington and Third Aves. Bus—M101, M102, M103. Subway—6 to 103rd St. Sun 11:30am.

PARKS

Central Park (East and Central Harlem)
Bus—M1, M2, M3, M4, M10, M96, M106. Subway—B, C, 2, 3, 6 to 110th St.

Central Park, both a National Historic Landmark and the first New York City Scenic Landmark, is located between 59th and 110th Streets between Central Park West (Eighth Ave.) and Fifth Avenue, and is 843 acres in size. The northern area of the park is located in both East and Central Harlem. It is among the most famous parks in the world and was the first landscaped public park in the United States. The land for the park was purchased for $5 million in 1856 and consisted of swamps, bluffs, and rocky outcroppings. In 1857 the Central Park Commission held the country's first landscape design contest and selected the **Greensward Plan** submitted by Frederick Law Olmsted and Calvert Vaux, considered the founders of the landscape architecture profession in the United States. Entirely man-made, Central Park is one of the urban wonders of the world, a green oasis in the midst of the great concrete high-rise landscape of New York City. The building of the park was one of the nineteenth century's most massive public projects, with some 200,000 workers used to pull off this great feat. The park first opened for public use in the winter of 1859.

The park contains eighteen different entrances, nearly fifty fountains and monuments, twenty-one playgrounds, fifty-one sculptures, and thirty-six bridges and arches. There are 58 miles of pedestrian paths, 4.5 miles of bridle paths, 6.5 miles of park drives and 7 miles of benches (nearly 9,000 benches in total). Today there are 26,000 trees, including 1,700 American elms. It is visited by over 25 million people each year. Some of the favorite places to visit in the park are the **Great Lawn**, where the New York Philharmonic and the Metropolitan Opera hold two free concerts in the summer; the **Delacorte Theatre**, which is home to "Shakespeare in the Park"; **Strawberry Fields**, which is the garden of peace built in memory of Beatles member John Lennon; **Summer-Stage** at Rumsey Playfield, where music, spoken word, and dance performances are held during the summer; and **Wollman Ice Skating Rink**, to name a few.

In the portion of the park located in Harlem, you will find the **Conservatory Garden**, which is the only formal garden in Central Park; the **Harlem Meer**, an 11-acre lake that makes it the second-largest man-made body of water in the park; the **Charles A. Dana Discovery Center**, which is the park's only environmental educational center; the **Block House**, a fort still standing from the War of 1812; **Lasker Pool and Rink**; and **Duke Ellington Circle**, featuring the first monument in New York City dedicated to an African American and the first memorial in the United States honoring jazz music giant Duke Ellington.

Facilities: Baseball fields, basketball courts, bicycling and greenways, dog runs, fishing, horseback riding trails, ice skating rinks, swimming pool, nature centers, paddleboat, rowboat, and canoe rentals, playgrounds, recreation centers, restaurants, soccer fields, tennis courts, volleyball courts, zoos, and aquariums.

M arcus Garvey Park

Bus—M1, M7, M60, M100, M101, M102, M104, BX15. Subway—A, B, C, D, 2, 3, 4, 5, 6, Metro North to 125th St.

Marcus Garvey Park, one of the oldest parks in New York City, is located between 120th and 124th Streets between Fifth and Madison Avenues, and is 20 acres in size. In approximately 1835, the park's land was acquired and the park opened in 1840. Originally named Mount Morris Park (for which the surrounding neighborhood's historic district is named), in 1973 the park was renamed in honor of Marcus Garvey (1887–1940), who was a publisher, journalist, entrepreneur, and crusader for Black Nationalism and who, in 1919, established the Universal Negro Improvement Association. The park is home to the

only surviving fire watchtower, which was designed by Julius Kroehl and erected in 1856. It was declared a landmark in 1967 because of its unique post-and-lintel cast-iron construction, which provided the prototype framing for the modern-day skyscraper, and was placed on the National Register of Historic Places in 1976. The park is also home to the **Pelham Fritz Recreation Center**, which contains a state-of-the-art physical fitness center, a 1,700-seat amphitheater (which was a gift from Broadway musical giant Richard Rodgers, who grew up across from the park in the early 1900s), and the **Harlem Little League**, which won the Mid-Atlantic Championship in 2002. The Amphitheater is the site for two popular annual events—the Charlie Parker Jazz Festival in late August and the two-day Dance Harlem Festival in September.

Facilities: Basketball courts, two dog runs, Olympic-size pool, playgrounds, recreation center that houses a fitness center containing cardiovascular equipment and a weight room, baseball field, barbecue area, African drumming circle, senior citizen program, computer resource center, and amphitheater where summer cultural events are staged.

T homas Jefferson Park

Bus—M15, M116, Subway—6 to 110th St. and 116th St.

Thomas Jefferson Park is located between 111th and 114th Streets between First Avenue and FDR Drive, and is 15.5 acres in size. Although the park was planned and named by the **Board of Aldermen** in 1894, the land for the park wasn't acquired until 1897. It opened on October 7, 1905, to provide organized play for the children of "Little Italy," the name for the surrounding neighborhood which was overcrowded with tenements. The park is named after **Thomas Jefferson** (1743–1826), who

was the third President of the United States, the author of the Declaration of Independence, and one of our Founding Fathers. The park is home to two sculptures that were installed in the park in 1995: **Tomorrow's Wind**, created by African American artist **Melvin Edwards**, and **El Arbor De Esperanza** (Tree of Hope) by artist **L. Brower Hatcher.**

Facilities: Basketball courts, dog runs, pools, playground, barbecue areas, baseball fields, handball courts, running tracks, soccer fields, and a recreation center that contains a physical fitness center and offers boxing, fencing, martial arts, and aerobics classes.

GARAGES

117th Street Corporation
220 E. 117th St., between Second and Third Aves. 7am–12am/Indoor/Valet/Credit and Cash.

Aspire One
1860 Park Ave., at 127th St. 7am–8pm/Outdoor/Valet/Cash-Only.

Champion 126 LLC-Parking Garage
162 E. 126th St., between Lexington and Third Aves. 24 Hrs/Outdoor/Valet/Credit and Cash.

East 105 Street Parking
156 E. 105th St., between Lexington and Third Aves. 24 Hrs/Indoor/Valet/Credit and Cash.

HV & M Parking Corporation
1325 Fifth Ave., between 111th and 112th Sts. 24 Hrs/Indoor/Valet/Cash-Only.

Imperial Parking
480 E. 101st St., between First and Second Aves. 24 Hrs/Indoor/Valet/Credit and Cash.

Lease Parking
158 E. 108th St., between Lexington and Third Aves. 24 Hrs/Outdoor/Valet/Credit and Cash.

Manhattan Parking
440 E. 102nd St., between First Ave. and FDR Drive. 24 Hrs/Indoor/Self/Cash-Only.

Merit Parking
12 E. 107th St., at Fifth Ave. 24 Hrs/Indoor/ Valet/Cash-Only.

Metropolitan Storage
1918 First Ave., at 97th St. 24 Hrs/Outdoor/Valet/Cash-Only.

385 E. 97th St., between First and Second Aves. Mon–Fri 7am–6pm/Outdoor/Valet/Cash-Only.

MPG MP 97
266 E. 97th St., between Second and Third Aves. 24 Hrs/Indoor/Valet/Credit and Cash.

Park & Go
179 E. 108th St., between Lexington and Third Aves. 24 Hrs/Indoor/Valet/Cash-Only.

Parking Guys 99pm
1559–1563 Lexington Ave., between 99th and 100th Sts. 6am–12am/Outdoor/Valet/Credit and Cash.

Rapid Park 334 Parking
302–04 E. 96th St., between First and Second Aves. 6am–1am/Indoor/Valet/Credit and Cash.

Taino Towers Garage
221 E. 122nd St., between Second and Third Aves. 24 Hrs/Indoor/Valet/Cash-Only.

SERVICE STATIONS

BP Service Stations
1890 Park Ave., at 129th St.

255 E. 125th St., between Second and Third Aves.

Getty Service Station
348 E. 106th St., at First Ave.

Shell Service Stations
1599 Lexington Ave., at 102nd St.

1855 First Ave., at 96th St.

2276 First Ave., at 117th St.

LIBRARIES/INTERNET

Libraries with Free Internet

125th St. Branch
224 E. 125th St., between Second and Third Aves. (212) 534-5050. Mon and Wed 11am–6pm, Tue and Thu 11am–7pm, Fri 11am–5pm, Sat 10am–5pm.

Aguilar Branch
174 E. 110th St., between Lexington and Third Aves. (212) 534-2930. Mon and Wed 10am–6pm, Tue and Thu 10am–7pm, Fri 12pm–5pm, Sat 10am–5pm.

WI-FI

Internet Café

Net Plaza Café Internet
206 E. 116th St. (212) 876-5407. Bus—M101, M102, M103, M116. Subway—6 to 116th St.

POSTAL SERVICES

U.S. Postal Service/Hellgate Station
153 E. 110th St., between Lexington and Third Aves. (212) 860-1896. Mon–Fri 8am–5pm, Sat 8am–4pm.

U.S. Postal Service/Lincolnton Station
2266 Fifth Ave., at 138th St. (212) 281-9781. Mon–Fri 8am–5pm, Sat 8am–4pm.

U.S. Postal Service/Triborough Station
173 E. 124th St., between Lexington and Third Aves. (212) 534-0865. Mon–Fri 8am–5pm, Sat 8am–4pm.

UPS Store #6166
30 E. 125th St. between Madison and Fifth Aves. (212) 722-8203. Mon–Fri 8am–8pm, Sat 10am–4pm.

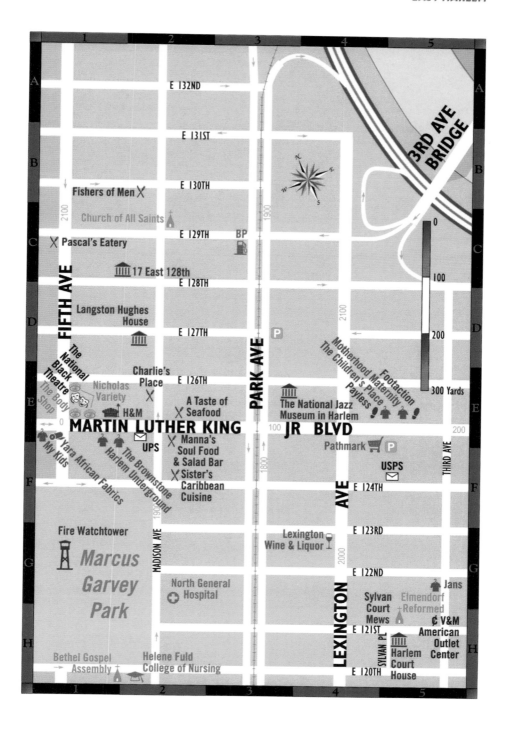

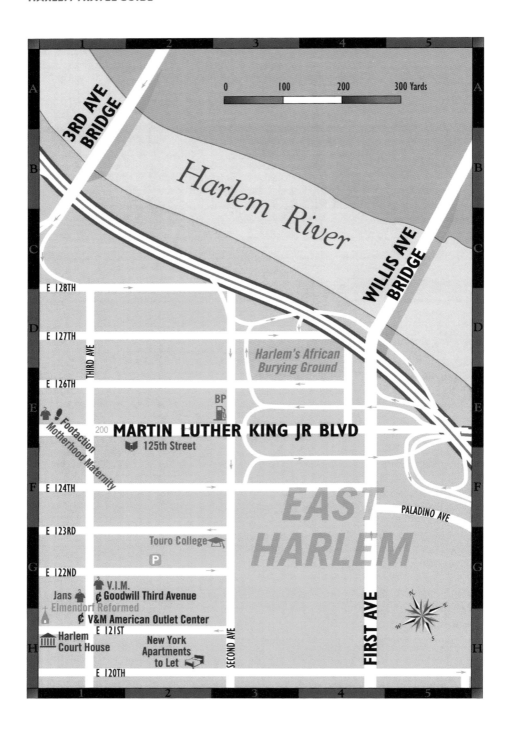

East Harlem Map A1

17 East 128th, C2
A Taste of Seafood, E2
Bethel Gospel Assembly, H1
BP, C3
Charlie's Place, E2
Church of All Saints, C2
Elmendorf Reformed, H5
Fire Watchtower, G1
Fishers of Men, B2
Footaction, E5
H&M, E1
Harlem Court House, H5
Harlem Underground, E1
Helene Fuld College of Nursing, H2
Jans, G5
Langston Hughes House, D2
Lexington Wine & Liquor, G4
Manna's Soul Food & Salad Bar, E2
Marcus Garvey Park, G1
Motherhood Maternity, E5
My Kids, E1
Nicholas Variety, E1
Pascal's Eatery, C1
Pathmark, E4
Payless, E4

Sister's Caribbean Cuisine, F2
Sylvan Court Mews, G4
The Body Shop, E1
The Brownstone, E1
The Children's Place, E5
The National Black Theatre, E1
The National Jazz Museum in Harlem, E3
UPS, E2
USPS, F5
V&M American Outlet Center, H5
Yara African Fabrics, E1

East Harlem Map A2

125th Street Branch NYPL, E2
BP, E3
Elmendorf Reformed, H1
Footaction, E1
Goodwill Third Avenue, G1
Harlem's African Burying Ground, D3
Harlem Court House, H1
Jans, G1
Motherhood Maternity, E1
New York Apartments to Let, H2
Touro College, G3
V.I.M., G1
V&M American Outlet Center, H1

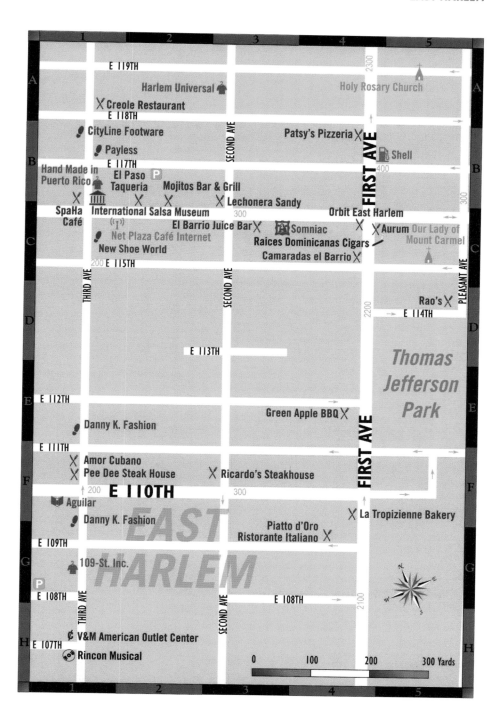

Thomas
Jefferson
Park

EAST
HARLEM

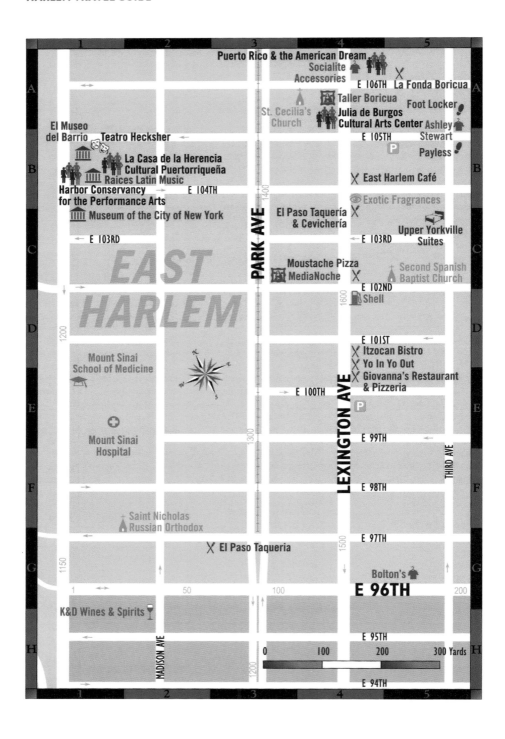

Puerto Rico & the American Dream
Socialite
Accessories
E 106TH   La Fonda Boricua
Taller Boricua
St. Cecilia's   Julia de Burgos   Foot Locker
Church   Cultural Arts Center   Ashley
E 105TH   Stewart
El Museo
del Barrio   Teatro Hecksher
Payless
La Casa de la Herencia
Cultural Puertorriqueña
Raices Latin Music   East Harlem Café
Harbor Conservancy   E 104TH
for the Performance Arts   Exotic Fragrances
Museum of the City of New York   El Paso Taquería
& Cevichería   Upper Yorkville
E 103RD   E 103RD   Suites

EAST
Moustache Pizza
MediaNoche   Second Spanish
Baptist Church
E 102ND
HARLEM   1600   Shell

1200   E 101ST
Itzocan Bistro
Yo In Yo Out
Mount Sinai   Giovanna's Restaurant
School of Medicine   & Pizzeria

E 100TH
Mount Sinai   E 99TH
Hospital

THIRD AVE
Saint Nicholas   E 98TH
Russian Orthodox

E 97TH
1150   El Paso Taqueria   1500

Bolton's
1   50   100   **E 96TH**   200

K&D Wines & Spirits   E 95TH

MADISON AVE   1200   E 94TH

PARK AVE   1400

LEXINGTON AVE   1300

0   100   200   300 Yards

1   2   3   4   5

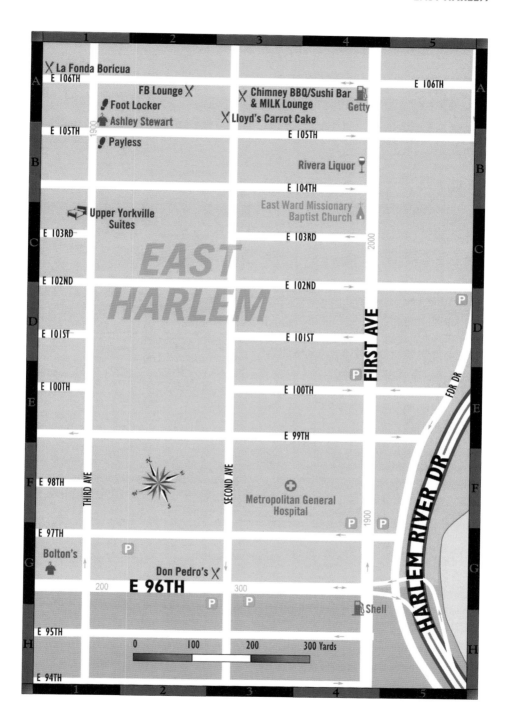

East Harlem Map B1

109-St. Inc., G5
Aguilar Branch NYPL, F5
Amor Cubano, F5
Art for Change, H4
Casa Latina Music Shop, B4
CityLine Footware, B5
Creole Restaurant, A5
Danny K. Fashion, E5
Danny K. Fashion, F5
Duke Ellington Circle, F1
Gran Piatto d'Oro, B1
Hand Made in Puerto Rico, B5
International Salsa Museum, B5
Kiosk, C3
Madison Avenue Wines, B2
New Shoe World, C5
Ottomanelli Bros, E1
Payless, B5
Pee Dee Steak House, F5
Piatto d'Oro II Ristorante Italiano, A1
Pro Trends II, B4
Puerto Rico & the American Dream, H4
Rincon Musical, H5
Savoy Bakery, F5
Socialite Accessories, H4
SpaHa Cafe, B5
St. Paul's Church, B4
USPS, F4
V&M American Outlet Center, H5
Virginia's Guest House, E3

East Harlem Map B2

109-St. Inc., G1
Aguilar Branch NYPL, F1
Amor Cubano, F1
Aurum, C4
Camaradas el Barrio, C4
CityLine Footware, B1
Creole Restaurant, A1
Danny K. Fashion, E1
Danny K. Fashion, F1
El Barrio Juice Bar, C3
El Paso Taqueria, B2
Green Apple BBQ, E4
Hand Made in Puerto Rico, B1
Harlem Universal, A3
Holy Rosary Church, A5
International Salsa Museum, B1
La Tropizienne Bakery, F4
Lechonera Sandy, B3
Mojitos Bar & Grill, B2

Net Plaza Cafe Internet, C1
New Shoe World, C1
Orbit East Harlem, C4
Our Lady of Mount Carmel, C5
Patsy's Pizzeria, B4
Payless, B1
Pee Dee Steak House, F1
Piatto d'Oro Ristorante Italiano, G4
Raices Dominicanas Cigars, C4
Rao's, D5
Ricardo's Steakhouse, F3
Rincon Musical, H1
Shell, B4
Somniac, C3
SpaHa Cafe, B1
Thomas Jefferson Park, E5
V&M American Outlet Center, H1

East Harlem Map B3

Ashley Stewart, A5
Bolton's, G5
East Harlem Cafe, B4
El Museo del Barrio, B1
El Paso Taqueria & Cevicheria, C4
El Paso Taqueria, G3
Exotic Fragrances, B4
Foot Locker, A5
Giovanna's Restaurant & Pizzeria, E4
Harbor Conservancy for the Performance
    Arts, B1
Itzocan Bistro, D4
Julia de Burgos Cultural Arts Center, A4
K&D Wines & Spirits, H2
La Casa de la Herencia Cultural
    Puertorriquena, B1
La Fonda Boricua, A5
MediaNoche, C3
Mount Sinai Hospital, E1
Mount Sinai School of Medicine, E1
Moustache Pizza, C4
Museum of the City of New York, C1
Payless, B5
Puerto Rico & the American Dream, A4
Raices Latin Music, B1
Saint Nicholas Russian Orthodox, G1
Second Spanish Baptist Church, C5
Shell, D4
Socialite Accessories, A4
St. Cecilia's Church, A4
Taller Boricua, A4
Teatro Hecksher, B1
Upper Yorkville Suites, C5
Yo In Yo Out, D4

East Harlem Map B4

Ashley Stewart, A1
Bolton's, G1
Chimney BBQ/Sushi Bar & MILK Lounge, A3
Don Pedro's, G3
East Ward Missionary Baptist Church, C4
FB Lounge, A2
Foot Locker, A1

Getty, A4
La Fonda Boricua, A1
Lloyd's Carrot Cake, A3
Metropolitan General Hospital, F3
Payless, B1
Rivera Liquor, B4
Shell, H4
Upper Yorkville Suites, C1

MUSEUMS

M orris-Jumel Mansion

65 Jumel Terrace, at 161st St., between Jumel Terrace and Edgecombe Ave. (212) 923-8008. www.morrisjumel.org. Wed–Sun 10am–4pm. Suggested Admission: Adults $4, Students and Seniors $3, Friends of Morris-Jumel Mansion and Children under 12 when accompanied by an adult: Free. Guided tours and a gift shop. Bus—M2, M3, M100, M101. Subway—C to 163rd St.

MORRIS-JUMEL MANSION

Morris-Jumel Mansion, Manhattan's oldest house (built in 1765 by British Army **Colonel Roger Morris**), was headquarters to General George Washington in September and October of 1776 during the Battle of Harlem Heights. After Washington's departure, the mansion played host to a succession of British and Hessian military leaders, served briefly as an inn for weary travelers, and finally returned to its role as country house. In 1819 the mansion was purchased and restored by French wine merchant **Stephen Jumel** and his wife, Eliza. When Stephen Jumel died in 1832, his wife later married Aaron Burr, but the marriage only lasted two years. Eliza owned the house until her death in 1865, and after a twenty-year court battle, the 130-acre property was divided and sold. In 1903 owners **General Ferdinand P. and Lillie Earle** persuaded the city to purchase the house and preserve its rich history. Today, the house is a museum that features twelve period rooms from the eighteenth and nineteenth centuries with furniture and decorations from the various owners and guests who lived there. They have workshops, lectures, exhibitions, a classical music series with the Brooklyn Baroque in autumn and spring, and a jazz series with **Marjorie Elliot** and Parlor Entertainment in the summer.

M useum of Art and Origins

430 W. 162nd St., at Jumel Terrace. (212) 740-2001. www.museumofartandorigins. org. By appointment. Suggested Admission: $10 for Adults, $5 for Students, Children free, $5 for non–U.S. residents. Bus—M2, M3, M100, M101. Subway—C to 163rd St.

Museum of Art and Origins exhibits consists of a vast collection of African masks, figures, and implements of many tribes and periods.

The Hispanic Society of America Museum and Library

Audubon Terrace, Broadway between 155th and 156th Sts. (212) 926-2234. www. hispanicsociety.org. Free. Tue–Sat 10am–4:30pm, and Sun 1pm–4pm. Tours (212) 926-2234 ex. 209. Tours at Two: The Hispanic Society offers free 45-minute tours of the building and collections at 2pm on Saturdays. Gift Shop. Bus—M4, M5, M100, M101, BX6. Subway—1 to 157th St.

EL CID SCULPTURE, THE HISPANIC SOCIETY OF AMERICA.

The Hispanic Society of America Museum and Library was founded in 1904 by **Archer M. Huntington,** adopted son of railroad baron **Collis P. Huntington**, to promote, preserve, and educate individuals on the arts and cultures of Spain, Portugal, and Latin America. It officially opened in 1908 in the beautiful Beaux-Arts building on Audubon Terrace that Huntington built and later added in its courtyard several grandiose sculptures created by his artist wife, **Anna Hyatt Huntington**. The collections boast over 200,000 items, including paintings, sculptures, decorative arts, prints, photographs, and textiles. The scope and quality of these items are second to none outside of the Iberian Peninsula. The library offers a treasure trove of over 250,000 books and periodicals.

GALLERIES

Rio Penthouse Gallery

10 Fort Washington Ave., between 159th and 160th Sts. Bus—M4, M5. Subway—1 to 157th St.

Located on the penthouse level of Broadway Housing Communities' building, this gallery features exhibitions of works by Latin American and African American emerging artists. The gallery also organizes programs that feature the works of poets, writers, musicians, dancers, and photographers.

THEATERS AND CULTURAL INSTITUTIONS

The Malcolm X & Dr. Betty Shabazz Memorial and Educational Center

3940 Broadway, between 165th and 166th Sts. (212) 568-1341. www.theshabazzcenter. net. Wheelchair accessible. Mon–Fri 9am–4pm. Bus—M2, M3, M4, M5, M100, M101, BX7. Subway—A, C, 1 to 168th St.

The Audubon Ballroom was built in 1912 by **William Fox**, creator of 20th Century Fox, who commissioned architect Thomas W. Lamb, known for his fanciful design of theaters, to design it. During its long, rich history the Audubon was used as a ballroom, vaudeville house, movie theater, synagogue, and meeting hall. However, it is also known as the place where, on February 21, 1965, Malcolm X was assassinated. Malcolm X was a Muslim minister, public speaker, and human rights activist who first rose to prominence when he was the principal spokesman for the Nation of Islam, an African American version of Islam developed by its leader, the Hon. Elijah Muhammad.

In 1945 **Malcolm Little** was sentenced to prison and it was there that he embraced the teachings of the Nation of Islam and changed his name to Malcolm X. After his parole in 1952, he quickly rose to the position of minister of information, and became the outspoken national spokesman for the organization. On January 14, 1958, he married **Betty X** and they had six daughters.

In early 1964, Malcolm X left the Nation of Islam and founded Muslim Mosque, Inc., a religious organization, and the secular, Black nationalist Organization of Afro American Unity, which held its weekly meetings at the Audubon Ballroom. During a hajj or pilgrimage to Mecca in 1964, he changed his name to El-Hajj Malik El-Shabazz.

In the 1990s the ballroom, not protected by landmark designation, was slated to be demolished by Columbia University, which had plans to build a biotech research center at the site. However, through the efforts of the late Dr. Shabazz and with the support of the community which had mounted protests against the building demolition, two-thirds of the original facade and a portion of the original ballroom were retained and redesigned into a state-of-the-art facility to honor the lives and legacies of Malcolm X and Dr. Shabazz. Located in the lobby are multimedia kiosks which offer testimonials, interviews, videos, and still images of events that occurred during their lives. There is also a life-sized statue of Malcolm X, and on the second floor where he was assassinated, a mural was installed that depicts his life journey from birth to death. This is a must-see! Check out the organization's calendar to see what other noteworthy events have been scheduled.

ACCOMMODATIONS

useum Bed and Breakfast
430 W. 162nd St., at Jumel Terrace. (212) 740-9999. Bus—M2, M3. Subway—C to 163rd St.

In this landmark brownstone/museum in the **Jumel Terrace Historic District**, you'll have the opportunity to stay in rooms that feature a rotating exhibit of art and artifacts from Africa, Asia, the Americas, and Europe. With a variety of views that range from sculpture garden to a nineteenth-century Belgian Block street to Yankee Stadium, the rooms also include the modern conveniences of air-conditioning, cable TV, Internet access, and some kitchen appointments. Room rates range from $130 to $170.

Sylvan Guest House

12 Sylvan Terrace, at 161ˢᵗ St., between St. Nicholas and Jumel Terrace. (646) 515-2552. www.sylvanguesthouse.com/sylvan/sylvan_terrace.html. Bus—M2, M3. Subway—C to 163ʳᵈ St.

Tucked away in the Jumel Terrace Historic District, the Sylvan Guest House is a landmark townhouse with modern-day furnishings. Accommodations include a two-bedroom duplex, a two-bedroom suite, and a studio. Each space is appointed with modern furniture, full kitchens, and bathrooms with large bathtubs and/or showers. Among the other amenities are luxurious bedding, complimentary high-speed Internet access, and local telephone service. Room rates vary according to room configuration, so please check the Web site or call for details.

SYLVAN TERRACE STREETSCAPE

LIVE ENTERTAINMENT

Marjorie Elliot/Parlor Entertainment

555 Edgecombe Ave., Apt. 3F, at 160ᵗʰ St. (212) 781-6595. Sun 4pm–6pm. Bus—M2, M3. Subway—C to 163ʳᵈ St.

If you ask those in the know where to find the best jazz in New York City, you will be referred to **Marjorie Elliot's Jazz Parlor**, where you can enjoy a free Sunday afternoon of jazz performed by some great musicians who play free of commercial pressure. Ms. Elliot, an actress/playwright and stride piano player, has been holding these free concerts at the northern tip of Harlem for more than sixteen years at 555 Edgecombe Ave., which is historic not only because of its architectural beauty but also because of its cultural significance. It was home to some of the brightest and most talented in the African American community. The roster of who used to live here reads like a Who's Who of Afro Americana: Count Basie, Paul Robeson, Thurgood Marshall, Lena Horne, **Coleman Hawkins**, **Erskine Hawkins**, **Canada Lee**, **Teddy Wilson**, Mary Lou Williams, Joe Louis, **Johnny Hodges**, **Don Redman**, **Andy Kirk**, Charles Alston, and Dr. Kenneth Clark. Today, the address is famous because of the music that issues from apartment 3F every Sunday. So, unlike traditional jazz performance spaces and clubs, this unassuming haven for America's classical music features fifty padded folding chairs set up in Ms. Elliot's makeshift jazz parlor living room and kitchen. Make reservations to be certain you will be seated.

ADDITIONAL INFORMATION

JANUARY
Three Kings Day Parade and Community Celebration
January 6. Parade start—11am, at 106th St. and Third Ave.; ends Park Ave., at 115th St. at La Marqueta where children receive gifts, toys, and books.

First Saturday after January 6. 3pm–5pm. A free community intergenerational family celebration is held at El Museo del Barrio, 1230 Fifth Ave., at 104th St. Visit www.elmuseo.org or call (212) 831-7272.

This colorful and festive parade, organized by El Museo del Barrio, features live camels, sheep, and stilt walkers. Three Kings Day is celebrated on January 6 in Latin America and Puerto Rico to commemorate the day the three kings visited baby Jesus. It is the day children receive gifts, after leaving hay for the animals beside their beds the night before.

Dr. Martin Luther King, Jr., Service and Celebration
Held the Monday closest to January 15. Set aside for the national holiday, 10am.
Convent Avenue Baptist Church, 420 W. 145th St., at Convent Ave. Visit www.conventchurch.org or call (212) 234-6767.

Sponsored by the Baptist Minister's Conference of Greater New York and Vicinity, the Dr. Martin Luther King, Jr., Service and Celebration is the oldest New York City worship service that honors the life and legacy of the slain civil rights leader on his birthday, January 15. Each year a prominent speaker is selected to give an address, and of course there is gospel singing.

FEBRUARY
Black History Month
Annual celebrations of Black culture featuring theater, dance, music performances, and more; various Harlem locations during the month; www.welcometoharlem.com.

MARCH
Women's Jazz Festival (in celebration of Women's History Month)
Weekly during the month of March. 7pm. Schomburg Center for Research in Black Culture, Langston Hughes Auditorium, 515 Malcolm X/Lenox, at 135th St. Visit www.nypl.org/research/sc/sc.html, www.telecharge.com, or call (212) 491-2206.

The Schomburg Center celebrates Women's History Month with an annual month-long series of extraordinary jazz concerts that feature extremely talented female artists. Past performances have included Carmen Lundy, Tamar-kali, Gerri Allen, and the Spellman College Jazz Ensemble, just to name a few.

APRIL
Earth Day Celebration
WE ACT for Environmental Justice. Visit www.weact.org or call (212) 961-1000.

WE ACT for Environmental Justice, one of the pioneers and founders of the national EJ movement, sponsors Earth Day in Harlem annually with a community fair that features performances by local talent, green giveaways, locally grown food, and information on green/sustainable living.

MAY

The Cultural Animators Series
Friday through Sunday for two weeks. Riverside Church Theatre, 91 Claremont at 120th St. Visit www.theriversidetheatre.org or call (212) 870-6784.

An arts festival featuring film, dance, visual arts, drama, spoken word, dialogue, and music that is used as a catalyst to inform and ignite social change.

Festival Cinco de Mayo
First Sunday closest to May 5. 10am–6pm. 116th St., between Second and Third Aves. Visit www. cecomex.org or call (212) 289-6400.

The holiday commemorates the Mexican army's unlikely victory over French forces at the Battle of Puebla on May 5, 1862. In East Harlem the event is celebrated with a day-long festival that features Mexican food, arts and crafts, and live musical performances.

JUNE

The New York Family Arts Festival
Every weekend in June. The Riverside Church Theatre, 91 Claremont St., between 120th and 121st Sts. Visit www.theriversidetheatre.org or call (212) 870-6784.

This month-long free festival brings in various artists who share information about their cultures through music, dance, storytelling, film, and food. Geared for families, these artistic presentations are crafted as learning experiences about other cultures.

Hamilton Heights House and Garden Tour
First Sunday in June. 11am–4pm. Tour Start and Ticket Pick-up/Purchase: St. Luke's Episcopal Church at the corner of W. 141st Street and Convent Ave. Sponsored by Hamilton Heights Homeowners Association. Visit www.hamiltonheightshomeowners.org.

Selected homes and gardens in the Hamilton Heights Historic District are on tour once a year. These houses exhibit a wide variety of architectural styles, including Romanesque, Flemish, Tudor, and Italian Renaissance Revival, and offer a variety of exquisite details. Usually a weekend event; visit the Web site for details about other activities.

116th Street Festival
Second Saturday in June. 116th St. from Lexington to Second Aves., and Third Ave. from 106th to 122nd Sts. Visit www.116thstfestival.com or call (212) 348-8272.

The largest Latino Festival in New York, it is always held the Saturday before the Puerto Rican Day Parade. The 116th Festival draws a diverse Latino audience, covers more than twenty-eight blocks, and has three main stages that feature live music performances. There are games, food, and over 200 exhibits as well.

Museum Mile Festival
Second Tuesday in June. 6pm–9pm.

Nine of the country's finest museums on Fifth Avenue, including El Museo del Barrio and the Museum of the City of New York, which are located in East Harlem, are open free to visitors to enjoy this big block party with live bands, entertainment, art in the streets, and more.

The David Walker Memorial Harlem Skyscraper Cycling Classic
Father's Day Sunday. Marcus Garvey Park, 121st St. and Mt. Morris Park West (one block east of Malcolm X/Lenox), Registration starts 11am. Visit www.skyscraper-harlembikerace.com.

The city's oldest continually held bicycle race, the Classic is held on a three-quarter-mile circuit around Marcus Garvey Park. Founded in 1973 by the late David Walker, there are racing competitions for men, women, and professional cyclists. There is also a community race for children, teens, and adults. Prizes are awarded in all categories. This race has molded the careers of several generations of cyclists such as Nelson Vails, a silver medalist at the 1984 Olympics.

KingFest/Juneteenth Celebration
First Saturday closest to June 19. 2pm–6pm. Marcus Garvey Park Amphitheater (behind park recreation center located one block east of Malcolm X/Lenox at 122nd St. and Mt. Morris Park West).

Juneteenth, or June 19, 1865, is the day that slaves in Galveston, Texas, learned they had been freed—two and a half years after the issuance of the Emancipation Proclamation on January 1, 1863. Since that time Blacks in Texas have celebrated, and in recent decades the celebration has spread. The celebration in Harlem features singers, dancers, mimes, and speakers, as well as food vendors and community service providers. Earlier in the day a parade that starts at 116th St., between Fifth Ave. and Malcolm X/Lenox, winds its way to Marcus Garvey Park.

The Entertainers Basketball Classic (EBC)
Third week in June to third week in August, Monday through Thursday. 7pm–10pm. Holcombe Rucker Playground, 155th St. and Frederick Douglass Blvd. Visit www.insidehoops.com/rucker.

It's the basketball tournament of the summer, not just in Harlem or New York City, but in street basketball, period! The EBC replaced the **Rucker Basketball Tournament**, which Parks Department employee **Holcombe Rucker** established in 1956 to get kids off the street and involved in positive activities. The Rucker Tournament attracted some of the NCAA's and NBA's greatest players, including **Wilt Chamberlain, Earl "The Pearl" Monroe, Julius Erving, Bill Bradley**, and Kareem Abdul-Jabbar, and helped hundreds of kids get college scholarships. It also attracted some of the greatest street ball players, such as **Pee Wee Kirkland** and **Earl "The Goat" Manigault**. Rucker died in 1965, but the tradition he started continued. In 1974, the playground that hosted his tournament was named the "Holcombe Rucker Playground" in his honor. While the original tournament faded in popularity, the EBC took its place. The EBC started in the early eighties as a series of games between teams sponsored by rap groups. Since the **Sugar Hill Gang** phrased in one of their songs, "I wouldn't take a sucker or a ball from the Rucker," other rappers such as **LL Cool J** kept the Rucker's name alive, and it didn't hurt that the Rucker Tournament has been the subject of several films. The EBC has grown into the world's largest street ball tournament, complete with television coverage, sponsors, and a host of really entertaining nicknames. It is EBC tradition for game announcers to assign nicknames to players—but only after they've played well enough to earn one. **Kobe Bryant**—the only player to participate in the EBC after winning an NBA title—was "Lord of the Rings." **Rafer Alston** of the Houston Rockets was "Skip to My Lou," and former Arkansas guard **Kareem Reid** is known as "Best-Kept Secret." During league play, MCs give the action flavor through constant play-by-play and by teasing players for bad plays and perceived weaknesses. Otherwise, the park that seats 1,500 but overflows to more than 3,000 during the tournament is known for the high level of basketball played publicly, particularly for its street ball style.

Harlem Meer Performance Festival
Every Sunday from late June to early September. 2pm–4pm. Central Park's Charles A. Dana Discovery Center, 110th St., between Malcolm X/Lenox and Fifth Ave. Visit www.centralparknyc.org/site/PageNavigator/events or call (212) 860-1370.

The swinging sounds of blues, jazz, salsa, world, and gospel music reverberate every Sunday starting in June at the northeastern corner of Central Park. The festival showcases some of New York's top talents.

JULY
Reel Harlem Film Festival
Every Wednesday and Thursday in July. 8pm. Visit www.historicharlemparks.org.

The Historic Harlem Parks Coalition, made up of park advocacy organizations supporting Jackie Robinson, Marcus Garvey, Morningside, and St. Nicholas Parks, sponsors an outdoor film festival in July. Every week in a different park live entertainment precedes the screenings, which include both feature and documentary films about people of color. Check the Web site for locations and film schedule.

Jazzmobile
July–August. 7pm. **Wednesday**. Grant's Tomb, 122nd and Riverside Drive. **Friday**: Marcus Garvey Park Amphitheater, 122nd St. and Mt. Morris Park West behind the recreation center. Visit www.jazzmobile.org or call (212) 866-3616.

In the summer, Jazzmobile brings free jazz concerts via a mobile cart to neighborhoods all over Harlem. In addition, every Wednesday and Friday renowned jazz musicians perform at free concerts at Grant's Tomb and Marcus Garvey Park starting the second week in July. The Jazz Vocal Competition is held in July, too.

Harlem Book Fair
Third Saturday in July. 11am–6pm; 135th St., between Adam Clayton Powell Blvd. and Fifth Ave. Visit www.qbr.com.

The largest gathering to support the Black literary tradition brings Black writers and booksellers from around the world together in a free outdoor book fair. The free part of the fair is the artist talks, panel discussions, special readings, book signings, and live spoken word performances. The book bazaar that is located on two blocks features all kinds of books for sale by mainstream and independent book publishers.

Hats by Bunn Fashion Show
Mid-July, on a Sunday. 2283 Adam Clayton Powell Blvd., at 134th St. Visit www.hatsbybunn.com or call (212) 654-3590.

It might not be Fashion Week, but it is a free fashion show à la Harlem style—right on the sidewalk at Adam Clayton Powell Blvd. in front of Bunn's retail store. Hat designer Bunn shows off his new line of custom-made hats both for women and men, as his models strut the latest in apparel by Black designers to accentuate the hats.

Harlem SummerStage
July and August. Thu 5:30pm–8pm. Adam Clayton Powell Jr. State Office Bldg. Mall, 163 W. 125th St., at Adam Clayton Powell Blvd.

Harlem SummerStage, a summer concert series, features a diverse selection of arts and entertainment including music, dance, and spoken word, all offered free to the public. This series is organized in cooperation with the New York City Housing Authority and the New York State Office of General Services.

CityParks Theater presented by Time Warner
Tuesday through Saturday the last week in July. 8pm. Marcus Garvey Park Amphitheater, 122nd St. and Mt. Morris Park West behind the park's recreation center. Visit www.cityparksfoundation.org.

Free theater in the park is produced by the City Parks Foundation, which seeks out quality theatre productions for this series. Plays that have been presented in the past include Melvin Van Peebles' *Ain't Suppose to Die a Natural Death*, William Shakespeare's *A Midsummer Night's Dream*, and Chisa Hutchinson's *Dirt Rich*, which was the first play commissioned for this series.

AUGUST
Harlem Week
Month of August. Visit www.harlemdiscover.com/harlemweek.

Launched in 1974 as Harlem Day, the event has grown into a month-long celebration of the economic, political, and cultural history of Harlem. Events include Harlem Jazz Fest, Historic Black College Fair, Junior Tennis Classic, Gymnastics Gala, Family Unity Day Festival, Black Film Festival, Children's Festival, fashion shows, and much more at various Harlem locations. Check the Web site for the schedule and locations.

CityParks Concerts
Every Thursday starting the second week of August for three weeks. 7pm–8:30pm. Marcus Garvey Park Amphitheater, 122nd St. and Mt. Morris Park West, behind the park's recreation center. Visit www.cityparksfoundation.org.

This free concert series features R&B, hip-hop, and gospel music performances by popular recording artists, and has a large and loyal following. Some past performers include Jon B, Rev. Hezekiah Walker, and Cuba Gooding, Sr., just to name a few.

ROY HAYNES PERFORMING AT THE CHARLIE PARKER JAZZ FESTIVAL

Charlie Parker Jazz Festival
Fourth Saturday in August. 3pm–8pm. Marcus Garvey Park Amphitheater, 122nd St. and Mt. Morris Park West, behind the park's recreation center. Visit www.cityparksfoundation.org.

The Charlie Parker Jazz Festival annually assembles some of the finest musicians in the world who reflect renowned saxophonist Parker's musical individuality and genius, to celebrate his birthday on August 29. The free concerts take place in neighborhoods where Charlie Parker lived and worked, in Harlem's Marcus Garvey Park (Saturday), and the Lower East Side's Tompkins Square Park (Sunday).

African Diaspora Summer Film Series
Last Week in August—Friday, Saturday, Sunday. Riverside Church Theatre, 91 Claremont Ave., at 120th St. Visit www.theriversidetheatre.org or call (212) 870-6784.

A sizzling schedule of independent, foreign, animated, feature, and documentary films by and about people of color around the world. Sponsored by Riverside Theatre and ArtHattan.

Dance of the Giglio and Feast
Second Friday through Sunday in August. 115th St., between First and Pleasant Aves., Our Lady of Mount. Carmel Church. Visit www.eastharlemgiglio.com.

Imagine 125 men carrying a five-ton, five-story, hand-sculptured tower and a twelve-piece brass band on their shoulders, dancing these through their neighborhood in tempo to joyous Italian folk songs, and you have the Dance of the Giglio. This is Italian Harlem, and the tradition of honoring Saint Antonio, which started in Brusciano, Italy, in the 1880s continues in East Harlem, even though most Italians have left the neighborhood, which was once the largest Italian settlement in the country. Italian families return for this event every year. There is nightly entertainment, carnival-style rides and games, and mouthwatering Italian food specialties, in addition to the actual Dance of the Giglio which is held on the last day—Sunday.

SEPTEMBER
Dance Harlem and Praise! Dance Harlem
Second Saturday and Sunday in September. 4pm–6pm. Marcus Garvey Park Amphitheater, 122nd St. and Mt. Morris Park West behind the park's recreation center. Visit www.historicharlemparks.org.

DANCE HARLEM

Dance Harlem is a free outdoor dance festival that showcases the pulse, passion, and direction of contemporary African American modern and liturgical dance in New York City. The contemporary dance program, which is presided over by Tony Award–winning choreographer George Faison and AUDELCO Award–winning dancer Dyane Harvey, is held on Sunday and includes works by established companies and emerging choreographers. The liturgical program is held on Saturday and includes some of the best praise dance ministries in the tri-state area.

Harlem Renaissance Road Race
Third Saturday in September. Pee Wee Race—9:30am, Wheelchair/Physically Challenged Race— 9:55am, 5-Mile Run and 2-Mile Health Walk—10am. The races start in front of Harlem YMCA, 180 W. 135th St., between Adam Clayton Powell Blvd. and Malcolm X/Lenox. Visit www.harlemrace.com or call (917) 945-9764.

The Harlem Renaissance Road Race encourages the community, especially parents and their children, to come out and run or walk for the cause of health and youth mentoring in Harlem. The race is a 5-mile run and a 2-mile walk designed for beginners and experienced runners and walkers alike. The proceeds are used to sponsor scholarships for Harlem youth.

African American Day Parade
Third Sunday in September. 1pm–6pm. Adam Clayton Powell Blvd. from 111th to 142nd Sts. Visit www.africanamericandayparade.org or call (212) 348-3080.

Nearly a million people line Adam Clayton Powell Jr. Blvd. to watch dignitaries, celebrities, bands, and marching brigades from twelve states, including at least one band from an historically Black college, make the more than thirty-block trek to promote unity, dignity, and pride. Just about every community of African descent is represented in the parade, including representatives from the West Indian Day Parade, Panamanian American, and Senegalese Federation, just to name a few, along with Harlem-based community organizations.

Our Common Ground Festival
Last Saturday in September. 1pm–5pm. Morningside Park, 117th St. and Morningside Ave. Visit www.morningsidepark.org.

Our Common Ground has become a neighborhood tradition that celebrates the rich cultural diversity of the surrounding community. Sponsored by the Friends of Morningside Park, the festival features fun activities for the whole family, including live musical performances, a Double Dutch demonstration, basketball clinic, balloon art, puppet performance, face painting, pony rides, food, and more.

OCTOBER
Feast of St. Francis (Blessing of the Animals)
First Sunday in October. The Cathedral Church of St. John the Divine, 1047 Amsterdam Ave., at 112th St. Visit www.st.johndivine.org or call (212) 662-2133.

The Feast of St. Francis of Assisi, who is the patron saint of animals, includes the blessing of animals as large as elephants and camels that are brought into the sanctuary, along with cats and dogs. Call for event information and tickets.

Harlem Art Walk
Second Saturday and Sunday in October. Saturday and Sunday 9am–5pm. Visit www.casafrela. com.

Harlem Art Walk, a self-guided tour of artists' studios sponsored by Casa Frela Gallery, is a tribute to the diversity of artists living and working in Central Harlem. Discover new artwork, galleries and meet artists from Harlem's vibrant art scene. The more than one hundred participating artists range from emerging talent to internationally recognized figures. Their studios vary from traditional loft spaces to converted bedrooms. Their artwork spans between cutting-edge new media to more traditional styles of representation and abstraction.

Halloween Extravaganza and Procession of Ghouls
Last Friday in October. 7pm and 10pm. The Cathedral Church of St. John the Divine, 1047 Amsterdam Ave., at 112th St. Visit www.st.johndivine.org or call (212) 316-7540.

This is one of the city's most exciting Halloween traditions. Wear your costume and enjoy this annual Halloween event, which begins with the screening of a classic silent horror film accompanied by outstanding organ music, followed by the Grand Procession of the Ghouls, which features imaginative costumes, creatures, and special effects.

NOVEMBER
Dance Theatre of Harlem (DTH) Open House Series
Second Sunday from November through May. 3pm–5pm. Dance Theatre of Harlem, 466 W. 152nd St., between St. Nicholas and Amsterdam Aves. Visit www.brownpapertickets.com/event/47697 or www.dancetheatreofharlem.org, or call (212) 690-2800.

Each month from November through May the Open House Series showcases students from the DTH School, DTH Ensemble, and special guest artists.

African Diaspora Film Festival
Starts the last Friday in November and runs for seventeen days. Visit www.nyadff.org.

NYADFF is an international film festival devoted to showcasing films depicting the diversity and richness of the global Black experience. ADFF features an eclectic mix of urban, classic, foreign, and independent films, including many world and U.S. premieres. Films are screened in various venues around the city, including Harlem.

International Latin/Tropical Music Collector's Festival
Caribbean Cultural Center African Diaspora Institute. (212) 307-7420. www.cccadi.org.

This annual festival, held in East Harlem, is organized by the Caribbean Cultural Center to showcase the finds of collectors of Latin musical treasures. This day-long event features collectors, displays, a flea market, vendors, panel discussions, performances, musicians, dancers, scholars, radio personalities and DJs who spin original vinyl recordings, and live music, and it attracts thousands from throughout five northeastern states. Each year the festival focuses on a particular genre of Latin/Tropical music. To get details about location and time, check the Caribbean Cultural Center's Web site.

DECEMBER
Hats by Bunn Fashion Show
First Saturday in December. 3:30pm sharp. Thurgood Marshall Academy, 200 W. 135th St., at Adam Clayton Powell Blvd. Admission: Unwrapped Child's Toy for Abyssinian Baptist Church Toy Drive. Visit www.hatsbybunn.com or call (212) 654-3590.

Fashion show and sale featuring New York's most innovative designers. Hat designer Bunn unveils his winter collection.

The NuDance Festival
Second week in December. Riverside Church Theatre, 91 Claremont Ave., at 120th St. Visit www.theriversidetheatre.org or call (212) 870-6784.

The festival is held over four days where eight to twelve up-and-coming choreographers show new, original choreography. The dance works are innovative, cutting-edge, and definitely thrilling to watch in three evenings of performance. The fourth night, Choreographers in Creation, share works in process with a participatory segment for audience members.

Black Nutcracker
Third Friday in December. 7pm. Apollo Theater, 253 W. 125th St., between Adam Clayton Powell and Frederick Douglass Blvds. Visit www.uptowndanceacademy.com or call (212) 987-5030.

This legendary classic ballet is an African American version presented annually by the Uptown Dance Academy. Their version features a collection of dance styles, from classical ballet to hip-hop, cha-cha slide, and African dance on pointe, performed to the music of Tchaikovsky, Duke Ellington, the Commodores, and live African drumming.

David A. Walker Memorial Double Dutch Holiday Classic
Third Saturday in December. 1pm–4pm. Apollo Theater, 253 W. 125th St., between Adam Clayton Powell and Frederick Douglass Blvds. Visit www.nationaldoubledutchleague.com/ HolidayClassic.htm or www.ticketmaster.com, or call (212) 531-5305/5304.

Since the initial tournament in 1974, competitive Double Dutch, which was developed by former NY Police Dept. Community Affairs Detective David Walker (who passed in 2008), has expanded with citywide and national championships. Nearly 100,000 girls and boys—representing schools and community centers throughout the United States and the world—compete for team positions at the national and international events.

Clement Clarke Moore Candlelight Carol Service
Christmas Season. Church of the Intercession, 550 W. 155th St., at Broadway. Visit www.intercession-nyc.dioceseny.org or call (212) 283-6200.

Every Christmas season the church honors Clement Clarke Moore, the poet who wrote "A Visit From Saint Nicholas" and is buried in the cemetery across Broadway. A tradition since 1911, the famous poem is read by celebrity guests while children are sitting on the steps of the altar. Traditional Christmas carols are also performed. Call for date and time.

Kwanzaa Celebration
First Saturday after Christmas. 7:30pm–10:30pm. Apollo Theater, 253 W. 125th St., between Adam Clayton Powell and Frederick Douglass Blvds. Visit www.ticketmaster.com or call (212) 531-5305/5304.

The Apollo Theater presents its annual Kwanzaa Celebration with Regeneration Night, a multifaceted performance featuring the renowned Harlem-based dance company Forces of Nature Dance Theatre, and other artists. It is the largest Kwanzaa celebration in the city.

New Year's Eve Watch Services
December 31. Approximately 10pm–12am. Most churches in Harlem. Check the church listing and call to get details.

Most Baptist, African Methodist Episcopal, and Church of God In Christ denominations bring in the New Year in the traditional Southern African American way—on their knees praying it in. There is usually a "watchman" who calls out the minutes up to the New Year to "travelers." Some of the best gospel choir singing can be heard on this night, too.

New Year's Eve Concert for Peace
December 31. The Cathedral Church of St. John the Divine, 1047 Amsterdam Ave., at 112th St. Visit www.st.johndivine.org or call (212) 316-7540.

The New Year's Eve Concert for Peace has become a tradition at the Cathedral since Leonard Bernstein proposed the idea and, in 1983, conducted the first installment. Bernstein's choice of Copland's "Fanfare for the Common Man" as the opening work suggested that this meditation was to be both communal and personal. The Copland has remained the concert's signature piece, and classical choral and orchestral selections, hymns, and contemporary musical selections are all programmed to make this concert special.

FAVORITE PLACES TO EAT

1. Billie's Black
2. Creole Restaurant and Music Supper Club
3. Chez Lucienne
4. Covo Trattoria Pizzeria and Lounge
5. El Paso Taqueria
6. Green Apple BBQ
7. Hudson River Café
8. Il Café Latte
9. Kitchenette Uptown
10. Mojos
11. Patisserie des Ambassade
12. Ricardo's Steakhouse
13. Sezz Medi
14. Tonnie's Minis
15. Tropical Grill and Restaurant

THINGS TO DO IN HARLEM

I. Tour the historic Apollo Theatre
253 W. 125th Street between Frederick Douglass and Adam Clayton Powell Blvds. www.apollotheater.org/tours.htm. Reservations: (212) 531-5337, Email: billy.mitchell@apollotheater.org. General Admission: Weekdays $16/person; Weekends $18/person. Nonprofit Organizations: Weekdays $14/person; Weekends $16/person.

Tours are conducted only when there is a group of 20 or more Mon, Tue, Thu, Fri: 11am, 1pm, 3pm. Wed: 11 am only. Sat. and Sun: 11am, 1pm. Contact www.welcometoharlem.com to get on a group list.

Billy Mitchell, the Apollo in-house historian, gives a very informative, entertaining, and fun-filled hour tour about the Apollo's history and anecdotes about the entertainers who graced its stage. You are encouraged to perform, on stage, as if you are a star waiting to be "born." Don't forget to buy an Apollo souvenir, too.

2. Go Fishing at Central Park's Dana Discovery Center
110th St., between Malcolm X/Lenox and Fifth Ave. (212) 860 1370.www.centralparknyc.org/site/PageNavigator/programs_fishing. April through October. Picture ID required. Tue–Sat: 10am–4pm (Last pole distributed at 3pm). Sun: 10am–2pm (Last pole distributed at 1pm). Free for families and individuals. For groups of 5 or more, $20 fee and reservation required

Catch-and-release fishing (you are loaned a fishing pole, and you get bait free) at the Harlem Meer, which is stocked with a wide variety of fish. All fishing is on a catch-and-release basis only, meaning that all fish caught must be put back into the water immediately. The use of barbs on hooks and lead sinkers is strictly prohibited.

3. Attend Free Charlie Parker Jazz Festival
Marcus Garvey Park Amphitheater. Mt. Morris Park West, at 122nd St. behind Pelham Fritz Recreation Center. www.cityparksfoundation.org. Fourth Saturday in August, 3pm. Free

Annually on the fourth Saturday in August, jazz enthusiasts get a real treat—a day of world-class, free jazz to celebrate Charlie "Yard Bird" Parker's birthday (August 29). Check the City Parks Foundation Web site for the lineup, then bring a brown bag of goodies and sit back and enjoy.

4. Get Your Read On at the Harlem Book Fair
135th St., between Adam Clayton Powell Blvd. and Fifth Ave. www.qbr.com. Third Saturday in July, 11am–6pm. Free

This is your chance to perhaps see your favorite Black writer who might be participating in a panel discussion or reading from and signing his or her most recent novel. The largest book fair in the country that focuses on Black books, this day-long event features a book bazaar of publishers (mainstream and independent) that sell titles ranging from children's lit to chick lit.

5. Spend a night out at St. Nick's Pub for authentic jazz
773 St. Nicholas Ave., at 149th St. www.stnicksjazzpub.net. Mon–Thu: 9pm–3am. Fri–Sat: 9pm–4am. Sun: 7pm–10pm

This is the place to be for straight-ahead jazz, except Saturday night from 12pm–4am, when it's African night. Favorite nights—Mon, Tue, and Fri.

221

6. Take a self-guided tour of Spanish Harlem murals

First take the #6 subway uptown to 103rd St. As you leave the station, be sure to see the mosaic **Neo-Boriken**, 1990 (*Puerto Rican-Style*, 1990) by **Nitza Tufiño**, one of the artists who founded el Museo del Barrio.

103rd St., between Lexington and Third Aves.

- A 1998 mural by **Maria M. Dominguez** commemorates Latin jazz musician **Rafael Hernandez** and more recent local idol **Marc Anthony**.
- **Pedro Pietri**, a community activist and one of the founders of the Nuyorican poetry movement in the 1980s, is honored by artist **James De La Vega**.
- Another De La Vega mural, showing a mother holding her crying baby and the Puerto Rican flag, celebrates the 1997 Puerto Rican Day Parade.

103rd and Park Ave.

- Manny Vega's ceramic mural of a jibaro family working the land.
- James De La Vega's memorial to his father with the text, "Great men never die. They live forever."

PEDRO PIETRI MURAL

104th St., between Lexington and Third Aves.

- **The Spirit of East Harlem**, a four-story mural on the wall of Exotic Fragrances building (1645 Lexington Ave.), was painted by **Hank Prussig** with the aid of mosaic muralist Manny Vega between 1973 and 1978 and restored by Vega in 1998 and 2009 under the auspices of Hope Community, Inc. The mural portrays neighborhood people painting the building, playing dominoes, strumming a cuarto (Puerto Rican guitar), riding bikes, and sharing food with neighbors.
- De La Vega's mural of the famous rapper **Tupac Shakur**.
- De La Vega's mural of rapper **Biggie Smalls** and other famous people.

105th St., between Lexington and Third Aves.

- Off Third Avenue—mural of freedom fighters **Ernesto "Che" Guevara, Pedro Albizu Campos**, and **Lolita Lebrón**, with quotes from each, by **Vagabond and Tato Torres**.
- De La Vega's *The Last Supper*, with skeletons depicted as disciples. The text reads, "*No había cena* (There was no supper)."

106th St. and Lexington Ave.

- Poet Julia de Burgos is commemorated in mural by artist Manny Vega.
- *Moses breaking the tablets of the law* with the text, "*Cómo nos tienen*(Look at the conditions we're in)!" James De La Vega.
- **Saint Sebastien**, James De La Vega.
- De La Vega's *Last Supper* with text, "*Aunque a toditos no los puedo ayudar, los quiero mucho siempre en el corazón* (Although I cannot help you all, I'll always love you in my heart)." Someone later crossed out the word "not."

106th and Park Ave.—Graffiti Hall of Fame.

Many of the images created by the commercial graffiti group **Tats Cru The Mural Kings**. Inside a school playground.

GRAFFITI HALL OF FAME

109th St., between Lexington and Third Ave.—**Jimmy Hendrix** mural by De La Vega.

110th St., between Lexington and Third Ave.—De La Vega mural commemorating Puerto Rican icons activist physician **Ramón Emeterio Betances,** and the bibliophile for whom the Schomburg research library in Central Harlem is named, Arturo Alfonso Schomburg.

End tour at 110th Street and Lexington Avenue subway—before boarding the train find Manny Vega's mesmerizing ceramic mosaic (1997) related to the Afro-Brazilian religious experience.

7. Enjoy Target Free Sundays at the Studio Museum in Harlem
144 W. 125th St., between Adam Clayton Powell Blvd. and Malcolm X/Lenox. (212) 864-4500. www.studiomuseum.org

Thanks to generous support from Target, the Studio Museum offers free admission every Sunday between 12pm and 6pm. In addition to free admission, the Education and Public Programs Department has organized free programs and events geared to audiences—from hands-on family workshops to theater performances.

8. Attend the Ice Show sponsored by Figure Skating In Harlem
361 W. 125th St., 4th Fl. (646) 698-3440. www.figureskatinginharlem.org. April

Come cheer on the girls (ages six to eighteen) of Figure Skating In Harlem at their annual performance event—the Ice Show. Each year the show is designed around a musical theme and students have the opportunity to perform in colorful costumes to proudly demonstrate their newly acquired skills. It's quite a show! Go to the Web site or call to get location and admission fee.

9. Enjoy films under the stars at the Reel Harlem Film Festival
www.historicharlemparks.org. Every Wednesday and Thursday in July at dusk. Free

The Historic Harlem Parks Coalition (HHPC) is a coalition of volunteer advocacy groups representing Marcus Garvey, Morningside, St. Nicholas, and Jackie Robinson Parks that organizes an annual free outdoor film festival featuring independent films about the African American and African experience. Each screening is complemented by music and dance performances as preludes to the films. Visit the Web site to get the film lineup, schedule, and locations. Then pack your picnic basket and bring a blanket to enjoy great films!

10. Experience Black Dance at two-day Dance Harlem Festival
Marcus Garvey Park Amphitheater. Mt. Morris Park, at 122nd St., behind the Pelham Fritz. Recreation Center. 4pm–6pm. www.historicharlemparks.org, www.welcometoharlem.com. Second Sat and Sun in September. Free

Experience the pulse and passion of contemporary African American modern dance and liturgical dance at Harlem's hottest outdoor dance festival. On Saturday, the best liturgical dance ministries in the tri-state area perform. On Sunday, established, emerging dance organizations perform. Emcees: Tony Award–winning choreographer George Faison and AUDELCO Award–winning dancer choreographer **Dyane Harvey**.

DANCERS PERFORMING CAMILLE A. BROWN'S *SHELTER OF PRESENCE* AT DANCE HARLEM.

11. Treat yourself to an authentic Harlem House Party

Welcome to Harlem Tours. 2360 Frederick Douglass Blvd.. Between 126th and 127th Streets. www.welcometoharlem.com. 7:30pm–10pm. Price: $45 per person.

How special is this? A private jazz concert in a private brownstone, complete with hors d'oeuvres, dessert, and wine. The Harlem Jazz Concert Series is organized by Welcome to Harlem Tours, which specializes in unique and authentic tour experiences in Harlem. It's a house party you won't forget! Visit the Web site for the schedule.

TOURS

Welcome to Harlem Tours

Gospel and Brunch Tour

Any Sunday morning come uptown to enjoy the toe-tapping, hand-clapping, foot-stomping rhythms of soulful Black gospel music. Participate in a moving worship service and enjoy a walk through the Mount Morris Park Historic District to see some of Harlem's most beautiful and historic churches and brownstone townhouses along the way.*

Date: Sun at 9:30am, 3.5 hours. Price: Adults $65, Children 4 years or older $45.

Mount Morris Walking Tour

In 1971, the New York City Landmarks Preservation Commission designated the Mount Morris Park neighborhood an Historic District, making it one of the earliest districts in the five boroughs to be landmarked. The area from 118th to 124th Streets between Mt. Morris Park West and the east side of Malcolm X/Lenox enjoy the protection of landmark designation. However, a larger area encompassing sixteen blocks going north from W. 118th to W. 124th Streets and west from Madison Avenue to Adam Clayton Powell Jr. Blvd., which includes the Historic District, was placed on the National Register of Historic Properties. This area contains a remarkable cross-section of late nineteenth- and early twentieth-century residential and church architecture, representing all of the various eclectic styles associated with the Gilded Age. "Doctors' Row" (W. 122nd Street between Malcolm X/Lenox and Mt. Morris Park West), Mt. Morris Park West, and Malcolm X Blvd./Lenox from 124th Street to 120th Street demonstrate the remarkable survival of substantially unaltered nineteenth-century streetscapes, a rarity in most areas of Manhattan.*

Date: Mon, Wed, Fri, and Sat at 11am, 3 hours. Price: $35 per person.

Soul Food and Jazz Tour "Le Jazz Harlem"

While jazz has its origins in New Orleans, Harlem is easily considered the birthplace of jazz because the jazz tradition was established by musicians who flocked to Harlem in the early 1920s. As these musicians made names for themselves, the clubs they jammed in became "destinations" for visitors from near and far. That's why tens of thousands of visitors come here each year seeking clubs and performers who can replicate the immortal sounds, tunes, and rhythms of the likes of the Duke (Ellington, that is), Lena (as in Horne), Billie (as in Holiday), Ella (as in Fitzgerald), the Monk (that's Thelonious), Bird (as in Charlie Parker), Miles (as in Davis), Sarah Vaughan, and Billy Eckstein—just to name a few. Whether you're a jazz aficionado or you just like music, Welcome to Harlem has created a very special tour that will take you to Harlem's best jazz clubs.*

Date: Mon and Tue at 7pm, 5 hours. Price: $120 per person. **Car service to your Manhattan hotel included.**

Harlem Jazz Concert Series

At Welcome to Harlem we believe in making sure that your experience in our Harlem is one you will never forget. So, we created the Harlem Jazz Concert Series, a unique opportunity for you to enjoy a private jazz concert in a private brownstone, complete with hors d'oeuvres, dessert, and wine. Call it a **"house party"**—and welcome to our house!*

Date: Call for schedule, the party starts at 7:30pm, 2.5 hours. Price: $45 per person.

Shopping Tour

Harlem's 125th Street has reemerged as the preeminent retail corridor of upper Manhattan and we know all the best places to shop for the most unbelievable bargains. We'll take you to well-known retail stores as well as to unique boutiques that have everything from fine African woodcarvings, artifacts, fabrics, and clothing to contemporary styles in designer sportswear, dress-up casuals, and elegant attire. Regardless of your interests, you'll find bargains galore in Harlem and we are just the ones to show you.*

Date: Tues and Thu at 11am, 4–5 hours, Price: $40 per person.

Custom Tours and Holiday Specials

Even at Welcome to Harlem we know that you can't be all things to all people. But we want to try. If there's something special you'd like to do or see and we haven't mentioned it, just let us know. Or, if you'd like to take a little from this tour and a little from that tour, let us know that, too. We're here to make your time in our Harlem the most enjoyable, eye-opening, and special time you've ever had. And if you're coming to New York during the holidays, please ask us about special music or other seasonal events that are sure to be taking place. We love to celebrate and you're always invited!

Date, Time and Price are negotiable.

*Harlem Eats

We can top off any of our tours with a stop at one Harlem's world-renowned and locally beloved eateries. What better way to end your tour?

For more in-depth tour descriptions and reviews, go to www.welcometoharlem.com and click on tours. To get to Welcome to Harlem, take the A train to 125th Street and we'll get the party started. Prices are subject to change.

Welcome to Harlem

2360 Fredrick Douglass Blvd., between 126th and 127th Sts. (212) 662-7779. www.welcometoharlem. com. Bus—M2, M3, M7, M10, M60, M100, M101, M102, BX15. Subway—A, B, C, D, 2, 3 to 125th St.

Receive a 10% discount when you book with us, please use discount code travel2011. You must contact us online to redeem the discount. The discount may not be added to any other offer. This offer expires after 12/31/2011.

Harlem Lost and Found Tours!

"Going through Harlem with historian and preservationist Michael Henry Adams is like trekking through the forest with a native guide. Seeing Harlem through his eyes, you realize how, without him along, you would have missed half of all you passed."

Peter Hellman, *New York Magazine*

Michael Henry Adams, author of *Harlem Lost And Found*, will show you the real deal—the Harlem he knows and loves so well, that heretofore outsiders were seldom privileged to inspect. You will see and be seen, meet and greet, drink and eat, on bus or walking tours designed to give you a pleasurable, authentic, and memorable experience. Adams' tours allow you to speak with local people and go into private, painstakingly restored Victorian row houses. In venerable neo-Gothic churches you can witness soul-stirring gospel singing. In down-home, hole-in-the-wall joints on "Jungle Alley" you will hear jazz performances good enough to make you weep and laugh, at the same time!

Group Walking Tours for 10–50 people: $25 per person
Exclusive of prix fixe lunch or dinner at $20 and $30, respectively
(exclusive of cocktails, wine, tax, and tip)

Walking Tours and Private Tours for groups of 10 or fewer: $150 per hour
Exclusive of prix fixe lunch or dinner at $20 and $30, respectively
(exclusive of cocktails, wine, tax, and tip)

Tours and Other Services on Request—email mrmhadams@aol.com
- Teas, cocktails, and after-parties, with any or each—featured DJs, live music, or other kinds of entertainment can be arranged.
- Bus and limousine rates as well accommodations and weekend packages exploring the entire city are available.

Tour Themes

Hebrew Harlem: examines Harlem's history a hundred years ago, when Jewish immigrants left the overcrowded Lower East Side to become aspiring "Uptown Jews"; includes magnificent former synagogues and one-time homes of luminaries like Richard Rodgers, Lorenz Hart, and Harry Houdini.

Hibernian Harlem: explores spectacular Catholic churches, the home of 1890s Mayor Thomas Gilroy, and other landmarks associated with Irish American Harlem.

Holy Harlem: celebrates the abiding presence of faith in Harlem manifested by imposing churches and masterful music-making.

Heroic Harlem: see where Maya Angelou lives, and where Langston Hughes and other legendary African Americans lived.

Homo Harlem: pursue your "down-low" fantasies in the haunts of Countee Cullen, Alain Leroy Locke, Cole Porter, and Audre Lorde.

Hip Hop Harlem: rapper's delight!

Hidiho Harlem: all that jazz!

Highbrow Harlem: literary landmarks associated with everyone from authors Dorothy West to James Baldwin.

Holland in Harlem: established as a Dutch colony in 1636, abandoned and then reestablished in 1658, mementos of Harlem's Dutch moments survive to be rediscovered.

Dining

Central Harlem

5 & Diamond
2072 Frederick Douglass Blvd., between 112th and 113th Sts. (646) 684-4262. Cuisine: American Nouveau, Mediterranean. Dinner, Brunch. $$$$. Tues-Thu 5:30pm-10pm, Fri-Sat 5:30pm-11pm, Sun 5:30pm-10pm. All major credit cards. Bus—M2, M3, M7, M10. Subway—B, C, 2, 3 to 110th St.

bier international
2099 Frederick Douglass Blvd., at 113th St. (212) 280-0944. www.bierinternational.com. Cuisine: Continental, Beers from around the world. Dinner, Brunch. $$$. Mon-Thu 4pm-2am, Fri 4pm-4am, Sat 12pm-4am, Sun 12pm-2am. All major credit cards. Bus—M2, M3, M7, M10. Subway—B, C, 2, 3 to 110th St.

Chocolàt Restaurant Lounge
2217-23 Frederick Douglass Blvd., at 120th St. (212) 222-4545. www.chocolatlounge.com. Lunch, Dinner, Brunch. $$$$. Mon-Thu 11am-12am, Fri-Sat 11 am-2 am, Sun 11am-11pm. All major credit cards. Bus—M2, M3, M10. Subway—B, C to 116th St.

Frizzante Bistro & Bar
2168 Frederick Douglass Blvd., at 117th St. (212) 866-0525. Cuisine: Italian. Lunch, Dinner, Brunch. $$. Mon-Sun 11am-11pm. MC, V. Bus—M2, M3, M7, M10, M116. Subway—B, C, 2, 3 to 116th St.

Yatenga French Bistro & Bar
2269 Adam Clayton Powell Blvd., between 133rd and 134th Sts. (212) 690-0699. www.yatengabistro.com. Cuisine: French and American. Dinner, Brunch. $$$. Mon-Thu 4pm-1am, Fri-Sat 4pm-2am, Sun 4pm-1am. All major credit cards. Bus—M2, M7, M10, M102, BX33. Subway—B, C, 2, 3 to 135th St.

Apparel/Cosmetics/Salon/Spas

BBraxton (grooming and day spa for men and women)
1400 Fifth Ave., on 116th Street between Malcolm X /Lenox and Fifth Ave. (212) 369-3094. www.bbraxton.com. Tues-Wed 10am-7pm, Thu-Fri 10am-8pm, Sat 8am-8pm. All major credit cards. Bus—M2, M7, M18, M102, M116. Subway—2, 3 to 116th St.

Polished Fingertips (spa for nail care and other services including boutique shopping)
2198 Frederick Douglass Blvd., between 118th and 119th Sts. (212) 222-4466. www.polishedfingertips.com. Mon-Wed 10am-8pm, Thu-Fri 10am-9pm, Sat 10am-7pm. Sun 11am-5pm. All major credit cards. Bus—M2, M3, M10. Subway—B, C to 116th St.

West Harlem

Dining

Bettolona
3143 Broadway, between Tiemann and LaSalle Sts. (124th St.). (212) 749-1125. Cuisine: Italian. Lunch, Dinner, Brunch. $$$. Mon-Thu 12 pm-11 pm, Fri-Sat 12pm-12am, Sun 11am-4pm. V, MC, AmEx. Bus—M4, M11, M60, M104, BX15. Subway—1 to 125th St.

Mel's Burger Bar
2850 Broadway, between 110th and 111th St. (212) 865-7100. Cuisine: Burgers. www.melsburgerbar.com. Lunch, Dinner. $$. Mon-Thu 11am-12am, Fri-Sun 11am-1am. All major credit cards. Bus—M4, M60, M104. Subway—1 to 110th St.

East Harlem

Dining

Café Saint-Germain Bistro
1695 Lexington Ave., between 106th and 107th Sts. (212) 289-2466. www.cafesaintgermain.com. Cuisine: Gourmet Sandwiches, Salads, Smoothies. Lunch, Dinner, Brunch. $. Mon-Sat 10am-7pm, Sun 11am-7pm. All major credit cards. Bus—M101, M102, M103, M106. Subway—6 to 106th St.

Ceviche Tapas Bar
2312 Second Ave., between 118th and 119th Sts. (212) 828-8830. www.cevichenyc.com. Cuisine: Peruvian. Dinner. $$$. Mon-Sun 4pm-12am. All major credit cards. Bus—M101, M102, M103, M116. Subway—6 to 116th St.

Morel
2347 Second Ave., between 120th and 121st Sts. (212) 831-7305. Cuisine: Soul Food with a French and West Indies flair. Breakfast, Lunch, Dinner. Tues-Sun 7:30am-12am. Bus—M101, M102, M103, M116. Subway—6 to 116th St.

Food

Wild Olive Market (organic and gourmet food supermarket)
10 East 125th St., between Fifth and Madison Aves. (212) 369-2665. Mon-Fri 7am-9pm, Sat-Sun 8am-9pm. All major credit cards. Bus—M1, M7, M60, M100, M101, M102, BX15. Subway—2, 3, 4, 5, 6 to 125th St.

Shopping

East River Plaza
517 East 117th Street, between Pleasant and First Aves. Bus—M M101, M102, M103, M116. Subway—6 to 116th St. Free Target Shuttle—Lexington Ave. at 116th St. and 106th St.

Best Buy
(646) 672-9959.www.bestbuy.com. Mon-Sat 10am-9pm, Sun 11am-7pm. All major credit cards.

COSTCO
(212) 896-5873.www.costco.com. Mon-Fri 10am-8:30pm, Sat 9:30am-6pm, Sun 10am-6pm. All major credit cards.

Marshall's
(917) 492-2892. www.marshallsonline.com. Mon-Sat 9:30am-9:30pm. Sun 11am-8pm. All major credit cards.

Target
(212) 835-0860.www.target.com. Mon-Sat 8am-11pm, Sun 8am-10pm. All major credit cards

COMING SOON

Museum

Museum for African Art
1280 Fifth Ave., between 110th and 109th Sts. www.africanart.org. Spring, 2011

Dining

Harlem Tavern Neighborhood Bar & Grill
301 W. 116th St. at Frederick Douglass Blvd.

Red Rooster (by Celebrity Chef Marcus Samuelsson)
310 Malcolm X/Lenox between 125th and 126th Sts. Cuisine: American Comfort Food. Winter 2010.

RECOMMENDED BOOKS ABOUT HARLEM

Adams, Michael Henry. *Harlem Lost and Found An Architectural and Social History, 1765–1915.* New York: Monacelli Press, Inc., 2002.

Anderson, Jervis. *This Was Harlem: A Cultural Portrait, 1900–1950.* New York: Farrar Straus Giroux, 1982.

Bailey, A. Peter. *Harlem: Precious Memories…Great Expectations.* New York: Harlem Commonwealth Council, Inc., 2003.

Dodson, Howard, Christopher Moore, and Roberta Yancy. *The Black New Yorkers: The Schomburg Illustrated Chronology.* New York: John Wiley & Sons, Inc., 2000.

Dolkart, Andrew S., and Gretchen S. Sorin. *Touring Historical Harlem: Four Walks in Northern Manhattan.* New York: New York Landmarks Conservancy, 1997.

"Harlem Mecca of the New Negro," *Survey Graphic*, Vol. VI, No. 6 (March 1925); reprint, Baltimore: Black Classic Press, 1980.

Johnson, James Weldon. *Black Manhattan.* New York: Knopf, 1930; reprint, New York: Atheneum, 1972.

Lewis, David Levering. *When Harlem Was in Vogue.* New York: Knopf, 1982.

Schoener, Allon, ed. *Harlem On My Mind: Cultural Capital of Black America 1900–1968.* Metropolitan Museum of Art Exhibition. New York: Random House, Inc., 1968.

Wilson, Sondra Kathryn. *Meet Me at the Theresa: The Story of Harlem's Most Famous Hotel.* New York: Atria Books, 2004.

233

Harlem Street Sign/Stephen Finn, Spirit of Harlem Mural/Mario Burger, Adam Clayton Powell, Jr. State Office Building/Mario Burger, Adam Clayton Powell, Jr. Statue/Bruce Weese, Michael Jackson Mural/ Sam Lahoz, Harriet Tubman Statue/Mario Burger, Frederick Douglass/www.welcometoharlem.com, Craig S. Harris/Darrell Bridges Entertainment, Astor Row Historic District /Emilio Guerra, Mount Morris Park Historic District Streetscape/Emilio Guerra, Mount Morris Park Historic District/Craig O'Connell, Striver's Row Streetscape/Emilio Guerra, Striver's Row Gates/Mario Burger, 369th Regiment Armory/Jim Henderson-Wikimedia Commons, Alhambra Ballroom/Ken Roe-London UK, Graham Court/courtesy of Harlemonestop.org, Theresa Hotel/Emilio Guerra, Schomburg Center for Research in Black Culture/cia_b of www.writingwithmymouthfull.com, Arturo O'Farrill jams at Jazzmobile-Central Park Conservancy Concert/Imagezs of Us, Harlem 144 Guest House Interior/Erdene Green, Harlem 144 Guest House Backyard/Isaac Diggs, Chez Lucienne (1&2)/Sirin Samman, Harlem Wing and Waffle/cia_b of www.writingwithmymouthfull.com, Miss Maude's Spoonbread Too/Esther Tseng, Minton's Playhouse/Keith DeBetham, Mojo/courtesy of Mojo, B.O.R.N. Vintage Boutique/Sam Lahoz, Hats by Bunn/Sam Lahoz, My Kids/Sam Lahoz, N Harlem New York/RickyDay.net, Hue-Man Bookstore/Sam Lahoz, Makari/Sam Lahoz, Sade Skincare/Sam Lahoz, Atmos/Carl Chisolm, Grandma's Place/Trevaughn Bynum, Mother A. M. E. Zion Church/Emilio Guerra, Abyssinian Baptist Church/Hozel Williams, Ebenezer Gospel Tabernacle Church/Emilio Guerra, Ephesus Seventh Day Adventist Church/Emilio Guerra, Mount Morris Ascension Presbyterian Church/Emilio Guerra, Mt. Olivet Baptist Church/courtesy of Harlemonestop.org, Salem United Methodist/Emilio Guerra, St. Aloysius Roman Catholic Church/ Emilio Guerra, Jackie Robinson Park Building/Emilio Guerra, Jackie Robinson Park Flowers/Jacquie Connors, The City College of New York – Shepard Hall/Bill Summers, Cathedral of Saint John the Devine/ courtesy of Cathedral of Saint John the Devine, Morningside Park/Emilio Guerra, Grant's Tomb/James Morrissey-Wild Coyote Studio, Harlem Sunrise/Mario Burger, IRT Subway Viaduct/Tore Berg, The City College of New York – Great Hall/Bill Summers, Harlem Stage Gatehouse/Vaughn Browne, Edgecombe Avenue/Emilio Guerra, West Harlem Buildings/Emilio Guerra, West Harlem Streetscape (1&2)/Craig O'Connell, Bailey House/Emilio Guerra, West Harlem Streetscape/Emilio Guerra, Alexander Hamilton Statue/Mario Burger, Hamilton Theatre/Ken Roe, London UK, Nicholas C. and Agnes Benziger House/ Emilio Guerra, Our Lady of Lourdes Roman Catholic Church/Emilio Guerra, Harlem Stage Gatehouse Interior/Vaughn Browne, Artistic Director Virginia Johnson and Eddie J. Shellman in Giselle/Dance Theatre of Harlem archives, Columbia University Low Library/Samuel Shapiro, The City College of New York – Townsend Harris Hall/Bill Summers, Sugar Hill Harlem Inn (1&2)/courtesy of Sugar Hill Harlem Inn, Hudson River Café (1&2)/courtesy of Hudson River Café, Famous Fish Market/cia_b of www.writingwithmymouthfull.com, St. Nick's Pub/Mario Burger, The Church of the Intercession/Jim Henderson-Wikimedia Commons, Convent Avenue Baptist Church/James Morrissey-Wild Coyote Studio, Old Broadway Synagogue/Emilio Guerra, Riverside Church/James Morrissey-Wild Coyote Studio, The Cathedral Church of St. John Devine and Peace Fountain/James Morrissey-Wild Coyote Studio, Morningside Park (1&2)/Jacquie Connors, Riverside Park River View/Dave Cook-Eating In Translation, Riverside Park/Monica Brady, River Bank State Park (1&2)/James Morrissey-Wild Coyote Studio, St. Nicholas Park Stairs/James Morrissey-Wild Coyote Studio, St. Nicholas Park/Emilio Guerra, West Harlem Piers Park Sunrise/James Morrissey-Wild Coyote Studio, West Harlem Piers Park/Jim Henderson-Wikimedia Commons, Graffiti Hall of Fame/Kristin Oftebro, East Harlem River/Emilio Guerra, East Harlem Building/Craig O'Connell, La Marqueta/Uucp-Wikimedia Commons, East Harlem Streetscape/ Emilio Guerra, 17 East 128th Street/Emilio Guerra, Harlem Court House/Emilio Guerra, Marcus Garvey Park Firewatch Tower/Mario Burger, Saint Nicholas Russian Orthodox Cathedral/Christopher de la Torre, Julia de Burgos Latino Cultural Center/Emilio Guerra, New York Apartment to Let (1&2)/ courtesy of New York Apartment to Let, Creole Restaurant and Supper Club (1&2)/courtesy of Creole Restaurant and Supper Club, Yo In Yo Out/Sam Lahoz, Harlem Underground/Sam Lahoz, The Brownstone/Michael Jones, St. Cecilia Church/Emilio Guerra, Church of All Saints/Christopher de la Torre, Holy Rosary Church/Christopher de la Torre, St. Paul's Church/Christopher de la Torre, Central Park Harlem Meer/Emilio Guerra, Central Park Duke Ellington Circle/Jim Henderson-Wikimedia Commons, Marcus Garvey Park Stairs/James Morrissey-Wild Coyote Studio, Marcus Garvey Park/

Valerie Jo Bradley, Thomas Jefferson Park (1&2)/James Morrissey-Wild Coyote Studio, Morris-Jumel Mansion/James Morrissey-Wild Coyote Studio, El Cid Sculpture, The Hispanic Society of America/ Emilio Guerra, Sylvan Terrace Streetscape/James Morrissey-Wild Coyote Studio, Charlie Parker Jazz Festival/Marcus Garvey Park Alliance archives, Dance Harlem and Praise! Dance Harlem/Steven Schrieber, Fried Chicken/Keith DeBetham, Soul Food Sign/Keith DeBetham, Pedro Pietro Mural/Mario Burger, Graffiti Hall of Fame/Kristin Oftebro, Dance Harlem/Steven Schrieber.

Front Cover Photo Credit

West Harlem Streetscape/Emilio Guerra

Back Cover Photo Credits

Craig S. Harris/Darrell Bridges Entertainment
Firebird/Dance Theatre of Harlem archives

Maps courtesy of Eurekaa Cartography

Made in the USA
Charleston, SC
24 January 2011